Connecting with Christ and His Word

CLICK

Holy Bible

Includes:

52 lessons for the whole year and resources for teaching each lesson for adolescents from 12 – 17 years and youth from 18 – 23 years.

BOOK 6

Click - Connecting With Christ and His Word, #6

Published by: Mesoamerica Region Discipleship Ministries

Monte Cyr - Discipleship Ministries Coordinator

www.discipleship.MesoamericaRegion.org

www.SdmiResources.MesoamericaRegion.org

ISBN: 978-1-63580-185-9

All of the scripture verses quoted are from the NIV Bible unless otherwise stated.

Translated into English from Spanish by: Monte & Bethany Cyr

Editor - Patricia Picavea

Printed in Guatemala

Mesoamerica Region

Table of Contents

Unit Five • People of God

Unit Six • Friendship

Unit Seven • Building My Identity

Unit Eight • Special Dates

Presentation

It's important to recognize that the teaching ministry for adolescents and youth is a very serious job; more if we understand that it's at this stage where they'll make decisions that will affect the rest of their lives. Many of the people around us made the decision of what profession they were going to study and practice, who they were going to marry, in which church they were going to congregate and where they were going to serve, at this stage. Consider how many of the members of our churches made their most important spiritual decisions in adolescence or youth.

The fact that you or your church acquired Click to teach shows the importance you're giving to the formation of the Christian life of adolescents and young people.

All the lessons in this book are based on the Holy Scriptures and prepared and written by an international team of pastors and youth leaders. We want you the teacher, and your students, to enjoy this wonderful experience of teaching and learning.

Click 6 has eight units that cover 52 lessons in total, to be used for a whole year. Each unit doesn't have the same number of lessons since it varies according to the objective and theme of each one.

We understand that each age has its characteristics. That's why Click has been designed to teach adolescents from 12 to 17 years old and young people from 18 to 23 years, more effectively. The Bible lessons are the same for both groups, but the introductory dynamics and activities for the student are different. You can adapt them according to the needs and facilities of your local church or the place where they meet.

In each lesson, you'll find the following sections:

- The objective of the lesson: What is expected to be achieved in the lesson.
- The Connect section, which is the introduction to the topic. Here you'll find the Introductory Activity for each age group.
- The Navigate section is the development of the lesson.
- The Review/Apply section is where the practical activity is located. You'll find the answers to each activity within the activity, usually the answers are underlined or in parentheses. Be aware that through this activity, you'll be able to provide feedback and x the lesson objective in the minds and hearts of your students.
- The Challenge at the end of each lesson is a personal challenge to the students for them to work on during the week. The idea is to motivate the student to live what they learned.
- Finally, you'll find Attention! boxes at the beginning of each lesson. The Attention! boxes are reminders to review the previous lesson's challenge.

It is our hope that through this material you can guide your students to continuous growth; go ahead ... get started now.

Patricia Picavea

Editor in chief, Ministries Publications

Aids

for the teacher

A

Intelligently reaching out to youth is vital to the growth and development of the church. Most of the evangelical leadership will agree with this statement. On the other hand, being a Sunday School teacher is a privilege that God gives us, and at the same time, constitutes a great responsibility. The privilege of teaching comes from having been taught first and from the mandate that we've received from Jesus to teach others (Matthew 28:20). If we understand the dynamics of teaching well, we won't be frightened by the responsibility, but will enjoy the privilege, and constantly train ourselves to form Christ in others. We encourage you to study each lesson carefully in advance. That way you'll have a better mastery of each subject, and without a doubt, it will be a time of spiritual growth.

Lesson Preparation

1. Pray to the Lord for wisdom and discernment to understand the Bible study passages and apply them first to your life. Don't forget to pray for your students to be receptive to the teaching of God's Word.

2. Prepare a distraction-free place to study the lesson with a table or desk. It's important to have some supplies such as: paper, pens, pencils, eraser, etc.

3. To the best of your ability, in addition to the Click book, have a dictionary, a Bible dictionary, and some good Bible commentaries on hand.

4. Read the Click lesson as many times as necessary at the beginning of the week. This will help you prepare the materials you may need for the class and keep an eye out for news and other information that you might include in the lesson you're preparing.

5. Look in the Bible and read each passage listed.

6. Read the objective of the lesson to know where to lead your students.

7. Write on a piece of paper the points that will be developed, the title of the first point, and develop your own summary as you study the lesson. Write and highlight the biblical quotes that will be read during class.

8. Write down the meanings of unfamiliar words so that you can better understand the lesson and explain it to people who will eventually ask you.

Lesson Presentation

1. Get to your class location early. It's important that you're already there when the first person arrives.

2. Change the position of the chairs (semicircle, circle, groups, etc). This will make the group more comfortable to participate and not feel like everything is too routine.

3. Before starting the lesson, welcome your students. This will allow you to create a pleasant study environment. Take an interest in people and pray for those in need.

4. Begin the class with a prayer, asking the Lord that He would help all of you to understand His Word and give you the willingness to obey it.

5. Write on the board the title of the lesson and the memory verse. Read the memory verse with your students several times. Once the lesson begins, write the main points of the lesson on one end of the board. This will allow the class to see the sequence of points that you're teaching.

6. Make the introductory activity as attractive as possible.

7. Keep an order in the development of the topic. Write the title of point 1 and begin to explain it. Use the board as a teaching resource to record key words, answers to questions, etc. When you finish item 1, write the title of item 2 and so on.

8. Please take a few minutes to discuss how everyone can apply the biblical truths to their daily lives.

9. Invite them to attend the next time you meet. Encourage them to invite other people to the class.

10. End the class with a prayer.

Other suggestions

1. Goals and Awards: You can offer a simple award for students who learn all the memory verses and say them to the class, and attend the class on time.

2. Certificate: If you want the students who were faithful or didn't miss more than one or two classes in the study of the unit, you can give them a certificate with the name of the corresponding unit. This can show that they're making progress in their learning and can motivate others to attend faithfully.

3. Enjoy the class and let your students do so too. Trust the Lord and pray that He'll bring every word to the hearts of your students.

A Relevant Book

Attention! Start by asking about what your students did during the week. You can start by giving them an example of how you put the Word of God into practice.

Accept x

Objective: Reaffirm in the young people the value and relevance of the Bible as the only manual for the Christian life.

Memory Verse: *Your word, Lord, is eternal; it stands firm in the heavens.* Psalm 119:89

Connect | Navigate

Introductory Activity (12 - 17 years).
- Materials: Newspapers
- Instructions: Divide the class into groups and give each of them newspapers. Then write the following words on a chalkboard: Fashion, technology, politics, violence, money, and fun. Then ask them to give and example of those words with news items that appear in the newspapers they were given. At the end of the dynamic, discuss with the students how these items have evolved or changed compared to five years ago.

Introductory Activity (18 - 23 years).
- Materials: Paper and pencils.
- Instructions: Divide your students into groups and assign each one the following topics: Changes in fashion; changes in electronics; and changes in communication. Tell them that they should explain the development of each of these themes in the last 8 or 10 years. Then together make a comparison between the validity of the biblical message over time and the themes they addressed previously. How current is the Bible today?

Connect | Navigate

The Bible is the best known book, having been translated into almost all languages, and published throughout the world. This marvelous book was written by more than 40 writers during a period of 1500 years; however, its coherence, veracity and importance remain to this day. The Bible contains a great deal of information about the natural world, which has been confirmed by scientific research and observations. Many historical events recorded in the Bible have been confirmed by extra-biblical sources. Historical research often shows great similarities between biblical and extra-biblical information on the same events. In fact, in many cases it has been recognized that the Bible is more historically accurate. However, we must keep in mind that the Bible isn't primarily a history book or a psychology text or a scientific publication. The Bible is much more than all that: it's God's description of who He is, what He wants, and what His plans are for humanity. It's there where the Bible's permanence and actuality lie. Change is moving from one situation or state to another. The world is constantly changing. Thus, there are changes in society, in concepts, in science and in everything that surrounds the life of the human being, who in him or herself is in constant change. Let's look at some changes that society is experiencing today:

1. Climatic and universe changes:

"Immediately after the distress of those days 'the sun will be darkened, and the moon won't give its light; the stars will fall from the sky, and the heavenly bodies will be shaken.'" (Matthew 24:29). Currently, we observe that the climate is constantly changing. The seasons and periods of rain are no longer the same as they were long ago. In the universe, the formation of stars and even new planets is constant. But we can also trust that the changes are controlled by God: "for he views the ends of the earth and sees everything under the heavens" (Job 28:24). The Bible also says: "Can you bring forth the constellations in their seasons?" (Job 38:32a). These, among many other verses, show us that God has control over these situations. So, although everything around us is constantly changing, we can trust that God doesn't change: "I the Lord don't change. So you, the descendants of Jacob, aren't destroyed"(Malachi 3:6). As a consequence, his Word doesn't change either.

2. Changes in humanity:

Mankind currently goes through many changes in his ethical, moral and even spiritual perception. It's increasingly common to see people with moral deviations. 1 John 2:17 clearly shows us that the desires of humanity change: "And this world is fading away, and these evil, forbidden things will go with it, but whoever keeps doing the will of God will live forever" (TLB). But it also affirms that the one who does the will of God is rewarded with eternal permanence. We see again that God, despite the fact that humanity is changeable, promises that his promises won't change. In the face of constant change in our life and environment, God shows us the permanence of his Word to give us strength and trust in him. Let's carefully study what has been mentioned.

Permanence of the Word

In 1 Peter 1:25, we're shown that the Word of God remains forever: "... but the word of the Lord endures forever." This verse says that the Bible is a book of constant application: "but the Word of the Lord will last forever. And his message is the Good News that was preached to you" (TLB). The Bible contains a great deal of relevant and accurate information. However, the most important message in the Bible is about redemption; that's perpetually applicable to all mankind. When human beings search the Bible for what they are, the Word of God will never be wrong. Cultures change, laws change, generations come and go, but God's Word is as relevant today as it was when it was written. Although it must be mentioned that not all Scripture necessarily applies explicitly to us today, we do need to keep in mind that all Scripture contains truths that we can and should apply to our lives today. In Matthew 24:35, it says: "Heaven and earth will pass away, but my words will never pass away," which affirms that although the world is constantly changing and will come to an end, the Word of God with its promises will be alive forever, and therefore, we can trust them since it's a faithful word: "This is the truth and everyone should accept it" (1 Timothy 4:9 TLB).

The Bible continues to speak to us today

The Bible continues to speak to us today The mere mention of the Bible makes us think of something very old, and of themes and stories from another era. And this is the greatest danger, that is, reading it like a book from the past. If that were the case, at best the Bible would be an interesting and instructive book, but it wouldn't go beyond there for the person who read it. However, we can affirm with certainty and with confidence that the Bible is much more than that because it's an always current book, like the Word it contains. In the Bible, God continues to speak to people here and now. Neither space travel nor electronic computers detract from the relevance of the Bible since its message is eternal. The Bible has to do with everything that happens in each person in the entire world.

Although it's a book that could be called religious, it's relevant to all reality since in it we find a variety of topics and advice that guide us throughout our lives. Perhaps few books are as realistic as the Bible. Born from the reality of the different times in which it was written, and embodied in it, the Bible has to be read, or rather, reread in the reality of our time and of each time. Reread it with ever new eyes, not to make it say what we want it to say, but for it to tell us what it has always had to say ... again.

Review/Application: Allow time for your students to write what these concepts mean to them (we've included an answer in italics):

- Change: (*Change is moving from one situation or state to another. The world is constantly changing. Thus, there are changes in society, in concepts, in science and in everything that surrounds the life of the human being, who in himself is in constant change.*)

- Permanence: (*Permanence is what lasts through time and doesn't change or disappear. The Bible is God's description of who He is, what He wants, and what His plans are for humanity. It's there where its permanence and relevance lie.*)

Have them connect the two concepts with what the scripture says and what they saw in the lesson.

Challenge: Take a few minutes of personal prayer to ask God to help you update His Word in your life. Take the time to apologize if you thought this was an outdated book. Finally, pray that this Word will be put into practice in your life.

Read it, Study it, Live it

Attention!

Start your class by asking them about what they've been up to during the week. You can start by giving them an example of how you have used the Bible!

Accept

Objective: That the young people will see the Bible as the only rule of faith and practice.

Memory Verse: *All Scripture is God-breathed and is useful for teaching, rebuking, correcting and training in righteousness,* 2 Timothy 3:16

Connect | Navigate

Introductory Activity (12 - 17 years).

- Materials: Books, magazines, a small shelf, pens, paper, dictionary
- Instructions: Depending on the number of students, organize them into small groups of three. Direct them to appoint a secretary to take notes. Ask them to answer the following questions:

1. What is a library?

2. What is it for?

3. Have you ever visited a library? What use did you make of it? Did you like it? Tell about the experiences you had when you visited the library.

Give enough time for them to answer. When they've answered, ask the group secretaries to present their work to the full group. Write the definition of "library" on the board: "An institution whose purpose is the acquisition, conservation, study, and display of books and documents. Place where there is a considerable number of books organized for reading." Compare it with the definitions given by the groups. Ask the scribes to help you place the books and magazines on the shelf. Encourage students to think of the Bible as a library.

Introductory Activity (18 - 23 years).

- Materials: Two cards, markers.
- Instructions: Have the cards handy, place one on the right and one on the left of the classroom. On the right, write "Ways to show love and interest in the Bible;" on the one on the left write "Actions that show a lack of love and interest in the Bible." On each card, students are to write down their ideas. Share the answers with the class.

Connect | Navigate

The people of God, in both the Old and New Testaments, had access to the sacred writings that men wrote under the inspiration of the Holy Spirit. These were carefully selected and compiled into a single copy.

In the beginning when the first part was formed, it wasn't called the Bible. It was known simply as The Law, The Prophets and The Psalms. Such sacred writings governed the life of God's people politically, economically, socially, and religiously. For more than two thousand years, these writings were considered sacred and special. They became what we know today as the Old Testament. As we all know, this happened before the first coming of our Lord Jesus Christ.

Later, as the years and centuries passed, other writings emerged after the redemptive work of Christ and his ascension. I'm referring to the time of the apostles and the early church when the gospels, the letters, the book of Acts and Revelation began to circulate.

The Christian church faithfully received the books of the Old Testament and held them in high esteem. It accepted them as the "Word of God", "Sacred Word", "Divinely inspired Word". It also began to produce it's own writings and saw them as a categorical word inspired by God. However, at the beginning, an exhaustive collection of the writings wasn't made. The history of the Christian Church records that it was Marcion, a Gnostic, who made the first collection of writings. This included only the Pauline writings from which he removed everything having to do with Judaism.

We, the sons and daughters of God, have before us the Holy Bible, the Word of God. We can access various translations or versions if we want. It's a great blessing to enjoy the beautiful content of the Bible. *Ask:* How can we show our love and concern for the Holy Bible and take advantage of its valuable teachings?

1. Daily Bible reading

The Lord Jesus came to the Nazareth synagogue. "He stood up to read,..." (Luke 4:16). "The Jews generally remained seated when they taught or commented on the Holy Scriptures or the traditions of the elders; but when they read, whether it was the law or the prophets, they invariably got up; It wasn't lawful for them to even lean on something while they were reading." (Commentary on the Holy Bible. New Testament Volume III. Adam Clarke. CNP, USA: 1974, p. 116).

Jesus was given the book of the prophet Isaiah to read, and he read the prophecy that had to do with him and his ministry (Luke 4:18-19).

The Lord Jesus, in discussions with his adversaries the Pharisees and other leaders, assumed that they must have read and known the Holy Scriptures. He asked them: Have you not read what David did? (Matthew 12:3); Or, have you not read in the law? (Matthew 12:5); Haven't you read that at the beginning the Creator ...? (Matthew 19:4); Have you never read? (Matthew 21:16); Have you never read in the Scriptures? (Matthew 21:42); Have you not read what was told you? (Matthew 22:31); Have you not read in the book of Moses? (Mark 12:26); What is written in the law? How do you read it? (Luke 10:26).

The apostle Paul advised the young pastor Timothy to dedicate himself to reading. He said to them: "Until I come, devote yourself to the public reading of Scripture, to preaching and to teaching." (1 Timothy 4:13); while John the seer, writer of the Apocalypse, exhorted his readers thus: "Blessed is the one who reads aloud the words of this prophecy..." (Revelation 1:3)

We see, then, that the faithful reading of the Scriptures is of vital importance for the people of God. "Everyone should read the Bible. It's the Word of God. It contains the solutions of life. It's an account of the best friend that mankind has ever had; the noblest, kindest, and truest man who ever walked this earth" (Handbook Digest of the Bible. Henry H. Halley. Moody, p. 714).

The reading of the Holy Bible should be characterized by being:

Fervent

Fervor is: "Devotion, intensity in religious sentiment. Enthusiasm, ardor, efficiency with which something is done. Admiration, adoration towards something or someone" (Dictionary Consultor Espasa. Calpe, S.A, Madrid: 1998, p. 161).

The Christian Bible reader should be excited and encouraged that he or she isn't just reading any old book about God. In the style of the believers of the time of Ezra and Nehemiah, they must make sense of what they read (Nehemiah 8:8).

Helpful

The sincere reader of the Holy Bible takes advantage of its teachings because they are a guide in all aspects of life (2 Timothy 3:16-17).

Supportive

The Word of God is food that sustains and nourishes one's spiritual life. The soul hungry for God and for doing good will be satisfied (Matthew 4:4).

God uses his powerful Word to sustain us every day (Psalm 119:28,116; Hebrews 1:2-3).

2. Thorough study of the Bible

In addition to the good habit of reading the scriptures, we must study them. This implies more effort and work, but it's worth doing because that way we'll get to know them much better.

The responsible study of the Word involves investment of time, memorization of its beautiful texts and stories, use of tools that facilitate the assimilation of its content, and the application of a suitable study method.

The purpose of Bible study, in addition to assimilating the content, is to understand it.

The following guidelines can help achieve this purpose:

What does the passage actually say? Does the passage contain any specific teaching about God, mankind, the world, the church…? Does it contain an example to follow, a warning, or a promise? Is any action required in light of the passage?

3. Application of the Bible to everyday life

We know well that the Bible is God's message to humanity, and that the impact it has on people's lives results in transformed lives. Its effects are long lasting. We'll see some of those below.

It transforms our lifestyle: Whoever follows the teachings of the Word will surrender to Christ. The Lord then works a glorious change in the heart so that life will never be the same again (2 Corinthians 5:17). Once in Christ, we continue to grow and develop. The Bible plays an important role in this growth and development.

It helps us to be better:

a). Better sons and daughters of God: As such we'll honor and please the Lord with a public testimony, holy and clean (Philippians 2:15).

b). Better families: All members of the family will work to maintain the unity of the family nucleus (Ephesians 5:1,4).

c). Better citizens: We'll respect and obey the legitimately constituted authorities in our countries (Romans 13:1,7).

Review/Application: Direct your students to read the Bible verses and fill in the blanks:

1. Hebrews 4:12 "For the Word of God is alive and active."

2. 2 Thessalonians 3:1 "...pray for us that the message of the Lord may spread rapidly and be honored..."

3. Psalm 119:105. "Your word is a lamp for my feet, a light on my path."

4. John 6:63. "The words I have spoken to you—they are full of the Spirit and life.

5. 2 Timothy 3:16. "All Scripture is God-breathed and is useful for teaching, rebuking, correcting and training in righteousness,..."

6. Psalm 119: 9. "How can a young person stay on the path of purity? By living according to your Word."

Challenge: Get into groups of three and discuss the importance and the need to share the Word of God with young people who don't know the Lord. Get New Testaments, visit these young people, invite them to come to church, and give each of them a copy of the holy book.

I Promise You!

Natalia Pesado • U.S.A.

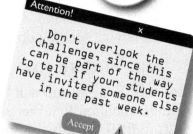

Attention!

Don't overlook the Challenge, since this can be part of the way to tell if your students have invited someone else in the past week.

Accept

Objective: That the youth will know God's promises and how He fulfills them at the right time.

Memory Verse: *Let's hold unswervingly to the hope we profess, for he who promised is faithful.* Hebrews 10:23

Connect | Navigate

Introductory Activity (12 - 17 years).

- Materials: Write the following promises on rectangles of paper (Matthew 11:28; John 14: 1a; 14:16; Romans 8:28; Psalms 23:1; 91:1; 91:7; etc.). Then cut the verse in half to make them incomplete (example: "those who love him" - "all things God works for the good of"), Bibles.

- Instructions: Place the pieces of paper with some of the promises mixed up and upside down on a table or on the floor. Have the students take a piece of paper and look among their classmates to complete the promise written on it. When finished, each pair will read their promise and talk about what it says. If young people don't know much about the Bible, you can put the reference up so they can look it up.

Introductory Activity (18 - 23 years).

- Materials: Blackboard and chalk, or large paper and pencil.

- Instructions: On the board, write the word "Promise" in large letters and ask your students to describe what the word means to them (you can write the concepts on the board that they describe). After a few minutes, write the title "A Broken Promise" on the side and do the same exercise described above. In closing, encourage your students to think about the beauty of never-failing promises.

Connect | Navigate

Throughout their existence, a person receives numerous promises, for example: promises of marriage, employment, housing, educational or financial results, gifts, visits, scholarships, etc. Some are fulfilled and others aren't. Today we'll see the true value of a promise.

1. The meaning of a promise

In the dictionary, the word "promise" is described as "a declaration that something will or won't be done, given, etc., by one;" or "an express assurance on which expectation is to be based:" (www. dictionary.com). A promise can also be understood as "a legally binding declaration that gives the person to whom it's made a right to expect or to claim the performance or forbearance of a specified act" (www.merriam-webster.com/dictionary/promise). In today's lesson, we'll study about the most special promises we can receive.

When we look around us, we can see that our social life abounds with promises. Students have a mutual contract (even though they haven't signed an official document) with their school teachers. For example, that the teachers will teach them the subjects, and if the students fulfill their tasks and demonstrate in the exams that they have learned the content, they trust that their teachers will give them a good grade and finally a completed education degree.

The promises we receive from God are also an agreement that if we're obedient and trust Him, He will fulfill His part (1 John 2:25; Acts 2:33,39). In these wonderful verses, we can see very clearly and specifically that God promised eternal life to those who believe in Jesus, and that he also promised the help of the Holy Spirit. The special meaning of God's promises is that they are an expression of his eternal love for us, they demonstrate his clear intention to save us, and he is the one who initiates his promises to us, seeking our positive response. We can be sure that God longs to bless us.

2. The value of a promise

In our life, we're and will be surrounded by many promises that we make and receive. Unfortunately, we must mention that many promises aren't faithfully kept: some students don't make the necessary effort in their learning; or there are teachers who don't recognize the effort of the student; sometimes, the banks don't return the money to the people who kept it there; sometimes bosses fire people from their jobs, or landlords evict tenants. Sadly, courtships or marriages sometimes fail because of infidelity. We cannot deny that an unfulfilled or "broken" promise can bring a lot of sadness, disappointment, and pain to the heart of the person who expected to see that promise fulfilled. It's possible that these painful experiences are already part of the life of a young person, despite their young age.

We see that the value of a promise is closely related to the truthfulness of the word of the person who makes the promise. If a person lies or generally fails, the value of their promise will be non-existent. On the contrary, when a person always keeps what he promises, the promises that person makes are of great value, because although they aren't yet fulfilled, past evidence gives us complete assurance for the future that the person will keep his word.

In our case as children of God, we can see that God's promises are of such great value that it's incalculable, because no promise of God has failed. Unlike our trust in human beings who can fail, our trust in God's promises is beyond doubt. In Hebrews 11:1, we read: "What is faith? It's the confident assurance that something we want is going to happen. It's the certainty that what we hope for is waiting for us, even though we cannot see it up ahead." (TLB).

Let's also look at the passages in Hebrews 10:23 and 2 Corinthians 1:20. We note that the author of Hebrews mentions that we can trust God's promises because He is faithful and has never failed His to keep his word. Similarly, in his letter to Christians in the city of Corinth, the apostle Paul teaches them the best way to value God's promises, and that way is to receive them by saying "Yes" and "Amen" (or, "so be it"), trusting that God's promises are fully trustworthy; and that we can rest in them.

In conclusion, the value of a promise resides in the person who says it and in the great peace and trust it brings to the recipient.

3. The fulfillment of a promise

A promise achieves its value by the person who expresses it, and that value is also complementary to the fulfillment of that promise. When a promise is finally fulfilled, both parties who had agreed are completely satisfied that they received what they longed for ... the fulfillment of a promise

It requires total commitment and effort from the person to carry out what was promised; therefore, for a person to fulfill her promise, she must be able to remember it and take the necessary action, sometimes for an extended period of time.

Many times, keeping a promise isn't easy. We could say that the more value a promise has, the more effort it will probably take to fulfill it, and therefore, these are the most special promises.

In our case as children of God, we can see that the promises that God made to us are unique and of incalculable value because their value is spiritual. The fulfillment of the divine promises is in God's timing. This time is known only to Him until He reveals it, and its timing is perfect, because it's determined by the perfect wisdom of God.

As human beings, it's very common that we tend to suffer from impatience, that is, we suffer from the feeling of urgency and / or despair about the time when things should happen.

A feeling of despair, which can overwhelm us in difficult life situations, must be submitted to God, and we must resist the tendency to despair or to think that God's promises have to be fulfilled when "I" think it would be better. In the same way, it's vital to resist the temptation to think that if what I want doesn't happen "now," God has failed us or doesn't care. This also applies to other aspects of our young lives, including dating, having children, becoming independent from parents, deciding to work or study, etc.

Finally, we see that in order to see the fulfillment of God's matchless promises, we need to have patience and faith. Trust that He is faithful and will do what He has said (Hebrews 6:12). We can trust that God's promises will be faithfully fulfilled at the perfect time.

Review/Application: Give them time to write down what each promise means to their lives.

BIBLE REFERENCES WITH A PROMISE	MEANING OF THE PROMISE
Jeremiah 29:11	God has a good plan for my life and future.
Haggai 2: 4-5	Jehovah is with me during the difficult times.
Psalms 25: 9; 32: 8	God can show me my professional field of study
1 Corinthians 10:13	God can help me overcome temptations
Philippians 4: 6-7	God can give me peace in the moments of greatest anxiety
James 1: 5	God wants to help me make very good decisions

Challenge: Have you thought about God's promises before today's lesson? Do you have any favorite promises? I encourage you to ask God to make you a promise for yourself or for a specific time in your life. These special promises are very useful when we share them with others. During this week, think about and choose a promise for your life.

Your "Hard Drive"

Ana Zoila Díaz • Panama

Objective: To promote memorization and application of the Bible.

Memory Verse: *My son, don't forget my teaching, but keep my commands in your heart,* Proverbs 3:1

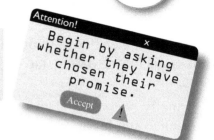

Attention!

Begin by asking whether they have chosen their promise.

Accept

Connect | Navigate

Introductory Activity (12 - 17 years).

- Materials: Posterboard/large pieces of paper with the following words, mind, book, television, magazines, heart and spirit.

- Instructions: Take out each posterboard and ask if each word refers to an external unit or an internal unit. When they agree or after a while, present the answers as follows:

Mind: RAM memory. Internal unit.

Book: External unit.

Television: External unit.

Magazines: External unit.

Brain: Hard Drive. Internal drive.

Spirit: Internal unit.

Introductory Activity (18 - 23 years).

- Materials: Individual posters/large papers featuring all the words of two or more little-known or rarely-memorized Bible verses.

- Instructions: Presents the quote(s), and ask the students to memorize the verses. Then ask them to try to order the words of the verse or verses in the order they were memorized.

Connect | **Navigate**

We too can compare ourselves in some way with the computer memory, because we can store in our memory data that's there when we need it.

1. Like RAM, the mind can be a place where information is stored for a specified time, but when we disconnect from the information, it's lost and we forget everything we received in it. As a popular phrase would say: "Information enters through one ear and leaves through the other."

2. External units or devices can be the different sources of information that appear in our lives: books, what we listen to and even what we see. Many times we must resort to those external sources to remember what they say, but they aren't always at our fingertips.

3. The hard drive resembles our brain: If you save or file something on it, you have the security that it will be within reach when you need it. Therefore, it's internal. In this way, it's protected from everything external to prevent something from damaging it.

1. What do you keep on your "hard drive"?

Computer memory (RAM) is a temporary storage place for the files you use. Most of the information stored in RAM is erased when the computer is turned off. Therefore, your computer needs permanent forms of storage to save and retrieve programs and data files that you want to use on a daily basis. Storage devices (also called drives) were developed to meet this need.

The most common types of devices are:

• External drives: USB sticks, CDs, DVDs, portable hard drives, etc.

• Internal drives: Hard drives.

The hard drive is the most important storage system on your computer. In it, the program files and the files that you create with those programs are saved.

Our brain is a "hard drive", internal memory like a computer's. In this sense, memory is one of the necessary conditions for learning to take place, which occurs precisely when the content of memory changes. Thus, once a stimulus, data, explanation, etc. has been received, our memory goes from a state of not having data to another of having it. It can be said that learning is saving something in memory to remember it when necessary. Memory and learning, therefore, are closely related. Memory is the test of learning.

Memorization is an intellectual activity by which we fix and retain in our minds the knowledge that we must learn, and then remember it when necessary. However, we must mention that there is a difference between memorization and understanding. Memorization is learning by remembering, without understanding, like a parrot that repeats, but doesn't analyze. Understanding is learning by comprehending and analyzing.

According to the Bible, information is in the heart in a metaphorical way, and there we must keep the Word of God. It's full of exhortations to implant its truth in our hearts. King David wrote that a young person can keep their path pure by treasuring God's Word in their heart (Psalm 37:31, 119:9-11). And wise Solomon also referred to this in Proverbs 4:4b: "Take hold of my words with all your heart; keep my commands, and you'll live." or "Let thine heart retain my words: keep my commandments, and live."

The word "retain" comes from the Hebrew term which means "grasp, understand, capture". Memorizing Scripture gives you a firm understanding of God's Word, and allows the Word to captivate you. King Solomon also mentioned writing the Word "...on the tablet of your heart..." (Proverbs 7:3), and having the Scripture written within us so that it's "...ready on your lips." (Proverbs 22:18).

In Proverbs 3:1-2, we're shown King Solomon's advice not to forget the Word. Forgetting things causes us to make many mistakes. If you forget the way to get to a certain place, you'll most likely lose time that you could have used on other things. These verses advise us, then, to keep God's law, his Word, in our hearts because God knows that life flows or proceeds from him (Proverbs 4:23). Your heart is a place that must be kept safe, protected from everything so that you can guarantee the smooth running of your life. If you keep words of hatred or resentment, i.e. negative words in it, the chances are that your actions will be just as negative. But if you keep God's message for your life in your heart, God promises you length of days and peace for your life: Length of days because you'll not waste your time on things that aren't important. That is, you'll not waste your time on activities that God doesn't want you to do, nor will you waste your time on absurd decisions.

Colossians 3:16 motivates us to have God's Word dwell in us. This means that God wants his Word and direction to be present in all areas of our life. May this be the one that guides us and shows us the best way forward, even in the smallest things. Joshua 1:7 shows us that this leader was advised not to stray to either his right or his left from the Word. The right hand symbolizes the times of well-being in your life, but the left hand is the times of anguish or darkness. If you keep the Word of God in your brain, it will help you cope with all the situations in your life. You won't always have a Bible within reach, but if you engrave the message that's in it in your brain, it's sure to come to your aid in any situation you live.

2. Advantages of having the Word of God on your ''hard drive''

If you save your computer information on the hard drive and protect it, you guarantee that your machine works well and you get good results from the information. In the same way, God has promises for those who keep the Word and put it into practice. What are six benefits of keeping the Word, based on these study verses.

The promises that God offers to our lives in these passages are the following:

1. Proverbs 3:1-2: Length of days and peace, that is, more days to live to fulfill God's purpose and which will be days of peace.

2. Proverbs 3:3-4: Grace and good opinion before people and before God. People also notice if you put into practice keeping the Word and doing it. People will admire you and seek your help because you're guided by God. In the same way, God Himself will be proud of you doing it.

3. Joshua 1:7-8: Prosperity in everything you undertake. God speaks to you of good results in everything you do.

4. Colossians 3:16: Helps us help others. If your mind and heart aren't counseled through the Word, you won't have the right words for the needs of others.

3. It's not enough to know or store the Word ... You have to put it into practice.

The idea of saving information on our "hard drive" is to use it when we need it. It makes no sense to fill the memory of the disk with information that won't be useful for our work.

God asks that all the Word that we keep in our brain (heart) be put into action, in other words, that we act according to it. In Colossians 3:17, we're told about the action of doing, of acting. The Word put into practice is what really brings out the promises previously seen. So, if you don't put it into action, it wasn't your "hard drive" that you used, but your RAM memory, that's your mind, and which will become only momentary information.

Review/Application: Have the students list six benefits of keeping the Word, according to the following study verses (the answers are in lesson point 2):

1. Proverbs 3:1-2: *Length of days and peace, that is, more days to live to fulfill God's purpose and which will be days of peace.*

2. Proverbs 3:3-4: *Grace and good opinion before people and before God.*

3. Joshua 1:7-8: *Prosperity in everything you undertake. God speaks to you of good results in everything you do.*

4. Colossians 3:16: *Helps us to help others.*

Challenge: Take the following daily readings and try to memorize a verse from each reading. Next Sunday, we'll discuss how it has been helpful to memorize these verses during the week. Monday: Psalm 119:1-11; Tuesday: Psalm 119:12-22; Wednesday: Psalm 119:27-36; Thursday: Psalm 119:89-94; Friday: Psalm 119:97-105; Saturday: Psalm 119:129-138; Sunday: Psalm 119:151-163.

My Weapon

Objective: That the young people know that salvation is the helmet that protects their head, and the Word of God is the sword that the Holy Spirit gives them.

Memory Verse: *Take the helmet of salvation and the sword of the Spirit, which is the Word of God.* Ephesians 6:17

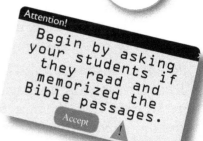

Attention!
Begin by asking your students if they read and memorized the Bible passages.

Accept

Connect | Navigate

Introductory Activity (12 - 17 years).

- Materials: Photos of a soldier ready for battle (can be taken from the internet or from a library book).
- Instructions: Show the students the photos you collected and ask them to share with you what they notice is different in the soldier than they would see in any other person walking in plain clothes.

Today, we'll study about what protects us as children of God.

Introductory Activity (18 - 23 years).

- Materials: Blackboard and chalk, or large paper and pencil.
- Instructions: Ask them to describe how an enemy attacks a soldier in a war (eg handguns, tanks, bombs, etc). Ask them to share the ways in which the enemy attacks God's children (doubts, temptations, painful trials, etc.). Write their responses on the board. Then ask them to tell how they can defend themselves against these attacks.

Connect | Navigate

When a soldier prepares to go into battle, he must ensure that he's going to be as ready as possible to survive the difficult situation he'll face. In general, soldiers prepare themselves physically (to be able to run and escape, to endure injuries, or walk through difficult terrain), they prepare emotionally (to be able to control the emotions of fear and anguish), and finally, they also prepare with weapons that can help them counter the enemy. In today's lesson, we'll study about innovative and infallible weaponry.

In the passage from Luke 4:1-14, we see that the author tells us in incredible detail the experience of Jesus' temptation in the desert. By reading the story, we can understand the tension in the environment and the tough battle between Jesus and the devil.

1. Strength in God's Word

From creation, God leaves a clear mandate on the institution of marriage (Genesis 2:24). This indissoluble unity was the original purpose of God. God didn't have in mind that couples should separate. He wanted them to persevere together. The sexual union made such a significant bond between the couple that they were no longer two but one flesh, reason enough to start a life together, to the point of leaving father and mother. Marriage in the time of Jesus and even before was more than a sentimental matter but a covenant of honor. Men generally married women from known families or relatives. The father who considered himself responsible had the duty to find a suitable husband for his daughter. The marriage wasn't a public celebration like today; there were no signatures on paper, only the word of honor. It was understood that this union would be respected for life.

As young people on the road of life, we cannot ignore or deny that there are many things that can destroy us (alcohol, drugs, tobacco, sex outside of marriage, sexually transmitted diseases, love disappointments, car or firearms accidents, gang involvement, educational and / or employment problems, etc). These situations can cause not only illness or physical death, but can also greatly affect our spiritual and emotional health, causing depression, anxiety or panic attacks, insecurity or low self-esteem, thoughts of suicide or personal harm, etc.

For these reasons, it's also important to know that God, our Creator, provided us with an exceptionally effective weapon to fight against these evils that attack us. This wonderful weapon is the Bible, the very Word of God. We must recognize that from the beginning of history, God used his word to create the entire universe (the one we know and even the part of the universe that we don't know, back in the galaxies). In Genesis 1, we can read about the amazing story of creation and how God used the word to create what we see; that is, his word is so powerful that it can make created things appear from nothing (vs. 3,11).

We see this same power highlighted in Luke 4:4 where we read that the Word gave Jesus the strength to overcome the temptation that the enemy presented. The enemy astutely knew that Jesus had gone forty days without eating, and that as a result he would be very hungry and physically and mentally weak. In those hard times of struggle, Jesus remembered and quoted the Word of God that was in his mind (v. 4). And in that moment, this same Word that Jesus mentioned strengthen him to not do what the devil suggested, but to follow God's will to continue seeking his presence.

We see, then, that the Word of God has the ability to provide us with strength in time of weakness. And this weapon will be at our disposal when faced with exhausting circumstances. We can be completely sure that reading the Bible and memorizing it will give us the ability to go on doing God's will. In our battle, we cannot win if we don't have our weapons ready.

2. Guidance in the Word of God

At other difficult times in our lives, we may face the need to make very decisive decisions. As young people, we must understand that although "the future" seems to be very far from the present, in reality each decision we make now is, from today, determining various situations of the future that we'll live in, whether it be a near or more distant future.

One way to understand this idea is to think of the seeds that are the beginning of any fruit. If you eat an apple, you'll be able to see some black seeds that you don't eat, and that we generally throw in the garbage. They certainly don't seem to be of much use. However, if those little seeds are planted in good dirt and receive fertilizer, water, and sun, in a while, a stem will begin to sprout, then that stem will strengthen and grow in height and thickness. It will produce branches with leaves. And eventually, that seed will end up turning into a big tree that will yield many new apples.

We can compare our life to a garden. The ideas that you drop into the soil of your heart and mind may seem like simple little seeds, but eventually they'll become big decisions like a tree that will be difficult to ignore or remove.

The enemy knows this process very well, and that's why he also attacks our decision-making center (our mind) to achieve the bad results of making us fall into painful and complicated situations. As young people, we have a specialized weapon to help us counterattack this strategy of our enemy. The Word of God is a wonderful weapon to help us make the best decisions. We can be sure that the Bible can help us in every situation we face, and that it will always be the best guide we can find.

The Bible can help you decide how to think and act about drugs, alcohol, and tobacco. The Bible can also guide you on how to proceed in your relationships with your friends and also in dating. It can help you enjoy a happier courtship and marriage than you can imagine.

In the same way, the Word of God can help you know how you can act in terms of violence, your studies, professional career, and / or job development. The Word also helps us fight situations of depression, anxiety, excessive anger, relationship and family problems. Let's read the Bible every day and especially mark those verses that give us advice for our life!!

3. The Truth in God's Word

The enemy wanted to confuse Jesus by reciting to him some Bible passages that apparently allowed Jesus to do what the devil asked him to do (Luke 4:9-11). This was an extremely complicated and difficult situation. How hard it must have been for Jesus, in these moments of weakness from prolonged fasting, to discern these words. Wonderfully, we see how once again the Word of God, memorized and internalized by Jesus, helped him give the final and forceful answer.

In your own lives as young people, you must remember that many times the enemy will use lies to attack you in this battle you face. Some lies that the devil uses repeatedly are the following: "don't worry, nobody will notice if you do it", "you're the owner of your body, you can decide what to do with it", "you aren't hurting anyone", "nobody loves you, you have no hope of being happy", or the most common, "nothing will happen". Have you ever felt that the enemy used any of these lies to bring you down? You don't have to share the answer with anyone, but it's useful to do this self-assessment to know where we should strengthen ourselves.

Thus, soldiers must analyze where the enemy can attack them in order to be prepared by practicing their tactics and preparing their weapons; likewise we must prepare ourselves to be ready when these kinds of lies come to confuse us.

The truth of God's Word is like a powerful flashlight that shines clearly for us to distinguish and discard the lies of the enemy. God's Word is what enables us to emerge victorious from the battle we face, just as Jesus did.

Review/Application:

Ask your students to look in their Bibles for some verses that can help with strength, guidance, or reminding them of a truth. They may ask for help from their classmates or from you.

ATTACK SITUATION	BIBLICAL WEAPON
Doubts about my future: calling, profession or dating/marriage and family	Jeremiah 29:11
Conflict with my parents	Exodus 20:12, Proverbs 23:22, Ephesians 6:1-3
Doubts about what to study in college	Psalms 25:9; 32:8
Addiction situations	Psalm 40, Ephesians 4:22-24, Proverbs 23:29-35
Feelings of anxiety, fear, or nervousness	Philippians 4:6-7, Psalm 27, Hebrews 13:5-6
Feelings of depression	Psalms 16 and 130, Ephesians 3:14-21

Challenge: I encourage you to take refuge, as never before, in the Word of God. It's your best weapon, and if you read it, study it and memorize it, you can be sure that the enemy won't be able to defeat you. Many adults who were previously youth your age can tell you about how God helped them in their youth through His Word. This week, find someone who wants to share with you their testimonies of how the Bible has been their weapon in overcoming a difficult situation.

Thank You, Grandparents!

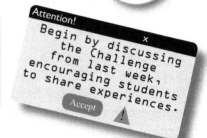

Objective: That students will value the role of grandparents within the family and their relationships with their grandchildren.

Memory Verse: *"Then Israel said, 'Bring them to me so I may bless them.'"* Genesis 48:9b

---

Connect | **Navigate**

Introductory Activity (12 - 17 years).
- Materials: Photos of older people (these can be hand-drawn drawings, magazine clippings, or photos from the Internet).
- Instructions: Ask your students to express what they think when they see the photos you show them. Ask them how they imagine themselves when they are elderly, and what they would like to do during that time of their lives. Then help them consider how God has designed this stage of life for his children.

Introductory Activity (18 - 23 years).
- Materials: Blackboard and chalk, or large paper and marker.
- Instructions: On the board, draw a vertical line dividing it into two equal sides. On one side, write the title "Disadvantages of old age"; and on the other, "Advantages of old age". Then ask them to reflect on both the positive and negative characteristics of being elderly. If they have difficulty expressing their ideas, suggest that they think of a grandparent or older person in the church.

Connect | **Navigate**

In recent years, children and youth have enjoyed receiving great attention and appreciation from society, including from the fields of politics, psychology, and medicine. This renewal includes the development of children's rights and specialization in health treatment for them. However, this change has also caused a certain devaluation of the elderly in our society, compared to ancient times when old age was considered with special respect and admiration. In today's lesson, we'll reflect on God's perspective of older people (Genesis 28:13, 32:9, 48:8-10, 15-16).

Senior adulthood is the time of life in which people have already experienced childhood and adulthood, and are in the final stage of their lives. According to different psychologists, senior adulthood begins around 65 years of age. At this stage of life, many elderly people stop formal working, and don't feel that they're an active part of society. Others may suffer from health problems, financial hardship, separation from their family, etc. which may result in loneliness or sadness. In the passages that we'll study today, we'll see that the Bible clearly teaches us about the important role that senior adults play in family and social life. And we'll also see what our role should be in the lives of the older people around us.

1. The Nature of Grandparents

In the passage of Genesis 48:8-10, we enter a very special scene: it's the part of the story in which Jacob had just found himself, after many years, with his son Joseph and with the children that Joseph had in Egypt: Ephraim and Manasseh. Over time, Jacob had become a grandfather.

We see in verse 10 of this chapter that "... Israel's (the name God gave Jacob) eyes were failing because of old age, and he could hardly see. So Joseph brought his sons close to him, and his father kissed them and embraced them." It's undeniable that the nature of old age includes certain difficulties. First, we see that old age changes a person's physical abilities. In Jacob's case, it was that his sight disappeared. In others, health and physical strength decline and cause various difficulties. There are older people who suffer from walking problems, body aches, sleeping or grooming problems, internal illnesses, etc.

Similarly, old age can affect how a person feels about himself. By not having a strong body like that of youth, an elderly person may experience sadness, fear and insecurity since they have to depend on others for many activities that they used to do alone. In old age, for lack of strength of the body, the person usually reaches a stage of retirement from formal work, and this brings with it a decrease in income. In this situation, the person may feel sad when they have financial need, fear when thinking about the future, insecurity when having to depend on others to cope with responsibilities, and finally, guilt when feeling "like a burden" to others.

In another aspect, we also see that older people often have a desire to share their time and affection with their family and friends. So, we see that Jacob was very affectionate with his grandchildren and kissed and hugged them. Being emotionally and physically connected is an important need of senior citizens.

By knowing the changes mentioned above, we can better understand the grandparents that God has placed in our lives, and avoid falling into the error of criticizing, mistreating or being inconsiderate to them. Rather, just as we see that Jacob's family helped him, we too should support our grandparents in their burdens and encourage them in their difficulties.

2. Honoring our Grandparents

In verses 12 and 13 of the same passage (Genesis 48), we see another wonderful scene from this family story in which Joseph shows special respect for his father who was already very old. The Bible says that "Joseph... bowed down" and introduced him to his children, that is, to Jacob's grandchildren. Bowing down or kneeling in front of a person is a sign of great respect for that person and an acknowledgment that that person has higher status than the person kneeling. This form of showing submission is widely used when a subject presents himself before his king. In this scene, we see that Joseph, being the highest ruler of Egypt besides Pharaoh, showed his father Jacob that he respected, admired, and recognized the honor that Jacob had as a father. Joseph's attitude is in opposite contrast to the attitude that younger people sometimes show to older people today.

Today, modern society has adopted a pervasive attitude of quickness, immediate gratification, and self-centeredness. These are ways of thinking that radically clash with the attitude that the Bible teaches us of peace, self-control and agape love. These attitudes present even greater difficulty for a young person when trying to relate to an elderly person who sometimes must move slowly, who needs the young person's patience and attention. As young Christians we must self-assess our personal attitudes toward people who are weaker, slower, and more in need than we are. If we find our attitude to be one of impatience, criticism, or mistreatment, we must ask God to change it with his supernatural power.

In the Bible, we see that older people, including Jacob in the aforementioned chapter, have a place of honor. In the dictionary, the word honor is defined as: a demonstration of appreciation made to a person by recognizing their virtue and merit; good opinion and fame; and esteem and respect for one's dignity. It's necessary to work intentionally so that our attitude towards our grandparents and other older people is a true demonstration of appreciation, genuine esteem, and respect for being the parents of those who gave us physical life.

We must recognize that this way of being won't always be easy, but the more we depend on God's help and the more we work to have an attitude of respect for our grandparents, the more we can do it! We can begin today thinking of practical ways to honor the older people in our lives, whether that's by obeying their wishes, spending quality time with them (including paying attention to them), doing something of their choosing with them, helping them in their lives with things such as home cleaning, garden cleaning or with their physical or financial needs.

Through this passage, God teaches us about the place of value and honor that older people should have in and outside a family.

3. The Instruction of Grandparents

Jacob spoke up and instructed his grandchildren about Jehovah and his works (Genesis 48:15-16). It's moving to see Jacob's teachings about the faithfulness and great protective power of God, just as we can see the honor and esteem that Jacob himself had for his previous generations by remembering them. In the final sentence, we see that Jacob blessed his grandchildren, asking God to give them a prosperous and happy future.

In the story of this biblical passage, we can see that grandparents, because of the great experience they have in life, are a wonderful source of instruction for those younger. Throughout the journey of life, the situations that a person faces make that person mature and have a unique knowledge of things. In our modern society, pride leads many youth to mistakenly think that the elderly "no longer have much to offer to others"; however, there's nothing further from the truth. The truth is that the elderly can be of great help to young and inexperienced people, since their advice can help them avoid an infinite number of problems, solve difficult situations, and bear certain burdens with responsibility and acceptance.

The key to success in experiencing the blessing of an older person's advice is to receive instruction with an open and humble attitude. It's necessary to spend time with the person and listen carefully to the stories and advice that that person can give us. God is very good and loving toward all his creatures, no matter what stage of development they're in. In the same way, God calls us to love our neighbor as ourselves (James 2:8), and of course, our neighbors are also our grandparents. Let's not miss out on the great blessings that God has for us through the teachings of our grandparents!

Review / Application: Ask your students to describe some ways they can put today's lesson into practice.

Ways to Give Honor	Ways to Learn
Don't talk critically about my grandparents to other people.	Spend time with my grandparents, learning from them how to do things.
Address my grandparents with respectful names and words.	Listen carefully and respectfully when they give me advice.
Etc.	Etc.

Challenge: Do you have an elderly person who is part of your life? I encourage you to make the effort this week to spend some special time with your grandfather or grandmother. If they live a long way away, call them or video chat with them for awhile. If they are no longer alive, invite a senior adult in your congregation to join you and a friend for coffee or visit them at their home.

Honor Your Mom

Attention!
Remember to ask your students if they visited an older person or their grandparents during the week and let them share how it went.
Accept

Objective: That students will value the role that mothers play in families.

Memory Verse: *"No discipline seems pleasant at the time, but painful. Later on, however, it produces a harvest of righteousness and peace for those who have been trained by it."* Hebrews 12:11

Connect | Navigate

Introductory Activity (12 - 17 years).

- Materials: Sheets of paper and pencils.

- Instructions: Ask your students to write down the word they use when they talk to their mother ("mom", " mommy, "mother", "boss", "lady", their name, etc.) and then make an acrostic with the word they use, using words that describe their mom.

- As you conclude, remind your students that in this life most of us will only have one mother, and that if she is alive, we should honor her now, and not wait until it's too late.

Introductory Activity (18 - 23 years).

- Materials: Sheets of paper and pencils.

- Instructions: Ask each student to write the name of a mother found in the Bible (Hagar - Ishmael's mother; Jochebed - Moses' mother; Naomi - Ruth's mother-in-law; Mary - Jesus' mother; Elizabeth - mother of John the Baptist, Eunice - Timothy's mother, etc.) and what her life has taught them.

- As you conclude, remind your students that the Bible gives us many examples of women who not only chose to become mothers, but who performed their role as mother with excellence.

Connect | Navigate

In many parts of the world, the issue of abortion has been on the table for public policy discussion. The parties of the left, especially, have proposed that "it is women who should decide to become mothers or not," because only they have the right to their body and to what they carry within it.

Of course this is anti-Christian! But, in addition to that, it's interesting to see that many women, despite the fact that in numerous countries the decriminalization of abortion has already been approved and unborn children are simply considered a nuisance, continue to decide to be mothers.

And thanks to that free decision to be mothers, many of us are here.

1. Let's Value Mothers More

Before we open the Bible, let's remember a few things women who decide to be moms go through:

- They are the ones that God has allowed to produce the "home" in which the embryo will grow into a human being.

- They must deal with cravings, dizziness, nausea and even pain that they were not used to. These will last almost from conception and for nine months.

- It is they who must take care of themselves at all times with physical exercise, nutritious diet, and sufficient sleep.

- Pregnancy can cause illness (for them and their babies) and even the death of the baby.

- They cannot eat just any food (doctors recommend that their daily food should include more vegetables) or self-medicate, since that can cause problems for the baby, and even death.
- The tone of their skin, their weight, their hair and even the smell that pregnant women expel radically changes (many of them even stop being exactly who they were after giving birth).
- They suffer labor pains ... To give us an idea, the biggest pain that men and women who aren't mothers can have is a toothache. But labor pains are three hundred times greater than that!
- They are the ones who have to give the baby their first care and food (like breast milk, suffering when the baby has to nurse to eat).

Think of your mom: Many of us live better lives than our mothers did when they were kids because they want to give us what they didn't have.

2. Honor Your Mother

When God gave Moses the 10 commandments, he included one that has promise; it's the first commandment with the promise to live many years on earth: "Honor your father AND YOUR MOTHER..." (Exodus 20:12, emphasis added).

It's interesting that on that date (1500-1400 BC), both parents were recognized in the law of God's people. The commandment doesn't say: "Honor your parents", but expressly states that they should honor both the male father and the female mother. This tells us that honoring our parents isn't simple, but specific, since as many people have seen, some children love their father very much (and they show it whenever they can), but not their mother, or vice versa.

So it's a matter of loving Dad and loving Mom; to always obey and honor them.

Do you remember the data we read at the beginning? It would be nice to honor mom! And even more when the Bible itself is demanding it.

The word that's translated as "honor" has at least two meanings:

A. It means to speak well of a person.

The Bible is telling us that it's our duty to speak well of our mother. It's true, she had to educate us and sometimes she wasn't the best at doing it, but our duty is to speak well of her. She may not have an academic education or big university degrees, but it's not our job to judge her, but to speak well of her.

B. It means speaking politely.

The Bible tells us with this verb ("honor") that it's not enough to speak well of her, but to speak to her with all of the respect possible.

Isn't it common that when she calls for our attention, or asks us to do something, we respond rudely? Watch out! We're attacking the Word of God.

Don't you think it's a double standard when we speak nice to a friend, but we don't do so with one of the people who loves us the most?

3. We Will Live Long Lives

Carl listens to his mom's instruction, but only does what he thinks is best. Mary does what her mom asks her to do, but only halfway and is angry because it's not what she likes to do. Carla does what her mom requests, but she expresses her disagreement every time she can. Robbie is always complaining to his friends because only he does chores at home. These and other examples indicate that we're generally not honoring our Mom.

In Ephesians 6:2-3, God gave a promise for children who honor their parents: "...so that it may go well with you and that you may enjoy long life on the earth.", and that's an echo of what the commandment God gave Moses says.

The Israelites were in the desert and were going to enter, at some point (according to God's promise), a rich and beautiful land. God was preparing them for when they would take possession of that land. In that new land, they were going to make their own government, have laws, build new forms of coexistence, etc. Therefore, they had to start living according to the will of God. And what better way to start living in harmony than by obeying at home!

God's will for your lives as young people is that you learn to respect the authorities, and you'll do so if you begin to respect and honor your mother. And you'll live many more years because your name will continue as a good memory among the people who knew you.

Many times we question our Mom before obeying her instructions, and sometimes we think the rules at home are unfair, but God's Word tells us that obeying is right. The obedience of children is one of the things parents want most. The mother seeks the best welfare of her family, striving to care for family members, especially children. She's aware of the activities of her children, their friends, school, their health, etc., and generally provides affection and attention to her children. Her desire is the well-being of her family and she looks for ways to provide it. Many adult children complain of having been treated unfairly, saying: "my sibling was her favorite child", "she spanked me for nothing", "she didn't love me" and many others. Maybe some of us have this view of our relationship with our mother and aren't convinced about obeying her. We need to ... it's God's will.

Cheer up! If we fulfill God's mandate, our life will be enduring, and our name will be remembered for many generations.

Review/Application: Ask your students to answer the following questions:

Based on today's class, what are the two meanings of "honor"?

1. _____

2. _____

If you are honoring your mom, congratulations! God will reward you.

But if you're failing in either of the two ways to honor her, how will you honor your mom starting today?

1. _____

2. _____

Brainstorm with your classmates ideas of how you can honor your mom.

Write down and Memorize Exodus 20:12 that urges us to honor our mothers, no matter who she is.

("Honor your father and your mother,
so that you may live long in the land the Lord your God is giving you".)

Challenge: Let's read Hebrews 12:11 and think about it. Let's examine our lives and recognize our failings before God, for it's Him that we must obey first.

This Is My Son!

Vivian Juárez • Guatemala

Start by asking how the Challenge from last week went.

Objective: That students know what God expects of them in their role in the family relationship.

Memory Verse: *"Children, obey your parents in everything, for this pleases the Lord."* Colossians 3:20

Connect | Navigate

Introductory Activity (12 - 17 years).

- Materials: White sheets of paper cut in half; pencils and adhesive wall tape.
- Instructions: Give paper and a pencil to each student. Then, ask them to write on their paper their answers to the following question: What does God expect of me regarding my role as a child in my family? Tell them that they can answer according to their opinion or according to the Bible if they know verses that speak to the topic. At the end, invite them to share their answers with the rest of the class and encourage them to talk about it for a moment. Then start the lesson.

Introductory Activity (18 - 23 years).

- Materials: White sheets of paper cut in half and pencils.
- Instructions: Give paper and a pencil to each student. Then ask them to write a definition of the word "child" in three to five lines. Next, choose five students to read what they wrote, and then brainstorm with all of your students to come up with a single definition for the word "child".

  Keep in mind that young people have a different concept than their parents do because of their maturity. Therefore, it's important that they be identified as children.

Connect | Navigate

Begin by asking the students to express what words they would like their parents to use to describe them to a stranger. (Here it's very likely that your students will express that they expect their parents to use words of admiration, affection or recognition). Then we suggest that you use those responses throughout the lesson so that they'll recognize that in order to receive those words they want from their parents, there are certain actions that they must take!

1. General Features

The book of Proverbs is without a doubt one of the best manuals a person can use to learn how to be a good son or daughter. With all the wisdom Solomon received from God, he was able to put together a series of advice and instructions that anyone could follow, not only to be a good son or daughter, but also to live each day wisely.

In Mark 1:11, you'll find the best recognition a father can give his child. Jesus had obeyed and honored his Father in everything, and God, like a proud father, wanted everyone to know that He loved His Son and was pleased with Him.

Perhaps the most taught responsibility regarding the role of a child is to be obedient to their parents. This duty, in addition to being a mandate from God, promises to bring much blessing to the child who fulfills it. But obeying isn't easy, especially during the time of adolescence when we seek to define our own identity and achieve a certain degree of independence.

It may be that for some of you, this aspect of the Christian life is creating many conflicts for you, especially if your parents haven't shown interest in knowing you, understanding you, and showing you their unconditional love.

2. The Best Example

Ask your students to define the word "obedience." When we read the Bible, we can find several verses that invite us to obey God, parents and authorities. When the Bible speaks of obeying, it leaves no room for considerations on the part of the person who obeys, that is, the command is clear. Obeying means giving up one's will to do someone else's will. This, due to human nature, can be a complicated matter, a difficult mandate to fulfill; but certainly not impossible. God in his love and mercy allowed Jesus, his Son, to give humanity the best example of obedience and honor towards parents.

For Jesus to obey wasn't a simple matter (Luke 22:42). Like every human being, He had to face the dilemma of choosing between doing what He wanted, and doing His Father's will. But Jesus chose obedience, and his Father couldn't have been more proud (Philippians 2: 9). Seeing obedience in our Lord Jesus, who is our role model, can help us understand the concept more clearly.

Obeying, especially in situations we don't understand, can be difficult. But Jesus showed us that this is possible. He is our best example, our role model.

3. Pleasing God through our obedience

Ask your students to make a list of where they have trouble obeying. Obedience, understood simply as a command, can increase the dislike of complying with it. In this regard, consider that your students may be facing situations in their family life where it's difficult for them to understand why they have to obey their parents. So teaching them that they should do it, because it's a command from God and nothing else, can make the problem worse.

Obedience to parents, beyond being a responsibility that each child has, brings with it a great blessing; since it's not only getting parents to see that they are respected (although this is important), but it's also knowing that our obedience to them pleases God (Colossians 3:20).

Whatever the living conditions of your students, they'll be shocked to know that with their obedience, they aren't only "looking good" to their parents; They're also building a better relationship with God because their heavenly Father will always be pleased with their obedience.

4. Being a blessing to our parents

Ask your students to write down four things they can do to make their parents proud of them. There is nothing better in the world than knowing that we're at the center of God's will, that what we do pleases Him and that He is happy with our behavior.

As Christians, we're called to be light and reflect Christ in all our ways of living. This point is very important, especially if you live in a non-Christian home. Your testimony as obedient children can impact the lives of your parents.

There's no better gift for a parent than to be proud of what their child does. Jesus left us an example of this because his Father was pleased with him (Luke 3:22). By obeying and honoring our parents, we aren't just fulfilling a command and pleasing the Lord; we are also being a blessing to our parents.

When seeing the obedience of their children, parents will be able to express with pride: "That is my son!" or "That is my daughter!" Also, if our parents aren't Christians, we can be the light that reflects Christ in our homes and helps our parents and / or the rest of our family members come to Christ.

At the end of class, they can say a prayer of commitment to God in which they express their desire to be better children and give testimony of their Christian life through their exemplary behavior at home. We suggest that you allow time for your students to pray individually. Then close with a prayer.

Review/Application: In Colossians 3:20, the Bible asks us to obey our parents in everything. Ask your students to:

- Make a list of the times or situations when it's most difficult for you to obey your parents.
- Write down four things you can do that will make your parents proud of your behavior.
- Write out Luke 3:22. ("... you're my Son, whom I love; with you I am well pleased".)

Challenge: You may have to face times when obeying won't be pleasant for you. During those times, remember the following:

- For Jesus, obeying wasn't easy, but his example will give you the strength to obey even under difficult circumstances.
- Obedience isn't only a commandment, but also a means of pleasing God.
- Your obedience is a blessing to your parents and a way to show that Christ lives in you.

Extreme Loyalty!

María de Carmen Rendón • Mexico

Objective: That students are convinced that God designed monogamy for the marriage relationship and Jesus reaffirmed it.

Memory Verse: *"So they are no longer two, but one flesh. Therefore what God has joined together, let no one separate."* Matthew 19:6

Attention!

Begin by starting a discussion about obedience and how it was applied during the week.

Accept

Connect / Navigate

Introductory Activity (12 - 17 years).

• Instructions: Share the following scenario: "Imagine that a friend agrees to go with you on Saturday to walk around the shopping center. But later, she tells you that she's not going to be able to go with you because her parents don't allow it. You decide to go anyway with your parents, and while your there, you see your friend with other friends".

After presenting the above scenario, ask the class the following: "How do you think you would feel if this happened to you? What would you do and what would you say? What would you call this action of your friend?" Allow your students to share their answers for a few minutes and then start the lesson.

Introductory Activity (18 - 23 years).

• Instructions: Divide your class into two teams. Then indicate to one of them that you're in favor of monogamy; while the other will be against it. Also, tell them that each team should present three arguments to support its position. Allow a few minutes, according to the time you have, for the members of each team to discuss and agree. In turn, each team will present their arguments. Then encourage discussion for five minutes and then begin the lesson.

Connect / Navigate

God made human beings, male and female, in his image and likeness (Genesis 1:27), and blessed them and made them stewards of his creation (Genesis 1:28). The Bible indicates that God evaluated his creative work as "very good" (Genesis 1:31). In chapter 2 of Genesis, the creation of man and God's decision to make him one wife to be with him forever are narrated.

However, this purpose of God was spoiled by the entry of sin into the world, and from then on, society and culture have taken it upon themselves to make people believe that it's okay to have more than one wife or husband, or to be unfaithful to one's wife or husband.

Dictionary.com defines monogamy as: "marriage with only one person at a time."

An investigation carried out by the UNAM (Autonomous University of Mexico) concludes that infidelity is on the increase, since "15 percent of women and 25 percent of men have had extra relationships at some time in their lives with people who aren't their spouse. And if only emotional infidelities are counted, that is, that didn't involve sex, the numbers rise to 35 percent in the case of women and 45 for men" (Infidelity is on the rise ... reveals research from the UNAM. Appeared in February 2012 and retrieved from http://www.jornada.unam.mx/2012/02/14/sociedad/039n1soc on January 13, 2014).

God knows what is good for people, and for that reason instituted monogamous marriage, and the Lord Jesus confirmed it (Matthew 19:4-6).

1. The best project for humanity

The institution of monogamous marriage arose from the mind and heart of God when he saw that the man he created needed a partner so that together they could manage his creation (Genesis 1:28-30). In Genesis 2:22-24, it's clearly indicated that man recognized woman as the only one among all the creatures formed by God who was of the same essence as him. For this reason, they together would form the unit that would carry out God's plans.

The declaration of God in the beginning (Genesis 2:24), and of the Lord Jesus later (Matthew 19:5-6), that man and woman were one flesh implies that marriage is meant to be monogamous. That is, the marriage union should be exclusive to two people of different sexes, where there is no possibility that another woman or man would be part of that marriage union or interrupts that union.

On the other hand, most people think that monogamy is solely and exclusively about sexual fidelity. This isn't so, since monogamy includes observing Christian values such as exclusivity, fidelity, commitment, respect, and honesty. These values constitute the "key element for monogamy, which means a dynamic surrender to a personal relationship and which also implies respect and consideration" (Sexology for Christians; Smedes Lewis. Caribe, Miami: 1982, p. 189). These values are taught and strengthened within a family where both the husband and the wife practice them on a daily basis for each other and for the whole family.

On the contrary, lies and tricks are the foundation of infidelity, and these are learned both in the family and through the media that present them as something natural or normal (infidelity, dishonesty and disrespect for the marriage bond).

These anti-values are bad because of their painful consequences, and because they hurt the person directly affected (the one to whom they are unfaithful) and also those around them (children, relatives, friends). But above all those, anti-values are harmful because they break the unity that God expects between husband and wife.

2. Jesus confirmed monogamy

A. United forever?

In the New Testament, Jesus Christ interpreted God's desire for man and woman in the marriage relationship to become one flesh so that no one could separate it without damaging it, without ending its existence as a marriage and without harming loved ones (Matthew 19:1-11).

In the passage just mentioned, the Pharisees are shown testing Jesus. Due to the great hostility they felt towards him, they wanted to find some theological error in him to discredit him and make him look like someone who contradicted the law of Moses. Therefore, they asked him if the man is allowed to divorce his wife for any reason. But Jesus didn't contend with them and limited himself to quoting the passage from Genesis 2:24 adding: "Therefore what God has joined together, let no one separate." And at the insistence of the Pharisees in this regard , the Lord concluded: "Moses permitted you to divorce your wives because your hearts were hard. But it wasn't this way from the beginning." (Matthew 19:8)

B. A hard heart

In the Old Testament, we see that monogamy was no longer a common general practice very early in human history. Among them, we can mention Lamech (Genesis 4:19), a descendant of Cain, who took two women for himself. From then on, sin continued to harden the hearts of humanity. Thus, we see many important men who had more than one wife: Abraham (Genesis 16:1-4); Esau (Genesis 26:34-35, 28:9); Jacob (Genesis 29:15-28, 30:1-13); Gideon (Judges 8:30); David (2 Samuel 3:2-5, 12:8, 15:16); and Solomon (1 Kings 11:1-3).

Men preferred to follow their personal desires rather than obey God (Leviticus 20:10-21; Deuteronomy 22:22-29), who also spoke to them through the prophets, letting them know that He condemns disloyalty, because it goes against his original plan: monogamy (Jeremiah 3:1; Micah 2:9; Malachi 2:14-16).

3. An example of fidelity

God feeds the birds and gives clothes to the flowers, are you not worth much more than they? (Matthew 6:26). We shouldn't be anxious about those things that God has promised to supply. Worry can damage our physical and mental health, affect the way we relate to others, and diminish our ability to trust God.

Planning and anxiety aren't the same. We too must do our part, provide for our future, but completely grounded in the truth that God cares for us. He must occupy our heart and he must be the one on whom we must have our vision, He is the Lord who has promised to take care of me. Worry is an expression of unbelief in the promise that God will add all that He already knows we need.

4. Monogamy based on trust and faith in God

Monogamy is the expression of faith that since God calls for a faithful and monogamous life, he will also accompany the fulfillment of the vows made by the spouses before God and the community of faith. Monogamy is believing that God will be with the marriage so that the couple grows together. Make your marriage relationship stronger and stronger, so that you can resist when you're tempted by external factors to consider the possibility of being unfaithful, He helps you to be loyal to the marriage vows. Without a doubt, monogamy is a challenge, not only to maintain sexual fidelity, but also to be loyal and responsible in doing everything possible to contribute to the development of the spouse, and a commitment to make honesty and exclusivity permanent values in the marriage relationship.

When it's time to get married, we propose that these values be part of our lives. In the marital relationship, people make a commitment, and if we fulfill it, we not only feel satisfied, but we'll develop as people and enjoy well-being, harmony and happiness.

In all interpersonal relationships, people make certain commitments. And if we fulfill them, we not only feel satisfied, but we grow as people.

Review/Application: Divide the class into four groups; and if they are few, in pairs. Assign each group three questions to answer. Then take time to have them share their answers with the rest of the class.

- How would you define fidelity? In what relationships should it be practiced?
- Is fidelity important?
- What is exclusivity in a relationship with a partner?
- How could one person show another that they have a unique place in their life?
- How can you show respect in a relationship?
- What happens when there is no respect between the couple?
- How would you define commitment?
- How did you feel when you kept a commitment?
- How did you feel when you failed to keep a commitment?
- What do you think of a person who isn't honest?
- How do you get to be honest?
- What difficulties are there in being honest?

Challenge: Choose one of the five values that support monogamy and decide to practice it consciously this week. Next Sunday, explain to your group how the implementation of this value went. Also, create a newspaper mural that displays the values that support monogamy. Then post it in a visible place in the church so that the faithful can see it.

Family Unity

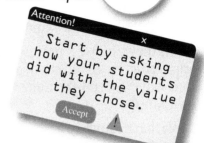

Attention! x
Start by asking how your students did with the value they chose.

Accept

Objective: That the young people will discover how they should behave in contributing to the unity of the family.

Memory Verse: *"Make every effort to keep the unity of the Spirit through the bond of peace"* Ephesians 4:3

Connect | Navigate

Introductory Activity (12 - 17 years).

• Materials: Paper (it can be scrap paper that's written or printed on) to be used to make boats or airplanes.

• Instructions: Place the sheets of paper on a table and ask each person to assemble as many paper boats or airplanes as possible in one minute. At the end of the time, acknowledge the winner. Then form groups of three or four and give the same instructions. Remember to recognize the group that won.

Once the activity is over, guide your students in reflecting on the activity by asking the following questions: Was there any form of organization? When did you make more boats or planes: alone or when you were in a group?

Then let your students know that, just like in a family, when we work together, we'll have better results. If the members of a family seek their own well-being and not that of others, or if they try to do what is easiest for them, the only thing they'll achieve is the destruction of the family.

Introductory Activity (18 - 23 years).

• Materials: Several spools of thread (it can be thread for sewing).

• Instructions: Divide your students into pairs and ask them to tie their wrists together with one strand of thread. Then instruct them to break free. Now instruct them to do it again, but this time use two strands of thread; and then have them try to break free again. Repeat the activity adding one more strand of thread each time until they cannot break the thread.

After finishing the activity, ask your students what they think about the activity. Then lead them to think about the family and how this applies.

Connect | Navigate

1. The importance of the family

Young people must bear in mind at all times the importance that God gives to the family so that they can value it. Today's society is taking away the value and relevance that it has. Family times are replaced by other activities, and young people, wanting to be up to date with society, allow themselves to be infected by these ideas and follows them.

To clarify this issue, ask students for examples of activities that replace family time. These can be the following: Being connected to the Internet; playing with the PlayStation; chat on iPhone, etc.

Then mention that you'll see what the Bible says about the family. In this part of the lesson, we suggest that you form groups to look up the Bible verses listed below and explain what they say about the family. Assign one verse per group (Genesis 1:28, 2:24; Deuteronomy 6:7; Matthew 1:24-25).

In Genesis 2:24, 1:28 we see that God establishes and blesses marriage. Therefore, marriage, which is where the family is born, wasn't a human invention, but was God's creation.

Deuteronomy 6:7 tells us that God knew the great influence that the family has on people and that society or people are formed in families. Therefore, he urged that in each house his law be repeated and learned, because he wanted a people who would recognize, love and worship him.

Matthew 1:24-25 points out that Jesus himself was born into a family already formed, rather than appearing on earth in surprising ways. So, it's valid to ask ourselves the following: Why did he do it that way? ... And the answer is because God recognizes how important it is for each person to be part of a family.

We have quickly seen the place that God gives to the family. He knows that family is the most important influence in our formation. However, when the young person enters adolescence, they often completely despise their family, preferring to be with others, even reaching the point of disrespecting their parents. Many become so rebellious that parents no longer have control over them, and this affects them so much that even their parents become depressed because of this problem.

This attitude shows that the young person isn't giving their family the place it deserves. And this is because they aren't submitting to the will of God.

2. Submit to God

When one enters the stage of youth, that's when it's most important to grasp the hand of God. Only in this way will it be possible to cope with these changes that produce reactions or attitudes that endanger the unity of the family.

If the young person submits to God's will, it will be easier for them to behave in a way that helps maintain harmony and peace within the home (Philippians 2:13). The young person who seeks God will have God's help to avoid being carried away by those rebellious and angry desires that occur in adolescence and bring division and disputes into the home. Only God gives us that self-control that we need so much (Galatians 5:23; 2 Timothy 1:7).

The young person usually thinks only themselves, without taking into account the concerns of their relatives. This is because they're often selfish, and that's the evidence of the lack of God in their life. By consecrating themself to God, the young person allows Him to work in their life through his Holy Spirit, thus achieving freedom from selfishness and caring more for others.

And how do we submit to God? Simply by seeking him daily in prayer and studying his Word. This is the only way we can be closer to our Lord. The youth who studies the Word of God acquires greater knowledge about the will of their Lord and this gives them greater responsibility and desire to put it into practice.

One of the great commandments is found in Matthew 22:37. Once the young person internalizes this commandment and puts it into action in their life, everything that God asks them to do will be much easier to fulfill. And among all the things that God demands of us is the duty we have as children to submit to our parents.

3. Submit to Parents

Ephesians 6:1-3 explains very well what the role of the child is within the home. And this is where the young person has many struggles, because due to their eagerness to want to do everything in their own way and feel free, they tend to break this commandment, rebelling against their parents.

In each family, there are usually rules, and all members of each family have to follow them in order to live in harmony. By following this commandment found in Ephesians 6, you're not only bringing unity and peace to the home, but you're also bringing blessing into your life. Verse 3 says: "...so that it may go well with you and that you may enjoy long life on the earth." God promises to bless children who fulfill this commandment. Obedience is the best gift that can be given to God and parents. Therefore, if the young person wants to help their family be united, they must be obedient and respect the authority that God has left with their parents.

Another way to contribute to this family unity is to pray for it. It's very important that we pray for siblings, parents, grandparents, etc. James 5:16 teaches that we should pray for each other. When we do, we're putting selfishness aside, and this pleases God. By praying for our family, we're showing God that we care about them, that we love them, and that we truly care. Furthermore, the second great commandment found in Matthew 22:39 says: "... Love your neighbor as yourself." That is why we must treat our family members with love, as if it were ourselves. Also Matthew 7:12 says that we should do unto others as we would like them to do to us.

If the Lord Jesus, being the God himself, was under the authority of his earthly parents, how much more should we, mere human beings, do the same!

In the Bible, we also find examples of families that were kept together thanks to the correct attitude of one of their members; However, we also find families that were divided by envy, selfishness or unforgiveness.

In this part of the lesson, ask the young people to look up the following scriptures and identify who did and who didn't seek unity in their family.

Exodus 2:1-9: Moses' sister did her best to keep her family together. When the princess of Egypt ordered her to bring a nurse for the child, she didn't hesitate to call her mother to take care of her own baby.

Genesis 7:7: Noah's sons didn't complain or protest about not staying in the place where they were born. They simply obeyed their father Noah and left everything. Their obedience helped maintain harmony and unity in the family.

Genesis 4:1-11: Cain wasn't a good example of a son/brother who sought unity in his family; on the contrary, he divided it by killing his brother.

Genesis 37:13-28: Joseph's brothers were carried away by envy and thus brought sadness and division to their family.

Finally, we must not forget that forgiveness is what will most help us to live in unity with the family. Regardless of the family that has raised and influenced us, we should never hold resentment against any of our relatives. Let's remember that Christ forgave us. Resentment only brings pain. Let's always seek unity in our home.

Review/Application: Allow time for your students to answer the following questions:

1. What do Genesis 1:28 and 2:24 tell us about the family?

2. How can I contribute to the unity of my family?

3. What does Ephesians 6:1-3 tell us about the family? (God gives the promise that if the children submit to their parents, everything will go well for them and they'll have a long life on Earth.)

4. What two great commandments are there in Matthew 22:37-39?

5. According to James 5:16, how else can we contribute to family unity? (Praying for our family members.)

Challenge: What has been your attitude towards your family so far? Do you think that you have done all you could to maintain bonds of love and oneness within it, or are you just being carried away by your selfish desires? I encourage you to seek God so that with his help, you can be part of this list of people who have contributed to the unity of their family with a correct attitude.

What Parents!

Objective: That young people value the role that parents play in the family.

Memory Verse: *"The righteous lead blameless lives; blessed are their children after them."* Proverbs 20:7

Connect | Navigate

Introductory Activity (12 - 17 years).

- Materials: Blackboard and chalk or equivalent.

- Instructions: Ask your students to come to the board and write a description of their ideal parent. Then ask (not waiting for a public response, just for their own reflection) if their parents live up to those ideals.

Introductory Activity (18 - 23 years).

- Materials: Pencils and blank paper.

- Instructions: Ask your students to divide the paper into two and on one side write the ideal relationship that should exist between parents and children, and on the other side make a list of threats to the harmony of the family. Then, just for their own reflection, ask what their relationship is like in their home and if the threats are destroying their home and therefore destroying the church of Christ.

Connect | Navigate

The Word of God tells us: "Children, obey your parents in the Lord ..." (Ephesians 6:1-4). And to us readers of the Bible in this century, it seems like a radical issue: Obey? Why do we have to obey?

But let's look at the context when Paul wrote this. The first Christians lived under the Roman Empire; what was customary in Rome was that the father had absolute power over all his children. He had the right to punish them as his anger allowed, without anyone being able to do anything to prevent it. The children were simply other pieces of his property. The father could sell his children as slaves if he believed that they were too expensive, or not worth it for him, or under certain conditions, he could even take their lives. This power of the father over his children lasted a lifetime. The child's life was worth little, as a letter dated 1 BC, written by a Roman soldier named Hilary, from Alexandria, Egypt, to his wife Alis reveals. In the letter he ordered her that if she gave birth to a boy, to let him live, but if it was a girl, to get rid of her.

Abandoning children to provide for themselves was customary in those days.

1. The Value the Word of God gives us

What Paul did was to dignify the place of children in the homes of the Christian community (and confirmed what Jesus Christ did in Matthew 19:14, when He asked the disciples to let the children come to Him). And his focus was towards a relationship within homes where there is genuine love, which is the basis of all relationships, where everyone also has a social and even spiritual duty.

The world at that time didn't value children, but the apostle Paul affirmed the infinite value of each child, as well as made a careful explanation of the mutual responsibilities of parents and children, which reinforced that value.

Paul exhorted children to obey their parents. The verb that's generally translated "obey" (hupakouo) is a compound word based on the word "listen" (akouo); therefore it has at its base the idea of "listen to" or "pay attention to" and therefore "obey". Much disobedience arises when children refuse to listen to the instructions given to them, as well as the reasons for those instructions.

In Proverbs 4:1-6, the writer links three generations and shows how love is transmitted mainly through personal influence.

2. Beware of our judgement!

When we're young and without the experience of being parents, we often severely judge what our parents do or don't do at home. But the truth is that they have had to learn to be parents to us. Parents don't have access to a manual where they can find answers to every situation they face as our parents. In many places, the father doesn't exert much influence on the family, since traditionally he is the one who leaves the home to work and bring home sustenance. On many occasions, the father figure is more of a kind of vigilante who will punish us if we don't do things correctly. And many times, we hear a phrase that isn't healthy at all in our lives, especially when he orders us to obey him and we angrily ask him "Why?", and he tells us, "Because I'm your father."

Parents often think they know everything, and that shouldn't scare us. The reason for this is because they have much more experience than we do, and what they want is to prevent us from doing badly (in school, in love, in life). Experience has provided them with wisdom, but it doesn't guarantee good treatment or eliminate their humanity, which is why many times they continue to make mistakes with us. The apostle Paul himself, inspired by the Spirit of God, wrote: "Fathers, don't embitter your children, or they'll become discouraged" (Colossians 3:21).

For some parents, they want their children to be better than they were, go further, achieve more triumphs, etc! Parents often project onto their children their aspirations and the achievements that they didn't reach. And they think that those places they dreamed of and those hopes that still nest in their hearts will be reached through their children (whether they are material goals, intellectual and even physical goals that children often don't want for themselves). And in most cases they seem to be "imposed" by parents on children. That's dangerous since we won't necessarily have the same goals and objectives as our parents. But we must seek God's will for our lives and fight for it with love and perseverance.

3. Obey the Lord

In his letter to the Colossians, Paul shows us the visible changes of the new life in Christ in relation to society, and especially in family relationships. To fathers, specifically, he spoke about the treatment of his wife and children; this relationship should be a reflection of the Christ-church relationship.

From the Old Testament, the Jewish people knew the commandment "Honor your father and your mother" which is the first commandment that includes a promise: "... so that you may live long..." (Exodus 20:12 ; Ephesians 6:2). However, it's not easy for children to fulfill this commandment since there are some parents who are difficult to honor.

One of the main causes of family disintegration in our society is the failure of some fathers to carry out the father's role in the family. Some of the problems this has led to are: violence, addictions, adultery and abandonment; and what is worse, when a father abandons his family, his son, as he grows up, will often do the same.

The Word of God guides us to the solution of this problem. In Ephesians 6:4 we're told, "Fathers, don't exasperate your children; instead, bring them up in the training and instruction of the Lord." And children are commanded to "obey your parents in the Lord"; which means that we have to listen to them and do what they ask us when we know that it pleases God.

Let's listen to the Word. We'll learn a lot if we begin to have the same relationship with our parents that God wants to have with each one of his children; Proverbs 23:26 says, "My son, give me your heart and let your eyes delight in my ways."

If there's love between parent and child, it's easy to comply with God's commandments, but there must be a mutual and individual commitment to God.

"Honor your father and your mother..." There's no pretext or excuse, it's a commandment, so we must seek, within the will of God, to honor them. And parents should imitate the loving father of whom Jesus Christ spoke of in Luke 15:11-32. It's not about a shallow smiling love, but something deep, like that of God towards us, a love that seeks to provide the affection that's so much needed, the protection that's needed, the security of a hug, the guidance and the example that we want so much in this life.

Let's look carefully at the story and note that, although the younger son thought he had reason to leave, when he was away, the reason to return was greater: the love of his father.

Review/Application: Ask your students to respond to the following:

1. How is your relationship with your parents? (If you're in good relationship with them, you could have some time to pray and thank God. If not, what better way to start improving the relationship than by interceding for them!)

2. If you're in a bad relationship with your parents, what steps could you take to improve that? (Spend time with them, ask for forgiveness, forgive them and tell them about God's love.)

3. Write what you learn from the following two biblical passages in your relationship with your parents:

   Proverbs 23:12-26   John 15:1-17

Challenge: Remember that God will judge parents and children for everything we do, say, and think. Don't forget to honor your parents with your life this week.

My GPS

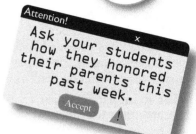

Attention! Ask your students how they honored their parents this past week.

Accept

Objective: That students will see the Word of God as the only guide to face the disturbing influences of the world and to maintain their personal relationship with God.

Memory Verse: *"All Scripture is God-breathed and is useful for teaching, rebuking, correcting and training in righteousness..."* 2 Timothy 3:16

Connect | Navigate

Introductory Activity (12 - 17 years).

- Materials: Bibles; Biblical concordances (sometimes found at the back of Bibles); markers (pen, pencils, etc.); cut-outs of 2 swords, a hammer and a lamp of foam or cardboard.

- Instructions: Divide the class to work in groups, or if there are few you can ask them to work individually. Next, distribute each of the shapes, and indicate that they should look for a verse where the Word of God is compared with each of the figures that were given to them. Once the verse is located, they must write it on their respective figure.

Then ask four participants (one for each shape) to read their verses and briefly reflect on the meaning of the assigned symbol. That is, in what way is the Word of God compared to the sword, the hammer and the lamp respectively? (Answers: Sword (Ephesians 6:17 and Hebrews 4:12); Hammer (Jeremiah 23:29); and Lamp (Psalms: 119:105).

Introductory Activity (18 - 23 years).

- Materials: Bible, sheets of paper and pencils.

- Instructions: Distribute the sheets of paper and pencils to the participants and ask them to make a list of the Bible verses that they know by heart, and underline the quote of their favorite verse.

Then ask a few volunteers to read their lists; others to recite their favorite verse; and others who say why their favorite verse if their favorite.

Connect | Navigate

The Bible calls itself "the Holy Scriptures" and "the Word of God". This wonderful book has been "inspired by God"; it's full of wisdom for practical life, and it reveals salvation to us through Jesus Christ.

However, sometimes we forget its importance and significance in our lives. It's necessary to always keep in mind that God has given us the Bible as the guide to know him and enjoy his blessings.

In this sense, it's very important to learn the Bible from our youth. Many of us have been raised in Christian homes and therefore have received biblical teaching from our childhood. That has become a good foundation for our personal relationship with God.

The Bible shows us everything we need to know about God and his purpose for us. It can also help us successfully deal with any problem and live properly. So, the Bible can be compared to a map or GPS that guides us so we won't get lost. How wonderful is the Word of God!

1. The Bible: Knowledge Plus Persuasion

It's one thing to appreciate the Bible because it has been taught to us from childhood; and another to be personally persuaded that it's the Word of God. We all need to take a personal position in relation to it.

In this regard, ask the following: What is your relationship to the Bible? A mere knowledge that you have learned? Or, is it the book that guides you in your daily actions?

The study passage for this lesson tells us precisely about the importance of the Bible for our Christian life. This is found in 2 Timothy 3:14-17.

Timothy was a young man raised in a believing home; hence he had been taught the scriptures from childhood (2 Timothy 1:5). In those days, believing families gave a high importance to the biblical teaching of their children. It's said that a boy of Jewish descent like Timothy began to be instructed in the Scriptures from the age of five. For this reason, Paul called him to "persist" in such teachings that he learned from his childhood: "But as for you, continue in what you have learned and have become convinced of, because you know those from whom you learned it, and how from infancy you have known the Holy Scriptures ..." (2 Timothy 3:14-15a). That is, it's necessary to persevere in those truths that we've learned in the Bible.

In addition to learning biblical knowledge from childhood, Timothy also experienced Christian "persuasion". The latter is produced by the Word of God through the mediation of the Holy Spirit, and leads us to repentance and new birth.

Also, in the verses just cited it's mentioned: "...you know those from whom you learned it..." This suggests that there were several influential people in Timothy's life who taught him the Word. One of them was Paul. His grandmother Lois and mother Eunice are also mentioned (2 Timothy 1:5). These people set a good example for him to follow.

After the above, ask the following: Who are the people who have most influenced your lives through the Word and Christian example? Allow a few students to share their own testimonies.

2. The Bible: The Map to Salvation

In public and private buildings where many people live or work, there are always plans or maps that indicate escape routes in case of emergency. These routes are also indicated on airplanes, ships and trains. Following these signs can be a matter of life and death!

A map is used so as not to get lost and to reach the correct destination. Likewise, now there are GPS's, small instruments that guide people to the destination they want to go by means of a voice that tells them where to go and a map that shows them the way.

In the same way, the Bible indicates the only safe route by which human beings can travel towards eternal life. Paul tells Timothy that the Scriptures (the Bible) "...are able to make you wise for salvation through faith in Christ Jesus." (2 Timothy 3:15b). In other words, obedience to biblical teachings enables you to live according to God's purpose, and ultimately to get to heaven.

There is no other way to be saved than by obeying the Word of God. This obedience must come from faith in Jesus Christ. That's to say, it's not by human effort but "by faith that's in Christ Jesus."

The world has what we might call "misleading signs" which try to divert us from God's path. These false indications lead us down wrong paths such as drugs, alcohol, cigarettes, worldly parties, pornography, theft, robbery, violence, etc. Therefore, we need the Bible as a map or GPS to guide us on the true path.

Furthermore, the Word has enough power to break any spiritual bondage in our lives (Hebrews 4:12).

3. The Bible: The "equipment" for our trip

Have you ever gone on an exploration trip or adventure? A useful team is needed to deal with the risks that may ensue. The great purpose God had in giving us the Bible is to provide us with the "equipment" necessary to live life as He originally designed it. Paul said in the aforementioned passage from Hebrews that the Bible is the weapon needed to live life correctly. This is by virtue of its nature: "All Scripture is God-breathed ..." (2 Timothy 3:16a). This means that God, the author of the Bible, empowered ordinary men with his Spirit to write it.

In this section of the topic, the teacher can prepare a picture or PowerPoint presentation about the meaning of the verse in 2 Timothy 3:16b. The following items are suggested:

The effectiveness of the Bible:

To teach in righteousness: Provides knowledge about the doctrine of God and how to live a holy life.

To rebuke in righteousness: Provides light to conscience and moral sensitivity when we sin or err.

To correct in righteousness: It provides repentance, discipline and rectification of the conduct towards the good.

To instruct in righteousness: Provides ongoing spiritual admonition that helps us persevere in faith.

We are constantly faced with different situations in our day to day activity in which we have to make important decisions. The world often offers us things that don't contribute to our well-being, but on the contrary, to our destruction. The Bible says: "There is a way that appears to be right, but in the end it leads to death." (Proverbs 14:12).

Think, for example, of the evil that drugs cause. Momentarily, they can provide pleasure and a sense of freedom, but finally, they become an addiction that enslaves and upsets to the point of destroying the user.

The wonderful thing about the Bible is that it contains teachings relevant to all human situations and needs. It provides us with the useful tools to be victorious in the face of any challenge and fulfill the will of God "...so that the servant of God may be thoroughly equipped for every good work." (2 Timothy 3:17).

Review/Application: Ask your students to define the following in their own words:

The Bible:_____

Christian persuasion:_____

Divine Inspiration from the Bible:_____

Rebuke in righteousness:_____

Correction in righteousness:_____

Instruction in righteousness:_____

Challenge: This week, read the following Bible passages that discuss the importance and effectiveness of the Bible: 1 Peter 1:23-2:3; Hebrews 4:12-13. Next, write down your personal thoughts about what the Bible means in your life.

Time With God

Attention!
Allow time for your students to share their thoughts about the Bible that they wrote during the week.
Accept

Objective: That students understand that God hears the prayer of a sincere heart, and responds to each request according to his will.

Memory Verse: *"As soon as you began to pray, a word went out, which I have come to tell you, for you're highly esteemed."* Daniel 9:23a

Connect · Navigate

Introductory Activity (12 - 17 years).

- Materials: Blackboard and chalk or equivalent.
- Instructions: Write the following question on the board: "What is prayer?" Then ask the class to give answers and write them on the board. Then as a group come up with a combined answer that takes into account the answers that the students gave earlier.

Introductory Activity (18 - 23 years).

- Materials: Chairs placed in a circle, blackboard and chalk or the equivalent.
- Instructions: Ask the class to sit in the chairs as they are arranged. Then ask the following question: "Does God answer all prayers?" Allow your students time to discuss this question for a few minutes. Then write important statements that emerged from the conversation on the board.

Connect · Navigate

Pray (praying, prayer) means: "to entreat, implore; to address God with adoration, confession, supplication, or thanksgiving." (www.Merriam-Webster.com).

On the other hand, prayer according to the theological dictionary is defined in this way: "It is the conscious act of man turning to God to communicate with him or to seek his help in time of need. Man can be driven to seek God by his desires, by emergencies or by his own insufficiency or inability to face difficult situations every day." (Beacon Theological Dictionary. CNP, USA: s / f, p. 479).

To come to a conclusion, share that we'll take some time during today's lesson to evaluate how God answered the prayer raised by Daniel.

1. Sincere Prayer

Daniel was a young Israelite who at the time of the captivity was taken to Babylon (Daniel 1:1-8). He was a young man faithful to God who in time became a counselor of kings. But despite all this, Daniel was never willing to give up his convictions. Thus, Daniel applied the commandments of God to his life and didn't change the good habits that he acquired, such as the habit of prayer, which he maintained despite the fact that it threatened his own life (Daniel 1:1-6:28).

Likewise, Daniel teaches us by his example that we shouldn't wait to be in a difficult situation to learn about prayer, and especially to put it into practice in our own lives.

The biblical commentators emphasize from Daniel's qualities, that he was a man who was close to the Word of the Lord. Therefore, he was able to identify that some of the prophecies in the books of Leviticus and Jeremiah corresponded to the times in which he was living.

In this regard, ask the following: When you approach the books of the Bible, do you understand the Word of the Lord? Can you identify, as Daniel did, the times in which you live and thus share the message of hope?

Daniel was a young man who lived a life of integrity who maintained a close relationship with God through prayer. Eventually, he did what he was used to doing: pray. In this way, Daniel submitted to a time of prayer for himself and for the people of Israel:

" While I was speaking and praying, confessing my sin and the sin of my people Israel and making my request to the Lord my God for his holy hill—while I was still in prayer…" (Daniel 9:20-21a).

Daniel was seeking divine intervention. The passage from Daniel 9:3 tells us of the desperation with which Daniel sought God's favor: "So I turned to the Lord God and pleaded with him in prayer and petition, in fasting, and in sackcloth and ashes." Daniel prayed with great fervor and asked according to divine purpose. Undoubtedly his prayer came from a sincere heart.

As we study Daniel's example, we see that he was a man of integrity, and that God heard his prayer. But in the Bible, we also find the case of other people who didn't have a close relationship with God and lived a less than holy life, but in a moment of distress, they cried out to the Lord and were heard. Examples of such cases are the following:

- The thief on the cross (Luke 23:40-43)
- The centurion (Matthew 8:5-13)
- The Pharisee and the publican (Luke 18:9-14).

2. The Answer to Prayer

James 4:3 says: "When you ask, you don't receive, because you ask with wrong motives, that you may spend what you get on your pleasures." In this sense, when contrasting Daniel's prayer with many of those we say, we'll find a difference. Daniel was able to pray by putting himself in someone else's shoes and assuming his own sin and that of the people (Daniel 9:20-21a). In other words, Daniel prayed for the sins of others and for their bitter consequences. He prayed for his people (Daniel 9:3-7)

Here it's necessary to pause to ask ourselves the following: Have we prayed for the things that hurt God's heart, or only those that hurt ours?

There are aspects that are very important to include in our prayer and which we often overlook. Such aspects are:

- Pray for knowledge of God's will (Colossians 1:9).
- To walk worthy of the Lord, to have a growing relationship with God (Colossians 1:10).
- To bear fruit and for it to remain (John 15:16).
- To have the power, endurance and patience to continue our Christian walk in the midst of trials (Colossians 1:11).
- To have joy and a good attitude (Colossians 1:12).

3. "Yes", "No", "Wait"

Ask: How does a parent respond to their child's request? They respond according to what they see as what is best for their child in his or her integral development, and according to their life experiences.

Ask: Does this differ from the way God answers our prayers? God will always look out for our best welfare. His Word says in Jeremiah 29:11-13: "'For I know the plans I have for you,' declares the Lord, 'plans to prosper you and not to harm you, plans to give you hope and a future. Then you'll call on me and come and pray to me, and I will listen to you. You will seek me and find me when you seek me with all your heart.'"

Our part is to believe this principle of God's Word, for the Lord desires our well-being, and He always hears us. God expects a sincere heart, full of faith and patience, knowing that we pray and are in His hands, and that He is always in control of everything (Hebrews 10:35-37). And when it seems to us that he delays his response, it's because he's doing what he knows is best for us and his plan.

At this point, the following question may arise: Why don't our prayers receive the answer we hope for? We don't know, but let me share Pastor Rick Warren's words:

"Friends, I have been studying the question 'why' for 37 years, and I am going to give you my polite answer: I don't know. And I will never know, because I am not God. And you aren't either! There are some things that we'll never understand until we get to the other side of death. Then everything is going to be very, very clear. God only knows. And if you don't get your response immediately, you should stop asking 'why?' because you're simply prolonging the pain." (http://rickwarren.org/devotional/spanish/dios-por-qu%C3%A9-me-est%C3%A1-pasando-esto#.U7xFvPl5P_E).

So if the answer to my prayer isn't what I expected or wanted, it doesn't mean that God doesn't listen to me. Let's remember that He always listens to us, wants our well-being, and His purposes are in relation to the advancement of the Kingdom. He sees the sincerity of our hearts. His Word says in 1 Corinthians 13:9,12: "For we know in part and we prophesy in part,... For now we see only a reflection as in a mirror; then we shall see face to face. Now I know in part; then I shall know fully, even as I am fully known."

To conclude, let's mention that God does answer all prayers, although not always in the way we hope. So sometimes he will say "yes" to our request; some times he'll say "no"; and other times, he'll say "wait."

Review/Application: Allow time for your students to respond to the following:

- How do you feel when you don't get a response from someone?

- Certainly, God answers all prayers. Do you feel that there is a prayer in your life that wasn't answered? Why?

- Give examples of two clear answers to prayers that have been prayed.

- Develop a prayer time in your life. Make a daily plan and include prayer time within this plan.

Challenge: What do you think about keeping a prayer journal that includes the things that touch God's heart? These could include:

- Our consecration to God.

- Conversion of the lost.

- Intercession for the needs of others

- Prayer for our leaders (parents, teachers, employers, president and civil authorities, etc.).

My Shelter

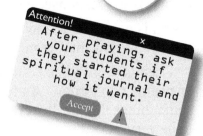

Attention! After praying, ask your students if they started their spiritual journal and how it went.
Accept

Objective: That students understand that even in the most difficult moments of their lives (sadness, bitterness or loneliness), God will always be by their side.

Memory Verse: *"I cling to you; your right hand upholds me..."* Psalm 63:8

Connect / Navigate

Introductory Activity (12 - 17 years).

- Instructions: Divide the class into two groups. When the groups are separated, ask them to form two lines. Tell them that each row should be located with its back to the other, keeping a distance of one meter between one row and another and half a meter between each of their respective members. Then tell them to turn around with their eyes closed, so that each of the members of each row is facing each other, without opening their eyes and in silence. Once in that position, (the two rows facing each other) ask the students to raise their arms, take a small step forward and extend their arms so that they hold hands with the person in front. Finally, ask them, holding hands, to open their eyes and hug each other.

Many of us need a sweet look and a hug, even if there are no words involved. Let's remember that God will always have his arms extended towards us to embrace us, so it's up to us whether or not we want to receive it.

Introductory Activity (18 - 23 years).

- Materials: White sheets of paper cut into four pieces and colored pencils.
- Instructions: Give the papers and pencils to the students. Then ask them to write the following sentence on their paper: "GOOD FOR A HUG". Then point out that at the end of the class, each of them should exchange their paper with someone they aren't very close with, or with whom they have had a moment of disagreement.

Keep in mind that young adults, although apparently more mature, often have a more difficult time approaching other people, especially when they have been offended. However, it's very important to keep in mind and mention to them that if God embraces us evil though we have sinned against him, who are we not to accept a hug from another person?

Connect / Navigate

Start the class by asking your students the following: Have you ever had to hide from someone? Who was it and why? What was your hiding place like? If someone wants to share, give them the opportunity to do so. Next, read Psalm 63 in a dynamic way, if possible from a contemporary version, to introduce the Word of God and so the application remains in the minds and hearts of the students.

In this Psalm, David found himself in adverse circumstances, fleeing through the desert away from his loved ones, surrounded by rocky mountains. However, his trust and hope were in God. Thus, the psalmist recognized that God was the only one who deserved his praise from dawn until dusk, and he also knew that worship and praise brought peace, security, and strength.

1. I know you're here

Every human being faces difficult situations at some point in life, and at the moment of feeling powerless, they seek refuge in something or someone. King David was no exception. In fact, he needed God, since he had problems with his children. His eldest son named Amnon had raped Tamar, his stepsister, and Absalom, her brother, ordered Amnon to be killed (2 Samuel 13).

Verses 1 and 2 of Psalm 63 says: "You, God, are my God, earnestly I seek you; I thirst for you, my whole being longs for you, in a dry and parched land where there is no water. I have seen you in the sanctuary and beheld your power and your glory." In the first place, and without a doubt, we can see that King David recognized who his God was, and he addressed Him confidently even though he was in a bad situation. His son Absalom had started a revolution in order to take the throne, turning part of the people against his father. That's why David fled to the desert. However, while far from the city, David knew that God was everywhere. Although he didn't have access to a sanctuary or temple, he was sure to find the Lord even in that inhospitable place. For that reason, David decided to seek him from dawn to see again the power and glory of God that he had seen and known before.

And the miraculous God that David met is the same God who is willing to lift us out of depression, sadness, anxiety, anger, etc. whenever we look to him.

2. Hide me in your arms

A shelter is a place of refuge that doesn't last forever because it's a temporary place where there's security and what's necessary to survive (food, shelter and protection). David, in the midst of his anguish, didn't stop praising and worshiping the Lord because he knew that they are weapons to attack the despair that was besieging him. In fact, the king was making his relationship with God his hiding place. The act of raising your hands is a symbol of surrender. When someone is attacked in an armed robbery, they are forced to raise their hands, this is done in order to immobilize the person who is being attacked. Also, showing empty hands gives the attacker assurance that he won't receive a counterattack. In verse 4 of Psalm 63, the writer mentions raising his hands in the name of the Lord of hosts, because he is sure that the Lord is the one who fights his battles and gives him the victory. In the moment of helplessness, surrender plays an important role. We aren't saying that God is attacking him, but that many times the attacks come as a consequence of our actions. Some are the harvest of a sowing, and other times, God simply allows this to test our faith, our faithfulness, as He did with Job. In this case, David was the victim of his own family. In the Bible, it's mentioned that because of his worship and praise of the Most High, David was like God, that is, according to his heart.

It was God who told Saul, through the prophet Samuel, that he rejected him as king and decided to anoint David as king of Israel in his place. We read this in 1 Samuel 13:14 which says: "But now your kingdom won't endure; the Lord has sought out a man after his own heart and appointed him ruler of his people, because you haven't kept the Lord's command."

In his youth, David was distinguished for being simple, humble, worshipping, exalting, obedient, courageous, and we could add many more attributes for which the Lord was pleased with him. However, David also had weaknesses as every human being has. One of David's was his attraction to women, of whom he was reciprocated, since he was physically handsome: "… He was glowing with health and had a fine appearance and handsome features…" (1 Samuel 16:12). At that time, it wasn't frowned upon for a man to have several wives. Therefore, David had them, but that had consequences for him.

His children (of various wives) were rebellious, and didn't have harmony with each other, as mentioned in the previous point. Added to the that, there were in this family, among other things, rapes, deceptions, murders and, to close with a "flourish", the usurpation of the kingdom by his son Absalom. These antecedents and others, which for time and space aren't mentioned here, led David to despair, to the point of having to flee to the desert to seek refuge. What was his war? The persecution by his son to destroy him (2 Samuel 17:1-2). But David, even in the face of all this, was confident that he would be victorious.

3. I'm satisfied to be with you

Who do I prefer to be with? If your mind is transported to a place of shelter for psychological, moral, emotional and spiritual well-being, apart from the physical conditions of the shelter, it's also necessary to have the company of someone who lifts our spirits, who gives us words of hope, who has the best ideas to get ahead, a person who gives us security, love and everything we need for that time of difficulties.

It doesn't matter what happened before, or what forced the person to come to a place like this, what matters is what follows and who they will be surrounded by from now on.

King David found asylum in the desert, possibly in a cave without the comforts of the royal palace, accompanied by his bodyguards and his warriors. Maybe there were a lot of them, but none met the requirements to comfort him because they were his subjects, and David needed someone superior. Psalm 63:5-8 says that God was his help, and that his right hand upheld him. God, it's the only one who provides everything necessary in all areas of human life, and David knew it.

This eternal refuge can be experienced from now on, and it's obtained with worship, praise, prayer and trust directed to the only one who deserves all of this, Jesus Christ our Savior and Lord.

Review/Application: Allow time for your students to reflect and answer the following questions.

• What kind of difficult situations have you faced or are you facing? _____

• How did you face those difficult situations? _____

• What personal lessons can you draw from Psalm 63? _____

• According to what you learned from Psalm 63, write a personal prayer. _____

Challenge: On planet Earth, there are shelters to go to in difficult circumstances. In today's lesson we learned that there is an eternal place for those who accept Jesus Christ as their one and sufficient Savior and Lord. This week, no matter what happens, go to Him as your only refuge.

Not Eating?

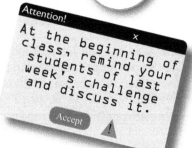

Objective: For students to recognize that Jesus taught about the need to fast.

Memory Verse: *Jesus answered, "It is written: 'Man shall not live on bread alone, but on every word that comes from the mouth of God.'"* Matthew 4:4

Connect | Navigate

Introductory Activity (12 - 17 years).

- Materials: White paper cut into heart shapes and markers.
- Instructions: Have the class read Matthew 6:16-18 and give each participant a paper heart and a marker. Then, allow time for them to write on one side of the paper heart two or three attitudes, which in their opinion, were in the hearts of the Pharisees while they were fasting; and on the other side of the heart, have them write down what should be in our hearts when we fast. Then let them share what they wrote with the class.

Introductory Activity (18 - 23 years).

- Materials: White sheets of paper and pencils.
- Instructions: Divide the class into groups and allow time for them to read the following Scripture verses and then complete the chart.
  a. Deuteronomy 9:8-11
  b. Deuteronomy 9:15-19
  c. Daniel 10:1-12
  d. 2 Samuel 12:15-2.

Biblical Passage	Name of the Person	When did they fast	Reason why they fasted

Then ask each of them to comment on which situation of the different characters caught their attention and why.

Connect | Navigate

In the Old Testament, people fasted mostly in times of deep trouble. Fasting was accompanied by expressions of sadness, such as crying, clamoring, dressing in mourning clothes, and wearing rough clothes generally made of goat skins (what was called "sackcloth"). Also, those who fasted sat on ashes and threw it on their heads (Esther 4:1-3; Psalm 35:13).

When the Bible talks about fasting, it always relates it to spiritual purposes. Fasting is a way to approach God by presenting our own bodies on the altar of worship as a living and holy sacrifice.

1. The effectiveness of fasting

During this class, we'll study in the book of Esther an event that illustrates the tremendous power of fasting. This book tells the story of the rescue of the Jewish people that occurred in the 5th century BC, during the great Persian Empire.

The Jews were scattered throughout the 127 provinces that made up this kingdom throughout the world. They had gone there as captives by the Babylonians, which was the dominate empire before the Persians.

Esther was an orphaned Jewish girl taken to the capital of the empire by her cousin Mordecai who had adopted her. By the providence of God, she "... had a lovely figure and was beautiful" (Esther 2:7). She was chosen from among many virgins by King Xerxes to be the queen in place of Vashti, his former wife, whom He had dismissed for disobeying an order he had given her (Esther 1:1-22).

An evil man named Haman, a favorite of the king, had obtained from him, under deception, a decree to exterminate the Jews (Esther 3).

When Esther found out, she, along with Mordecai and their people, did nothing but approach God in fasting and prayer. Read Esther 4:3-16, and ask: What was the fasting of the Israelites like?

God didn't leave the cry of his children unanswered, but completely changed the situation in which they lived, putting it in favor of his people.

Esther played a key role in this change. With great faith and wisdom sustained by the grace of God, she succeeded in helping her people win a great victory over their enemies. So much was the grace of God manifested in Esther that the king, "When he saw Queen Esther standing in the court, was pleased with her and held out to her the gold scepter that was in his hand. So Esther approached and touched the tip of the scepter. Then the king asked, 'What is it, Queen Esther? What is your request? Even up to half the kingdom, it will be given you.'" (Esther 5:2-3) In response, he granted everything she asked for in favor of her people.

As we see, fasting expresses a deep desire to obtain divine help. It's not an empty and meaningless practice, but it's highly effective. God promised to answer us when we cry out to Him: "Then you'll call on me and come and pray to me, and I will listen to you. You will seek me and find me when you seek me with all your heart." (Jeremiah 29:12-13)

2. The time of fasting

The question may arise: How long should I fast, or how often should I fast? In the Bible, we can find an appropriate answer. Let's study this in Matthew 9:14-17.

The various religious groups of Jesus' time frequently fasted. The Pharisees, for example, fasted on Mondays and Wednesdays. It's said that they liked to show themselves with "gaunt" faces in public. It seems that their interest was to be seen by the greatest number of people because those were the days when people went to the markets (Luke 18:12).

Then ask: According to Matthew 6:16-18, how should we fast according to Jesus?

The disciples of Jesus, unlike the Pharisees and the disciples of John, seem to not have been very fond of fasting. This disturbed the followers of John the Baptist who came to ask Jesus: "How is it that we and the Pharisees fast often, but your disciples don't fast?" (Matthew 9:14b). Jesus' response was profound and logical: "How can the guests of the bridegroom mourn while he is with them? The time will come when the bridegroom will be taken from them; then they'll fast" (v. 15). With this, the Master said something like: What should be the attitude of people who attend a wedding party? He was referring to the wonderful time in which they lived in the very presence of the Son of God.

The following verses further clarify Jesus' concept of fasting. Jesus responded with the following analogies or comparisons: "No one sews a patch of unshrunk cloth on an old garment, for the patch will pull away from the garment, making the tear worse. Neither do people pour new wine into old wineskins. If they do, the skins will burst; the wine will run out and the wineskins will be ruined. No, they pour new wine into new wineskins, and both are preserved" (vs. 16-17).

If new wine is poured into old leather wineskins that are stiff, the leathers will burst from the fermentation gas. The meaning of this wasn't that Jesus and his disciples down played fasting, but that they didn't share the legalistic way it was practiced in their time. After the ascension of Jesus, the early Christians practiced fasting as an important means of seeking God's direction and grace (Acts 13:2).

Fasting has great importance, and even more so in these last times that we live. The frequency of fasting depends on our need for God and our love for Him.

3. The food of fasting

Just as our body needs to be fed regularly, so does our soul. When one starts fasting to seek the face of God, this is precisely what happens: We feed on the presence of God and his Word.

Ask: If you had been hungry for 40 days and had the power to turn stones into food, what foods would you turn them into?

In Matthew 4:1-4, the passage that talks about the temptation of Jesus teaches this great spiritual truth: "After fasting forty days and forty nights, he was hungry. The tempter came to him and said, 'If you're the Son of God, tell these stones to become bread'" (vs. 2-3). Note that this was the first temptation, and it's here where the devil will always attack us first because of natural appetites and desires.

So Jesus was tempted by the devil on the basis of his physical need. The enemy wanted Jesus to give prominence to satisfying his natural hunger, but Jesus focused on the spiritual. He quoted Deuteronomy 8:3, when Israel was fed by God in the desert: "Jesus answered, 'It is written: "Man shall not live on bread alone, but on every word that comes from the mouth of God."'" (v. 4).

Today's culture has taught us to place greater importance on meeting our physical needs than our spiritual ones. Commercial advertising tries to sell us all kinds of fast food with lovely images. In our homes, sometimes there is an inordinate desire for food, and we even get used to gluttony!

Ask: How will we respond to God's call to sustain our spiritual selves? Spiritual fasting is an important part of that divine nourishment.

The most important thing about fasting is the spiritual motivation you have. God's response to fasting will correspond to that motivation in our hearts.

Review/Application: Allow time for your students to answer the following questions:

1. How many days did Esther and her people fast? (Three days.)

2. Was Esther's fast partial or absolute? (Absolute.)

3. What is your food during the fast? (The Word of God and prayer.)

4. Have you ever fasted? What was your experience like?

Challenge: Set aside one day this week for a partial fast. This means that you have to skip one or two meals. The best way to start the fast is to consume only fresh fruit juice. Even if you're doing your usual daily chores, stay in an inward attitude of prayer, worshiping the Lord. The most important thing is your spiritual attitude. At the end of the fast, eat a light meal, preferably consisting of fruits and vegetables.

Created to Praise

Objective: To teach students that regardless of the situation we're living in, we can and should praise God.

Memory Verse: *"I will extol the Lord at all times; his praise will always be on my lips."* Psalm 34:1

Connect | Navigate

Introductory Activity (12 - 17 years).

- Materials: White sheets of letter-size paper, pencils or pens.
- Instructions: Give a sheet of paper to each student and ask them to clearly write their names at the top. Then, each person must pass their paper to whoever is sitting on their right. Then, those people will write down positive characteristics, praises and good qualities of the owner of the paper they have in their hands. When finished, they pass the paper to those on their right, who do the same. This is repeated until the papers return to their original owners. Then, each person should read what was written on their paper and share with the group how they feel.

This activity serves to reflect on the importance of sharing the positive with people and how this is received.

Introductory Activity (18 - 23 years).

- Instructions: Ask the students to sit in a circle and each student will take turns standing in the center of the circle. Once in the middle, the other students will tell the person who is the focus of attention all the positive feelings and thoughts they have towards him or her. The person should only listen ... not speak. The impact of this dynamic is strongest when everyone stands in front of the person, touches them, looks them in the eye, and speaks directly to them. At the end of the dynamic, give everyone the opportunity to comment about the experience.

Connect | Navigate

Ask: How many times a week or a day do we praise and celebrate people around us with words? This probably seldom happens in our daily lives. And as Christians how many times do we praise and celebrate the name of our God? That is probably rare too. Sometimes we limit praise to Sunday worship when we praise the name of God through songs; other times, we base it on our situations or emotional states to do so.

Let's reflect on Psalm 34:1 and discover the resonance these words have in our hearts and actions.

Today the word "praise" is generally linked to the times of singing in our churches. Thus, when looking for the definition of "praise" we find the following: "the offering of grateful homage in words or song, as an act of worship; the express approval or admiration of; comment; extol." (dictionary.com). Such a definition shows us that praise is really linked to exalting the name of God with words and songs. In this regard, ask: What song or praise comes to your mind that exalts the name of God and fulfills that function?

So really at least once a week for about 20 minutes or so we praise the name of God; but is this enough? In addition, it's worth asking ourselves, with what attitude are we exalting the name of God? On autopilot? From the heart? Only when we're joyful and happy?

It's very important to reflect on the attitude with which we praise God, as well as the moments in which we do it. Today, many Christians in their churches wait for the time of praise to exalt the name of God, but what happens the rest of the days?

1. Praise at all times...

Psalm 34 tells us about the wonders that God did in David's life. The psalmist expresses the enormous gratitude towards the wonders that God had done for him. But when we stop to think about the context in which it was written, we'll realize with amazement that David didn't write it in his moments of glory and peace, but in the midst of anguish and persecution.

David was running from Saul, who wanted to kill him. This account is described in 1 Samuel 21. David fled to Gath, the land of the Philistines. There he appeared before King Achish, being recognized by the king's servants. This caused great fear in David, who pretended to be insane, so he was thrown out by the king and went to take refuge in the cave of Adullam.

When David escaped from this situation, he wrote Psalm 34. This makes us think that David wasn't really in an optimal moment of joy, peace and well-being. However, he praised the name of God.

Furthermore, that aforementioned situation wasn't the first time that David praised the name of God in the midst of his flight. There are eight psalms whose titles allude to David's persecution by Saul (Psalms 7, 34, 52, 54, 56, 57, 59 and 142).

Ask: Is it possible to praise God's name in the midst of a difficult situation like the one David was going through? If we think about the occasions when we've praised someone, they have surely been due to a feeling of deep happiness and gratitude.

Our praise to God must start from the recognition of God in our lives. The psalmist David teaches us in this Psalm that we shouldn't only praise God when we receive something special and pleasant from him, but it's also necessary to praise and bless the name of our God in the midst of pain or affliction.

2. Praise is born out of the recognition of who God is

Ask: Who is God? What is the most common response or responses? Young people and teenagers will probably answer that he is a deity, our father, our friend, our pastor, the Almighty, etc.

In trying to define who God is, we find the following: "Biblical doctrine begins with the understanding that God is the Creator. The first few pages describe God as the initiator and source of all things. His creative activity doesn't admit many other approaches to the basic definition. The Scriptures everywhere assume that God is a person who knows, feels and acts" (Beacon Theological Dictionary, CNP, USA: 1995). It's important to note that God is the initiator and source of everything, and that he is also interacting with humanity. By being created in the image of God, we share attributes with him such as feeling, thinking and knowing. Therefore, it can be concluded that the recognition that each person will have of God will be from the communion that they establish with Him. His power, majesty, love, sustenance and mercy are undeniable; however, humanity (even on many occasions, Christians themselves) in an absurd way miss admiring and feeling all that God is.

So when we actually meet God face to face, we'll only be able to exalt his name and acknowledge all that he is.

3. Praise is born of one's will

We've pointed out that God is still God even though the whole of humanity doesn't recognize him. In his infinite mercy, God has continually reached out to humanity throughout history to offer his great love, forgiveness and salvation; even reaching out through his Son Jesus Christ.

Although the process of salvation and redemption was born in God, and He works in the person through the Holy Spirit before conversion, at a certain point, the person must decide to believe in the Word, repent and accept God's gift of forgiveness.

Then, the life of the Christian is a continual decision to stand firm and seek God's will, joy, and reflection in their life.

This joy that the world cannot take from us (because it comes from God) can lead us to resemble David and be able to say in the same way: "I will extol the Lord at all times; his praise will always be on my lips," no matter what circumstances we're going through.

Difficulties will always be present as long as we live in this world where a battle is constantly being waged with evil and sin. But let's continue the race, shedding sin and running with patience, always keeping our eyes on Jesus (Hebrews 12:1-3). Seeing what Jesus Christ has done for us, we have many reasons to praise Him.

4. Praise infects others

Growing up, I believed that Christianity was only for biblical characters or older people. When I accepted Christ in my teen years and sought to grow in my relationship with God, motivated by the Holy Spirit, that thought changed. No one had told me that communion with God blurred my problems, fears, pain and suffering. This didn't mean that I was in a state of denial or that the problems were erased, but that God supported me.

These testimonies abound in Christians, and when we hear them, they infect us, and when we share them with non-believers, we'll probably see confused faces, but our joy will be undeniable.

King David said: "I will glory in the Lord; let the afflicted hear and rejoice" (Psalm 34:2). That happens within the body of Christ: We rejoice and rejoice with the brothers and sisters in faith who glorify the name of God and give thanks in the name of Jesus. In community worship, there is an appreciation of God for what he has done, for what he is doing, and for what he will do. This allows us to testify of the wonderful God that we have. Perhaps we've gone through or are going through difficult times where there is discouragement, pain or sadness. We must remember that God is still God; he continues working in our lives, giving us his love and sustenance, and is there for us. So let's keep praising his name.

Review/Application:
Allow time for your students to create an acrostic with the word "Praise".

> **P**rayerful heart
> **R**eflection
> **A**doration
> **I** am loved
> **S**inging songs to God
> **E**veryone worships together

Challenge: As we've learned in today's class, it's important to praise God at all times. Pick a son to sing to him daily, and practice praise during prayer time. For next Sunday, come ready to share with the group what it feels like to praise God in private.

True Worship

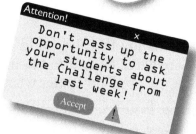

Objective: That students understand what is true worship of God.

Memory Verse: *"Yet a time is coming and has now come when the true worshipers will worship the Father in the Spirit and in truth, for they are the kind of worshipers the Father seeks."* John 4:23

Connect — Navigate

Introductory Activity (12 - 17 years).

- Materials: Sheets of paper and pencils.

- Instructions: Read as a group (or if you prefer, individually) the study passage in John 4:1-24. Then hand out the sheets of paper and pencils and ask your students to draw an aspect of the story that caught their attention. Then encourage a volunteer to explain the meaning of their drawing.

  Drawing helps students create mental images of what they're reading and sets the scene for what will be seen in class.

Introductory Activity (18 - 23 years).

- Materials: Sheets of paper and pencils.

- Instructions: Read as a group the study passage in John 4:1-24. Then hand out sheets of paper and pencils and ask them to answer the following guided questions:

1. Where did this meeting take place?

2. Who participated in this biblical passage?

3. When did this meeting take place?

4. What was the central theme of the talk between the woman and Jesus?

These questions will help students envision the topic globally before diving into it.

Connect — Navigate

If you've grown up as a Christian attending church, you've probably heard the term "worship" often. If you've had little time in church, you may have heard of worship in regards to church music. Or it may be that you associate "worship" with an artistic or sports figure. Today, we'll see that the worship of God includes a spiritual dimension and an element of truth.

1. The Stage

Today's lesson takes us to the gospel of John 4:1-24. There we read that Jesus was going from Judea to Galilee, but not before passing through Samaria. But in reality, the Lord could have gone the long way, through the eastern part of the Jordan. However, he decided to take the busiest shortest route, even if it meant crossing the territory of the unwelcoming Samaritans (John 4:9a).

His encounter with a woman at Jacob's well set the stage for a conversation with impressive statements from Jesus. First, He, a Jew, spoke to a woman and, what was worse, to a Samaritan woman. But he not only spoke to her, he asked her to give him a drink. Due to the historical animosity between Jews and Samaritans, the woman was shocked by Jesus' request (John 4:9b).

Later, Jesus began to speak of water in metaphorical terms (John 4:13-14), while the woman spoke of water in literal terms. When she saw the benefit of drinking the water that Jesus offered that would forever do away with her thirst, she asked him for a little. Perhaps she did it because she no longer wanted to go to the well to draw more water out (v. 15). According to the story, she went alone during a time when the well wasn't normally used, which makes us think that her society marginalized her.

When Jesus mentioned the matter of her husbands to the woman (vs. 16-18), she told him that he was a prophet. Then she herself, out of insight or by changing the subject, brought up the matter of worship (v. 20). For Jews and Samaritans, worship had to do with a physical place: the temple in Jerusalem and the temple on Mount Gerizim, respectively. Ask: For you, where and/or how should we worship?

2. The crux of the matter

And this is where the matter got interesting. Jesus made an emphatic statement: "You Samaritans worship what you don't know..." (v. 22a). The Amplified Bible translation says: "You [Samaritans] don't know what you worship." Actually, the problem with the Samaritans, or with some of us today, is that we believe that worship has to do with a place, or with a type of music, or with gestures, or with clothing; but in reality, it has to do with the knowledge of the being we adore, God Almighty. And the Samaritans didn't know him.

Musical fashions in the contemporary church have led many young people to view worship as a ritual to be practiced with specific rhythms, instruments, and movements. Thus, there are songs classified as "worship songs" that have certain metrics, and if a song departs from them, it's no longer a "worship" song. In a way, we've entered into the false belief of the Samaritans and Jews regarding worship. For them, worship had to take place in a specific place, and that place became the center of worship. They forgot who the very essence of what they worshiped was. That's why Jesus was so emphatic with the Samaritan woman, because they (Samaritans) had no idea who they were worshiping.

The Samaritans only accepted the Pentateuch, while the Jews had what we know as the complete Old Testament. In this part of the Bible, God's revelation of a promised salvation is manifested in the figure of the Messiah. And that Messiah, Jesus, revealed to us who the Father is. The Father is our reason for worship. He cannot be confined to a physical space like a temple or a mountain or limited to a rhythm or type of clothing.

The Father is Spirit. Verse 23 speaks of the worship of the Father in "spirit and in truth" (or as the Good News translation says: "offering him the true worship that he wants."). Thus, Jesus didn't define worship in physical terms, but in spiritual terms. True worship goes beyond anything that is known, and it isn't a question of ethnicity or location.

"God is spirit, and his worshipers must worship in the Spirit and in truth" (v. 24). In other words, the worship that God demands is worship that entails total surrender. According to Daniel Steel, in spirit "implies that we surrender our will to God, our thoughts and plans to those He has for us..." (Beacon Biblical Commentary. Volume 7. CNP, USA: 1985, p. 76). In truth (or in a true way) refers to the fact that "we aren't worshiping an 'image' of God, made according to our ideas ... Only Christ presented us to the real or 'true' God." (Beacon Biblical Commentary, Volume 7 CNP, USA: 1985, p. 76).

3. True worship that reveals

True worship reveals to us who God is and what He asks of us. In the preamble to what he said about worship, Jesus revealed to the Samaritan woman that He was the Messiah. The woman knew that the Messiah would reveal or explain all things to them. On that occasion, he revealed to her that true worship was one that centered on the Father, and that it had nothing to do with the material aspects that she had been taught.

When we genuinely worship the Father in spirit and in truth, "we share something of the nature of the worshipped person" (XXI Century New Testament Biblical Commentary. Hispano World, USA: 2003, p. 310). Thus, we're spiritual beings and our spirit enters into communication with the Father, who is Spirit. And in that communication, God, our Father, reveals himself and his will to us.

The verb that Jesus used for "worship" is proskynein, which literally means "physical prostration". Australian theologian Francis J. Moloney says that the use of this term is "the only appropriate way to worship God. The unconditional and absolute reverence of one's life towards God is the only acceptable act of worship" (El Evangelio de John. Verbo Divino, Pamplona: 2005, p. 153).

Worshiping him truly involves stripping ourselves of poses and preconceptions. True worship isn't about us, it's about God. It's surrendering everything, including ourselves, to Him. He is the center and the reason for all worship.

Review/Application:

1. Why did the Samaritan woman ask Jesus why he asked for water? (Because she was a Samaritan and He was a Jew; and Jews and Samaritans didn't use anything in common, they didn't interact at all.)
2. According to the woman, where did the Jews say to worship? (In Jerusalem.)
3. According to verse 22, what did the Samaritans worship and what did the Jews worship? (The Samaritans what they didn't know, the Jews what they knew.)
4. How will true worshipers worship the Father? (In truth and spirit)
5. What do these words mean to you today?

Challenge:
During the week, think about some ways you have worshiped God, whether collectively in church or alone. How would you change your worship knowing that those who worship the Father "must worship in the Spirit and in truth"?

Worship as a Family

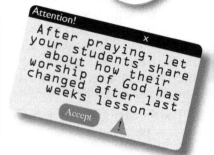

Attention!
After praying, let your students share about how their worship of God has changed after last weeks lesson.
Accept

Objective: That students understand that God's love is lived and reflected, first of all, in families; and that the Lord's desire is that every family worship him.

Memory Verse: *"...and all the families of the nations will bow down before him."* Psalm 22:27b

---

Connect | Navigate

Introductory Activity (12 - 17 years).

- Materials: Colored pencils and white sheets of paper.

- Instructions: Provide the students with the paper and colored pencils and ask them to draw a picture of a family based on what they consider a family to be.

  The idea is that at the end, they share about the different concepts that exist about family and this introduces the lesson.

Introductory Activity (18 - 23 years).

- Materials: Blackboard and chalk or equivalent.

- Instructions: Ask your students to think of an ideal family. Then, ask them to come to the front and write a single word on the board that they feel is the most important concept that distinguishes that ideal of family (love, respect, education, children, etc.).

  At the end, remind them that the most important issues in a family, whatever it may be, are the values that sustain it.

Connect | Navigate

There's no single absolutely correct model of what a family is supposed to be like. There are different types of wonderful godly families ... plural ... period. Even in the 66 books of the Bible, we don't find just one single model of family, but rather we're presented with a variety of family realities. Here are some examples: 1] Jesus' family consisted of a father - who would soon be absent due to death - a mother, an older son (Jesus) who left home, and younger brothers and sisters who questioned the work of the elder; 2] Jacob's family consisted of a husband (Jacob), two wives (who were sisters), two concubines and thirteen children; 3] The family in "The Parable of the Prodigal Son" consisted of a father and two sons; 4] Another family consisted of three single siblings (Martha, Lazarus and Mary); among many others.

But in Genesis 2:24, we read that God commanded the man to leave father and mother, (mentioning the basic family) to form a new family with his wife. In Ephesians 5 and 6, Paul gave a basic model of family: husband, wife, children.

Think of your family. Maybe it's not the one you want, or perhaps it's going through a crisis: it needs a member, it has become a fragmented family, or perhaps today it can even be considered a dysfunctional family ... But be that as it may, it's your family , and in the Word of God we find wise advice that you can put into practice today to improve the life of your family.

1. The Christian Life

John Wesley, one of the most outstanding people in the holiness tradition in the history of the Christian church, affirmed that worship "is not about a quiet time, a time of worship, but a devotional life, a whole life of worship." And that's exactly how Christianity works: it's not about a specific time and place where we act as Christians (the church, the public worship on the weekend), but about all of life, daily life, everyday life. It's in real life that we need to be Christians. It's in places where there's no faith that we need to be people of faith; it's in places outside the church and community worship that we need to live out all that we learn in them. Otherwise, we would only be affirming that the Christian religion is simply that: one more religion, and then the deepest convictions that support our beliefs and all our work would be meaningless.

It's necessary to live Christian convictions, what we've called values of the kingdom of God (love, justice, forgiveness, mercy, peace and joy, among others) not only in the building where we meet Sunday after Sunday to celebrate Jesus Christ, but live them for real during all hours of every day, in every week of the whole month, every year. And the most concrete way to live these Christian convictions is at home. Yes, where every day we share life with our family. Yes, with all the members that make it up.

Because, if what we sing publicly and what we read in the scriptures on Sundays at church is true, then we can put it into practice. John puts it another way: "Whoever claims to love God yet hates a brother or sister is a liar." (1 John 4:20a).

2. Who is my neighbor?

During the time that Jesus was among us physically, He taught that we should do good to others. In this regard, in Luke 10:25-37, an interpreter of the law questioned Jesus and insisted on asking him the following: "... who is my neighbor?"

This question is still valid because the original meaning of this word has to do with "the closest", the one that's close to me. And the people who are closest to us are those who live with us every day: Our family.

We love going to church! We love going to school or the company where we work! We are dazzled by our friends, neighbors, and colleagues with whom we spend a lot of time! But ... what about our family? What about those neighbors ... the people closest to us?

Let's not make the mistake of loving someone who is far from us, but not loving someone who is closest to us. We would be liars! Incongruous people like that boyfriend who called his girlfriend's mobile phone and said: "I love you. For you I'm willing to do anything! And I promise you that I will always do my best to be with you." Then she excitedly asked him, "Will you come to see me today, my love?" He ended by saying, "If it doesn't rain, then yes I'll come see you!"

3. The simplest and most difficult acts

Most of us suffer from this: We love others, but we want nothing to do with those in our own home. This situation was something that even Jesus himself suffered through (John 7:1-5). And it's logical, because we know those who live with us well, and we know that they aren't perfect. Precisely for this reason, we can today decide to love them as we love ourselves (Luke 10:27).

Here we put forth some ideas to be worshipers in the middle of our family. Although it's difficult to do them at first, you'll be able to see the results over time.

- At least one day a week, we can pray for each other. And if you're the only Christian in your home, that's even more reason that you should you intercede in prayer for them.

- Let's promise not to insult each other at home in any way: Not with physical blows, not with offensive words, or with gestures.

- Once a week we can open the Bible and read a passage of spiritual strength such as some of the psalms that have blessed many many people in the Christian faith: Psalm 1, 5, 23, 27, 34, 91, etc.

- When we travel together, let's take some time before leaving or returning to say a family prayer that the Lord will protect us, carry us and keep us well.

- Let's play Christ-honoring music during housework.

4. Family Worship

If you have a Christian family, you have a huge advantage in accomplishing this last point of the class: Family worship.

Worshiping God isn't just about singing hymns or singing the latest choruses; worshiping God isn't limited to religiously attending a church or holding many meetings with fellow members of the congregation. Worshiping God is something much deeper that always goes beyond the religious.

In Genesis 8:15-22, God told Noah to take his entire family (because the flood was over) and get out of the ark. Noah, as an act of gratitude, built an altar to the Lord by taking clean animals and making a sacrifice with them that was pleasing to God.

Today we could do the same; however, God doesn't want burnt offerings since the perfect sacrifice has already been made. Today God wants us to be the sacrifice, in our own flesh (Romans 12:1-2); that's to say that we're the living worship that burns on the altar ... And it would be wonderful if we didn't do it alone, but like Noah, with our entire family.

Surely, God will be pleased by our life and accept what we do. He may even give us a special promise.

Review/Application: Allow time for your students to write down what will be asked of them, and then share some of that in the group so that they can intercede for one another. In the end, encourage them to make a commitment to worship in their respective families.

Write the names of those who make up your family, their roles in it, and the needs they have right now.

	Name:	**Role:**	**Need:**
Example:	Andrew	Dad	To accept Jesus
	_____	_____	_____
	_____	_____	_____
	_____	_____	_____

Finally, make a commitment to be the one to initiate worship in your family. Here is a model of this commitment.

"I, _____ commit myself before God to worship God in my home, being an example in everything I do and say."

Challenge: This week, try to live out all of your religious beliefs at home. Don't forget some of the tips:

• At least one day a week we can pray for each other.

• Let's pledge not to insult each other in any way at home: not with offensive hitting, words or gestures.

• Once a week we can open the Bible and read a spiritual strength passage.

• When we travel together, let's take the time before we leave or come back to offer a family prayer.

• Let's play music that honors Christ during housework.

"We All Serve"

Objective: That students understand that the church functions as a body and that as such, each part or member of it has a specific function.

Memory Verse: *"...so in Christ we, though many, form one body, and each member belongs to all the others."* Romans 12:5

Attention!
Ask your students how they did living out their beliefs during the last week.
Accept

Connect | Navigate

Introductory Activity (12 - 17 years).

- Materials: A large piece of paper or blackboard, a marker or pencil, sheets of paper, and tape.

- Instructions: Draw the silhouette of a human body on the board. Cut the piece of paper into small pieces, and on each one write the spiritual gifts and functions, especially those that are clearly performed in your church (ushers, pastors, teachers, compassion, prayer, etc.). Put them all in a basket. Ask the students to each take a piece of paper and place it on the part of the body where they think it corresponds, according to their function, and briefly explain why they put it there. For example, the gift of prayer could be placed on the knees, because a person who prays spends a lot of time on their knees, or the gift of compassion could be placed on the heart, etc.

Introductory Activity (18 - 23 years).

- Materials: Sheets of paper and pencils or pens.

- Instructions: Cut the sheet of paper into small pieces, and write on each of them the name of all the participants in the class. Put all the names in a basket and ask the students to take one. If the name they got is their own, let them change it until they have one other than their own.

When everyone has a name, encourage them to write a gift they think that person has and explain how that person, with their gift, can contribute to the unity and harmony of the church or class. For example: "Manuel's gift is service; he's always willing to help", or "Ana is a person who reads the Bible a lot and she motivates the group to seek more of God." By the end of the round, everyone will have heard something positive about themselves.

Connect | Navigate

The city of Corinth was a place of unusual immorality "with all that could serve the pleasures of the senses ... it was one of the most lustful, effeminate, ostentatious and dissolute cities in the world" (Beacon Biblical Commentary, Volume 8. CNP, USA: s/f, p. 321). The Corinthian church couldn't keep itself out of all the sinful influence around it. That's why Paul in his letter to the Corinthians reminded them that they were "called to be [God's] holy people" (1 Corinthians 1:2).

Among all the problems the Corinthian church faced was failing to value the various gifts of the Holy Spirit, and considering some gifts to be superior to others. This had caused them to lose their sense of unity and service, belittling other ministries of the Holy Spirit that they considered less important.

1. One in Christ

Every Christian is a member of the body of Christ. We're all different, we live in different parts of the world and have different roles, but despite all this diversity, in Christ there is unity (1 Corinthians 12:12-13). For Paul, it was crucial that the Corinthians understand that. For that reason, he repeated the word "one" five times in just two verses. He made it clear that the emphasis was on unity.

In verse 13, Paul explains the common denominators that make us one in the church; namely, two experiences that are shared by all believers:

a. We were all baptized by one Spirit (12:13a).

Every believer shares this wonderful experience. This eliminates any differences that may exist between Christians, such as race, culture, position, etc. Both Jews and Greeks, slaves and free, men and women, rich and poor, we all share the experience that makes us one body, one church.

b. We were all given the one Spirit (12:13b).

Christians are united because we share the communion of the same Spirit that dwells in each one of us. In this fellowship, we share eternal life and the provision and mission of Christ (John 6:53-58), thus breaking down all barriers that can divide us.

2. Importance of diversity

"Even so the body isn't made up of one part but of many." (1 Corinthians 12:14). This analogy between the human body and the body of Christ teaches us that the body is a unity in diversity. In verses 14-26, Paul tried to make this message clear (even in a funny way), that each member of the body has a role and that all are important and necessary for its proper functioning. Personifying the different parts of the body, he conveyed the idea that each part, no matter how different, is important.

Indirectly, Paul presents two problems or tendencies in the church that prevent us from enjoying and valuing unity in diversity, and these are the inferiority and superiority complexes.

Do not **underestimate** our importance in the body of Christ (Low self esteem). Even though we think that we're inferior to others regarding gifts, it doesn't mean that we aren't a fundamental and important part of the body (vs. 15-16). Taking Paul's examples, it may be normal for the foot to feel inferior and unimportant relative to the hand. The hand plays instruments, welcomes visitors, even takes part in worship when we raise our hands. Even so, without the foot, we couldn't go to evangelize, participate in races, carry loads, keep the rest of the body in good physical shape, etc.

God expects us to do our part with what he has given us. Remember that every part of the body is important.

On the other hand, let's not **overestimate** our importance in the body of Christ either (pride). Paul tells us about the other extreme, when a member has a higher self-concept than he should have (v. 21). Paul gets closer and closer to the problems that existed among the Corinthians. The message needed to be clear: We are all important and no one is indispensable or more important than anyone else.

Paul rejects the erroneous way of thinking of the Corinthians, who valued and honored certain gifts more, considering them superior with respect to the "less important". They chose the most colorful gifts or ministries for selfish reasons, when the purpose of the gifts is to contribute to the growth of the body ... the church. If we believe ourselves to be spiritually superior or indispensable because of the gifts we've been blessed with, we may be straying from God's will. We must think better of it and ask God for forgiveness immediately, before it's too late.

Let's always take care and seek unity and we'll enjoy diversity in our church.

3. Different gifts, but the same body

Paul presents a list of gifts and responsibilities of the church (1 Corinthians 12:27-31). But first, he remarks that all are the body of Christ, although each one, a member in particular. And before starting the list, he makes another clarification "… God has placed in the church…" Members don't choose their office or choose their gifts. God is the one who sets people to do certain things in the church.

Paul divides the list in two. On the one hand, apostles, prophets, and teachers, and on the other, miracles, those who heal, who help, who administer, and the gift of tongues. Although he makes a clear division, this doesn't mean that he is distinguishing gifts, or that the list is organized in order of importance. No gift or office should be belittled or exalted above the others ... all are necessary. For this reason, he then makes a list of rhetorical questions, the obvious answers to which are negative: Not all are apostles, nor do all have gifts of healing (vs. 29-30). They are all valuable and we must accept, honor and respect them in the same way.

All members of the body of Christ have unique spiritual talents, abilities, and gifts. This variety of gifts enriches the church. Each part is vital and necessary for the proper functioning of the whole body. We are all called to do our part, to contribute our gifts and talents to the growth of the body. This means that we must all discover our spiritual gifts and serve in the best possible way.

Review/Application: Divide your students into groups and ask them to write definitions for the following gifts, and one or two practical functions in the church. (List taken from 1 Corinthians 12:28 and Romans 12:6-8). Then let them think about what their gift is within the church.

1. Administration: Ability to organize and direct activities, secretary, treasurers.

2. Exhortation: Ability to motivate people to live a true Christian life, counselor, teacher.

3. Distribute or Give: Ability to materially support the work through offerings.

4. Preside or Lead: Ability to guide a group with vision and concern, cell leader, pastor, teacher.

5. Mercy: Having compassion for the needs of others, compassionate ministries, giving food to the hungry, etc.

6. Prophecy or preaching: Ability to proclaim and apply the word of God, pastor.

7. Service: Ability to help others in a practical way, ushers.

8. Teaching: Ability to clearly communicate biblical truths to others, teachers, cell leaders.

9. Healing: Pray for healing, visit and pray for the sick.

Challenge: The church is like a big puzzle. No two pieces are the same. If they were, we wouldn't be able to see the finished image and that would mean one piece left over and another is missing. In the body of Christ, the same thing happens. There are no two identical members, therefore your gift is needed. Do you already know your gifts? Do you serve in your church, community, or neighborhood? Put your gifts at the service of God!

How Do I Serve?

Objective: That students understand that the talents and gifts that they possess have been given to them by God so that they can serve Him.

Memory Verse: *"For whoever has will be given more, and they'll have an abundance. Whoever does not have, even what they have will be taken from them."* Matthew 25:29

Connect | Navigate

Introductory Activity (12 - 17 years).

- Materials: Pieces of paper (5 x 7 cm) and pencils.
- Instructions: Each student will write on the piece of paper a list of their skills, such as public speaking, writing, singing, painting, etc. Then ask them to read and share how to use those skills to serve in the church.

Introductory Activity (18 - 23 years).

- Materials: Newspaper from the jobs section and blank sheets of paper and pencils.
- Instructions: Bring the newspaper sheets from the jobs section to the class and ask students to read aloud the profiles that are required for some jobs. Then ask them to create a profile of a servant of God and discuss whether they fill that profile to serve the Lord and whether they are serving effectively in the kingdom of God.

Connect | Navigate

A talent is a person's ability to understand and perform a certain activity. Talents can be acquired by genetic inheritance or by stimulation and learning. Whether we get them by inheritance or by learning, we must consecrate them to the service of God. What can we do to honor God with the talents He has given us?

1. Fulfilling the role of servants

We as children of God have the responsibility to serve him and watch over the interests of his Kingdom, and that's why he gave us abilities to effectively carry out the ministries that he entrusted to us. In Matthew 24:45-51, the Lord related a parable to teach how He wants to trust us as good servants.

A. The good and faithful servant

The Lord Jesus Christ promised to return for his church and no one knows when it will happen, but in the meantime, we must be doing what he told us to do. According to this parable, the good servant of God has the following characteristics:

Faithfulness: It consists of taking care not to defraud or betray the trust placed in us. The person is faithful in the presence or absence of the other person; executes exactly what was entrusted to him.

In the parable, the person who has these qualities is exalted. Faithfulness is exactly what God expects of his children. We must ensure that we don't break God's trust by serving Him with excellence, love, and gratitude (vs. 45-46).

Prudence: A prudent person is cautious and sensible in their attitudes and actions. This quality is necessary so as not to harm the interests of those who trust us. In our service to God, we need to put in all our effort so that we're effective and the Lord is pleased (vs. 45-46).

Reward: Every decision has a consequence. The servant who decided to be responsible, faithful, and wise was declared blessed and would be put in a position of greater authority. The Lord will reward by blessing those who serve him faithfully (v. 47).

B. The bad servant

According to this parable, the evil servant has the following characteristics:

Neglect: it's knowing what to do and not doing it. The bad servant is the one who doesn't do his part, thinking that his boss will take a long time to return, or that he won't hold him accountable and believes that he'll have time to correct his carelessness (v. 48-49).

Abuse: it's the misuse, excessive, unfair or improper use of something or someone. It can be the object of dishonest treatment of a person of less experience, strength or power (vs. 48-49).

The Lord has entrusted responsibilities to the church. Ask: Are you doing what God gave you to do? Have you been faithful and careful, or have you been negligent and irresponsible? People go to school or work even if they're sick, but not all go to church, and some neglect their area of service entrusted to them without excuse.

Reward: The bad servant had to face the consequences for his disloyalty and recklessness. When his master returned, he was severely punished and thrown out of his post. Christians who trust that they have a long time ahead of them and don't fulfill the opportunities of service that the Lord gives them will also lose the opportunity to be in his kingdom. It would be better for us to responsibly assume the role of servants of the Lord so that when He returns, he'll find us doing his will and serving him (v. 51).

2. Using and reproducing talents

The talents that the Lord gives us must be used and reproduced. In Matthew 25:14-30, we find the parable of the talents. Talents were a measure of change used in transactions. But the vital teaching of the parable includes aspects beyond economic value.

A. Trust, ability and responsibility

Each talent represented a fortune placed in the hands of the servants: The man deposited not only wealth but also trust in each one of them. Intellectual, artistic, professional, administrative, manual, counseling skills, etc., are gifts/talents received from God to be used to please God, and not just to earn money. The Lord gives gifts/talents according to God's plan. God entrusted us with talents by giving us the ability to perform certain activities, but He also gave us the ability to use them for his best interests. The Almighty doesn't need anyone, but with love he gives us the honor of serving him.

God gives you responsibilities according to the abilities that he's given you. You're not responsible for what you cannot do, but you're responsible for what you can do. Responsibility is the human capacity to answer for our actions. When receiving talents, qualities or aptitudes and abilities, sometimes we have the false idea that God is very far away and doesn't realize what we're doing. However, Jesus taught that he will return and then each one will give an accounting of what they did or didn't do with what they received. In the church, we constantly suffer from the lack of responsibility of some people, so the service of others is overloaded. Failure to comply doesn't exonerate us from liability.

Ask: Why do you think we can serve well in secular tasks and not in Kingdom ones? Perhaps because in secular tasks we have a boss or a teacher who has power over us and if we don't comply we can lose work, study, etc.

Talents must be developed, corrected, perfected and put at God's service. William Carey, a missionary in India, said, "My business is the Kingdom of Heaven. I'm a shoemaker just to cover my business expenses." That humble man, full of love for the Lord's work, said the following words in one of his sermons: "Expect Great Things From God. Try Great Things For God". (Missionary Lessons of Dr. Carey http://www.rlhymersjr.com/Online_Sermons_Spanish/2006/021906PM_LeccionesMisioneras. html).

B. Different actions

The first two servants assumed a dynamic, active attitude because they immediately took action to carry out what was asked of them, and the result was evident because they doubled the capital received (vs. 16-17).

The only effort of the negligent servant was to hide the capital received (v. 18). Many Christians don't undertake anything in the church because before trying it, they already decided that it won't work. The pessimistic attitude not only prevents them from working, but also from seeing results. The bad servant excused himself by putting the blame for his irresponsibility onto his boss. Ask: What excuses do fellow church members make when they don't fulfill their responsibilities? What excuses have you used for not using your gifts and talents in the service of the Lord?

Each faithful servant received praise and increased his capital, but the negligent servant lost what little he had. If you want to have God's blessing, you must use the gifts and talents that He gave you instead of hiding them and making excuses (vs. 21-18). The Word emphasizes the reality that the day will come to render an account before God of the use of our time and of our abilities and skills, without excuse. The important thing won't be the amount of talents received, but the results of having invested in the Lord's Kingdom.

Review/Application: Questions for group discussion:

1. Think of a person in your congregation (if you want you can say their name) who is characterized by their willingness to serve and do what is asked of them and they do so with pleasure. What effect has their example had on your life? Are they loved and respected? Would you like to be like them? Why?

2. According to Matthew 24:30-51, what are the characteristics of those who aren't faithful in doing the work that God has entrusted to them? (They are lazy, pessimistic, negligent, and irresponsible.)

3. What can be the results of neglect in serving God? (Disapproval and rejection on the part of God and the church.)

4. What will be the results of faithfulness in serving God? (We'll feel that we're doing God's will and we'll be recognized by Him as his faithful servants. We'll have more responsibility.)

5. What practical lessons does the parable of the talents have for your life?

6. What are you willing to do as a result of studying this lesson?

Challenge: Make it a duty to help in the church. You can do this by talking to your Sunday school teacher or another leader, asking how you can help. This could be preparing materials for the next lesson, setting up, contacting class members, etc.

In and Out

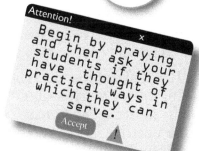

Attention!
Begin by praying and then ask your students if they have thought of practical ways in which they can serve.
x
Accept

Objective: That students recognize the importance of fulfilling the ministry to which God has called them, inside and outside the church.

Memory Verse: *"Watch your life and doctrine closely. Persevere in them, because if you do, you'll save both yourself and your hearers»* 1 Timothy 4:16

Connect / Navigate

Introductory Activity (12 - 17 years).

- Materials: White sheets of paper, pencils, individual chairs.
- Instructions: Ask your students to form pairs, and each will interview the other asking: If you had to lead or start a ministry in the church, what would it be? Each pair will come forward and introduce their partner and say what they wrote about that person.

Introductory Activity (18 - 23 years).

- Materials: Individual chairs to organize equipment, cards with signs.
- Instructions: Bring to the class cards with names of different ministries that can be developed in the church: evangelism, discipleship, compassion, prayer, visitation, administration, education, music and worship, etc. Post them in different parts of the classroom, and ask each student to sit near the ministry sign that catches their attention the most. Then each group will talk about how they could develop a ministry inside and outside the church. They'll share their ideas with others in the group.

Connect / Navigate

Let's define the word "ministry." In the Old Testament, the Hebrew term "sharat" was used, which means to minister, serve, officiate. The Latin term minister in turn is derived from the adjective "minus" which means less or less than. The minister was the servant or subordinate who was in the service of his master. In the New Testament, the most used term for minister was "diakoneo", which means to be a servant, assistant, serve, assist, minister. It's mainly translated with the verb "serve." (Expository Dictionary of Old and New Testament words. W.E. Vine. Caribe, 1999, Colombia, page 554).

These definitions help us understand that developing a ministry in the church implies a serious commitment to serve God and the people around us

1. To develop a ministry, you must first be a servant

In the New Testament context, being a servant was synonymous with being a slave in the service of one's master. This implied total submission to the will and orders of their master. In the Christian life, being a servant means first being a Christian and accepting the lordship of Jesus Christ as King and Lord. To understand servanthood is to be willing to humble yourself before God and decide to serve him. Timothy was a young man who had known Christ since childhood, and despite the persecution situation, he was willing to serve God (2 Timothy 1:5; 2:1-3). Every Christian is called to serve in the church, since this is a living organism; each one is empowered by the Holy Spirit to develop a specific ministry within his work (1 Corinthians 12:12-27).

2. To minister, you must prepare

Paul invited Timothy to be a good minister of the gospel. In 1 Timothy 4:6-16, he mentions some qualities one must cultivate to be a good minister.

Prepare for the task: "If you point these things out . . .", This implies preparation, study. Thus, Timothy would be a) Nourished with the words of faith, and b) have good doctrine. The minister of the Lord doesn't have to be a great teacher, but they must know the Word of God and what they believe in.

Recognize false doctrine: "Have nothing to do with godless myths and old wives' tales...". The King James version says: "refuse profane and old wives' fables". The Message says: "Stay clear of silly stories". Sadly, many evangelical Christians who serve God in various ministries don't know true doctrine, don't know how to differentiate between a false doctrine and a biblical one. And it's unfortunate how so many people go to certain congregations where the Word of God isn't taught. Those who serve God must know God through his Word.

Be godly: "… train yourself to be godly…". There are Christians who are good athletes and others who are almost bodybuilders, but they don't practice holiness. It doesn't mean that Paul is against physical exercise, he only warns Timothy that it must not occupy the first place in his life since there are things of greater importance. For liberal Christians, piety is fidelity to religious duties. "But in the Bible it has a broader meaning. In its Hebrew expression (hesed), it implies mutual, effective and faithful help to brothers, sisters, relatives, friends, allies, etc. Mercy isn't such if it's not expressed in specific acts of mercy. Another kind of piety must respond to God's mercy for his people, faithful obedience and the loving worship of man to God." (Biblical Vocabulary, Xavier León Dufour. Follow me, Barcelona: 1965, p. 615). In the past, there were many godly men and women, but today they are very rare. Churches need men and women of this stature. Paul himself says that godliness has promise for this present life and for the life to come.

Work and suffer: Generally jobs (except that of a minister of Jesus Christ), are jobs that have an established schedule of entry and exit. After working the established hours, the employee can go home quietly, sleep without interruptions, if he works from Monday to Friday, he can have Saturday and Sunday to rest or go for a walk with his family, etc. But the minister's job is very different. Paul says to Timothy: "… be strong…, Join with me in suffering…, No one serving as a soldier gets entangled in civilian affairs…,competes as an athlete…" (2 Timothy 2:1-8). If the minister didn't receive a good preparation, at the first battle he'll immediately leave his ministry. To serve God, you have to pay a price, you have to dedicate time and effort.

Be an example: Paul clearly mentions that whoever wants to serve God needs to live a life of integrity, as an example to others, in their way of speaking, in their conduct, in love of neighbor, in faith and purity of heart. There is a very common saying that goes, "Actions speak louder than a words." So that no one despises you or considers you too immature or inexperienced to develop any ministry, it's necessary to demonstrate it with a good testimony. The testimony of a young Christian is decisive for his success in any ministry he develops; not mattering the age, but total surrender to Christ.

Stay busy: To develop a ministry, you have to work at it. Paul, although he knew that Timothy was very young, invited him to prepare and practice. Don't think that you need to know a lot to start serving. Just start. Read, find out what you're going to do, learn from others, teach others, and serve the Lord.

Take care of your ministry: Timothy had received the laying on of hands to be ordained as a minister of the church, (what today we would call being ordained) to shepherd a congregation. This implied a great responsibility for a young man. Therefore, Paul's recommendation was: Take care of the gift that's in you and use it to bless others. Today we must value serving God. When we're given a ministry to serve in the church, we must do so with joy and gladness and not be irresponsible since we'll give an account to God of what we did with the gifts that He gave us. Take your ministry seriously. Serving God is a privilege, not an obligation.

3. To serve, you have to be ready for anything

A. Minister within the church.

There are ministries within the church that serve for the edification of the body of Christ, that is, to promote the spiritual growth of those who are believers or interested in the gospel. There are usually many possibilities to serve within the church, such as being teachers, ushers, participating in music, singing, discipling, prayer, administration, leadership, etc. Most Christians are involved in developing these ministries.

B. Minister outside the church

The ministries that are most needed in the church are those that have the purpose of reaching others, and these should be developed to reach outside the four walls of the church. Among them we can find the ministries of evangelism, visitation, compassion, discipleship, cell leaders, preachers, church planters, missionaries, etc. Sometimes churches don't grow because all ministries are focused on keeping those who are already within the church and not winning those who don't know Christ.

Today we must reflect on our spiritual life and ask ourselves, Am I truly a child of God? Am I willing to be a servant? What spiritual gifts has God given me to serve Him? How am I developing my gifts? In what ministries can I get involved inside or outside the church?

Review / Application: Allow time for the students to read the passages, reflect, and respond:

1 Timothy 4:7-8 - Why should Timothy ignore gossip and put aside physical exercise to dedicate himself to fulfilling his ministry? (Because to fulfill his ministry, he had to give God the first place in his life, put aside what was distracting him, such as gossip, false doctrines, philosophical theories, sports, etc)

1 Timothy 4:12 - In what areas of your Christian life must you work at in order to develop a ministry in the church? (In my testimony, how I behave, the exercise of my faith, how I speak, how I am living, in my relationship with my neighbor, etc.)

In what areas of ministry would you like to serve God inside or outside the church?

Challenge: God continues to speak to us about service and to share what we've received from him. Keep meditating on it, and this week, if you already have a ministry, think about how to develop it, and if you aren't serving yet, don't wait. This week put your hands to work and start now.

Servant or Master?

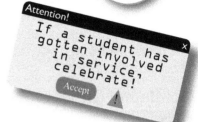

Attention! If a student has gotten involved in service, celebrate! Accept

Objective: That students see service as part of their Christian life.

Memory Verse: *"and whoever wants to be first must be slave of all."* Mark 10:44

Connect | Navigate

Introductory Activity (12 - 17 years).

- Materials: Drawings or pictures of people helping others (crossing the street, carrying something heavy, caring for a sick person, giving money, comforting someone who is crying) or posters that mention some kind of service.

- Instructions: Ask your students to express how they feel when they see these scenes; Reflect on how God works with us in our need and how we should serve others in the same way.

Introductory Activity (18 - 23 years).

- Materials: Blackboard and chalk or large paper and marker.

- Instructions: On the board, write on one side: "Helpful person" and on the other side: "Selfish person." Ask your students to describe the characteristics that each of these people usually have. At the end, reflect together on the differences that have been mentioned and the influence that these characteristics can have on the interpersonal relationships of these people.

Connect | Navigate

True Christian service is intrinsically related to its original meaning, that is, it includes attitudes of humility, sacrifice, and active love. We must recognize that these characteristics aren't to be temporary in the life of the young person, but must become a daily lifestyle in which they live consistently serving God and others, answering the question: Am I a servant or a master?

1. The attitude of humility in ministry

In the verses before the study passage for today (Mark 10:35-45), we see that Jesus had been traveling to Jerusalem and teaching the people along the way (Mark 10:1, 17:32). In Mark 10:29-31, we observe that Jesus made it clear to the disciples that in the kingdom of God, the order of importance is completely opposite to the order of importance that exists in our human society (v. 31).

Paradoxically, we note that just a few verses later, two of Jesus' disciples made a request that was in contradiction to what the Master had just said. In Mark 10:37, we read that brothers James and John asked Jesus: "Let one of us sit at your right and the other at your left in your glory." We note in these words that the brothers were thinking about their own future well-being, and that they showed an attitude of pride in thinking that they deserved a more prestigious place than the other followers of Jesus. Unfortunately, this attitude is one that's repeated, even today, in many of the current followers of Jesus. This attitude remains in the contemporary church when a young Christian seeks to feel praised or flattered by others, or works only to feel they are in a higher place than others, or treats others with contempt or inattention when that other person is less recognized in the social environment of the congregation, youth group or community.

Jesus was very patient and clear with his disciples, yet they still struggled with an attitude of pride. He clarified that in the kingdom of God, only God knows how things will be organized and this shouldn't be our responsibility or concern (v. 40). Instead, what is of utmost importance for a young Christian serving in Jesus' name is to have an attitude of humility on a daily basis, for example: consistently thinking about how others feel, what others need, and what can you do about it. Your constant prayer as young Christians serving in the church should be that Jesus Christ will release you each day from an attitude of pride. May your way of speaking, looking, dressing, and relating to others always be a true reflection of the humble attitude of Jesus. It's necessary that we pray to God that around us, people will always feel received, loved and blessed by Him. We must recognize that this won't be easy in our human nature, which always tends to personal pride, but when we submit to reading the Word, unceasing prayer and the purifying work of the Holy Spirit, we can be humble Christians and extremely sensitive to the needs of others (Luke 1:37).

2. The willingness to sacrifice in ministry

In the following verses of our study passage for today, we see that Jesus shared something difficult with the disciples who wanted to lead. Jesus said: "'You don't know what you're asking,' Jesus said. 'Can you drink the cup I drink or be baptized with the baptism I am baptized with?'" (Mark 10:38). (Here Jesus was referring to what he had just said in Mark 10:33-34, which was his torture and death on the cross).

Jesus made it clear to his followers that Christian ministry wasn't centered on the privileges and / or blessings that come with that path, but rather it's a journey that requires a clear and decisive willingness to sacrifice for others. This sacrifice requires a lot from the young Christian, including personal time, family time, work time, money and other material resources, and also often emotional suffering and discomfort. It's important to understand that in this journey of sacrifice for others, there won't always be the expected reward of human recognition from leaders; there won't always be the expected result of gratitude or growth in those for whom the sacrifice is made; and finally, understand that many times it will be a path of loneliness, pain and weariness. This kind of service is in total opposition to the general trend of modern society, which is always seeking pleasure rather than suffering for others.

In cases where the young Christian doesn't possess a willingness to sacrifice for others, whether at home, in church, or at school, people will notice his selfish tendency. It will be sad and probably other young people will follow that example of thinking first of themselves and not thinking of other people in the congregation, much less of those who are still unconverted. This situation keeps many churches stuck on themselves and with a chronic lack of spiritual vitality.

By understanding these difficult realities of daily service to God, young Christians who serve (in different areas) can ensure that they are 100 percent dependent on the strength of Jesus for their ministry. As they seeks to study Jesus' example in the Bible and plead with the Holy Spirit to fill them with his love and wisdom, young Christians can be empowered for ministries of true sacrificial love that transforms lives and pleases the Lord. Jesus told his faithful followers that they would suffer and bear many of the same things that He suffered (Mark 10:39). He also told them, "And surely I am with you always, to the very end of the age." (Matthew 28:20).

3. The action of service in ministry

Finally, in Mark 10:43-44, Jesus spoke to the disciples about the importance of serving others. The Lord mentioned that many secular leaders of that time abused their position of authority over others for their own benefit (v. 42). We can notice that in our contemporary society, this situation continues. People's desire for power leads them to seek, by any inexcusable means, a position of authority, and from there they forget the needs of others.

On the contrary, Jesus taught that we must characterize ourselves by a constant action of service to others, and not by seeking others to serve us. This action must be exactly that, an action, and not simply words that are said without making them a reality. The action of service requires great effort on the part of the young Christian, because as human beings, we tire ourselves physically, mentally and emotionally. When this burnout happens, it's easy to fall into an attitude that expects or demands that others do the work (for example: cleaning the church and bathrooms, visiting the discouraged or sick young people, going out to deliver evangelistic brochures around the neighborhood, preparing the necessary things for the worship service, working in the kitchen, going to get those who don't have transportation to church, seeking shelter or food for those who don't have it, praying for those who are in need, etc.).

The young person who wants to serve must bear in mind that in order to be a servant as Jesus taught, it's also necessary to seek the same training that Jesus sought. In the Scriptures we see that Jesus regularly set aside time to be alone with God and pour out his sad or worried heart to his heavenly Father in prayer. We observe that Jesus shared time alone with his close companions to eat and rest from hard work, that he had time to fast, and also time to eat; Furthermore, Jesus enjoyed time with family and friends (the wedding at Cana of Galilee, John 2:1), and also with children (Mark 10:14). Today, young Christians will benefit from taking care of their physical body with exercise and basic medical care; also taking care of their mind and heart by taking time to be alone with God, rest, have fun, and enjoy time with their close family.

Humility, sacrifice, and service are closely related characteristics that are also essential and indispensable in true Christian service. We have also noticed that this kind of service, full of spiritual vitality, is only possible when God is the center of all effort, and the young person simply does what the Lord Jesus asks daily. "For we're co-workers in God's service..." (1 Corinthians 3:9).

Review/Application: Allow time for them to think of practical examples from their daily lives that demonstrate the corresponding attitude (answers are by way of examples).

TEACHINGS OF JESUS	MY RESPONSE
Attitude of Humility	• Talk to those I don't feel comfortable with.
	• Don't speak ill of others; rather say positive things
Willingness to Sacrifice	• Give offerings instead of buying something for myself.
	• Share my food with another person.
Service in Action	• Help with the housework of an elderly or sick person in the neighborhood.
	• Raise funds for a family in greatest need..

Challenge: What is your perspective on Christian ministry? What experiences or examples have you had with your leaders? Have you ever wanted to serve in the church or are you already doing so? Remember that God created you for a special plan. He says in Jeremiah 29:11, "'For I know the plans I have for you,' declares the Lord, 'plans to prosper you and not to harm you, plans to give you hope and a future.'" Don't hesitate to share your doubts and questions with me, your Sunday school teacher.

One Option?

Objective: That students compare the characteristics of the servant of God with the characteristics they currently have.

Memory Verse: *"Those who have served well gain an excellent standing and great assurance in their faith in Christ Jesus."* 1 Timothy 3:13

Attention!
Don't forget to ask about last week's Challenge!
Accept

Connect | Navigate

Introductory Activity (12 - 17 years).

- Materials: Sheets of paper (rectangular size 20x10 cm., White or colored), pencils or markers and clips for each student.

- Instructions: it's important that you arrive at the classroom early, prepare in advance, and make sure you have all the necessary supplies on hand. Arrange the chairs in a circle. When the students arrive, welcome them, ask them to sit down on one of the chairs. Choose one of your students to be your helper to give the others a piece of paper, a pencil, and a clip. Ask each student to write on their paper a characteristic that they think a servant of God should have. As they finish writing, each one will come to the front and clip their paper to the clothes of the person you designated as your assistant.

Make a list of the different characteristics that people wrote down.

According to your own thoughts, these are the qualities a servant of God should have. Compare your own lives with the characteristics or qualities of a servant that you all wrote down. Ask: How much are you like him/her?

Introductory Activity (18 - 23 years).

- Materials: Copies of a paper with different boxes where you'll write the qualities of each of your students (if you have 10 students, you'll make a chart with 10 boxes) and a pencil.

- Instructions: Give each of your students a copy of the paper with the boxes of characteristics and ask them to go find the person who they believe has the characteristic listed in the box and have that person sign in the box. The first one to fill the entire table with different signatures will be the winner, but everyone must fill each of the boxes with signatures.

We all have special characteristics that make us different and valuable to others.

Connect | Navigate

The apostle Paul wrote that we're open letters that are read by everyone, (2 Corinthians 3:1-3). In other words, all the time the people around us are reading our letters, seeing our testimony, our way of behaving, etc. Ask: What do you think people might say about us as Christians? Do people see in us the qualities of a servant of God?

Ask: Has it ever happened to you that sometimes when it comes to doing something, you don't have everything you need to do it and you solve the problem by replacing one thing with another? When it comes to doing a good job, there's nothing more satisfying than having everything we need.

For example: if we're going to fix something, having all the tools we need, or if we're going to cook, have all the ingredients, or if we're going to make a craft, having all the materials. If we apply this to the spiritual life, we could say that God always has his chosen instruments, or tools, which he will use to do everything that He wants to do in our lives at this time. To carry out his plans, many times he uses young people who put themselves in his hands. But what kind of youth does God use? The Lord uses young people with certain significant qualities. For example, he used the following young people:

1. Joshua, a young man different from the others

a. From an early age, Joshua was characterized by a life of consecrated and dedicated service to God. "The Lord would speak to Moses face to face, as one speaks to a friend. Then Moses would return to the camp, but his young aide Joshua son of Nun didn't leave the tent." (Exodus 33:11).

b. Despite the negative thinking of his fellow spies, Joshua proved that he could make a difference in the midst of a rebellious, ungrateful and incredulous generation. He was a person committed to God, who had a different perspective than others in the different situations of life. From this perspective, he achieved the objectives set forth. "Joshua son of Nun and Caleb son of Jephunneh, who were among those who had explored the land, tore their clothes and said to the entire Israelite assembly, 'The land we passed through and explored is exceedingly good. If the Lord is pleased with us, he will lead us into that land, a land flowing with milk and honey, and will give it to us. Only don't rebel against the Lord. And don't be afraid of the people of the land, because we'll devour them. Their protection is gone, but the Lord is with us. Do not be afraid of them.' " (Numbers 14: 6-9)

c. When God looked for Moses' successor, he didn't need to go very far; it was a natural transition of leadership for the people.

d. For times as difficult as those of today, God will use "Joshuas" who have learned by serving their leaders and who think contrary to how people often think by saying "it isn't possible", "I won't achieve the objectives" or "I will never get ahead in the middle of this situation." People challenged by God, like Joshua, look to God for answers when they face difficulties.

2. Josiah was a young man with a good heart for God

a. "Josiah" in Hebrew means "the Lord supports me" or "Jehovah has healed". He was king of Judah between 639 and 608 BC, and instituted very important reforms for the entire nation. Josiah came to the throne at eight years of age, due to the murder of his father, Amon, and reigned for thirty-one years. He didn't imitate the evil that his ancestors did. We don't see in him involved in bad leadership as had been the case with earlier kings, but rather on the contrary, he was concerned about what he could do to help his people follow God. "He [Josiah] did what was right in the eyes of the Lord and followed the ways of his father David..." (2 Chronicles 34:2; 2 Kings 22:2)

b. Already at 18 years of age, Josiah showed great concern for the house of God, which until then was abandoned and not maintained. He set about to repair it. He put his complete trust in the construction workers, thinking highly of them (2 Kings 22:7). But, above all else, he had a great and deep fear of God. Scripture illustrates how he was saddened and anguished at the reading of the Word, which he heard for the first time (vs. 10-11), because the people were not obeying it.

- His heart melted
- He humbled himself before the Lord
- He tore his clothes
- Cried in God's presence

c. Something very interesting to highlight is that by listening to God, God listened to Josiah (v. 19). He turned to the Lord with all his heart, and as a result of such consecration, he was turned into an instrument that brought great spiritual revival to an entire nation. God still continues to use useful tools to produce revivals. These people understand that according to the impact they have experienced from the Word and the presence of God in their hearts, that will be the magnitude of God's blessing on an entire nation (2 Chronicles 34:3, 14-33).

How many times have we asked ourselves: Will ministry be an option for me? Will I, Lord, be the ideal person to develop this work? I once heard an author say that, "People don't reject the message, they reject the messenger." Could it be that due to the bad testimony of some messengers, the image of a good servant of God, who exemplifies with concrete characteristics what it means to be a good pastor, deacon, or a good evangelist, has been lost?

Today God wants to use you. For each job, God needs an effective tool to carry out his mission, like Joshua who learned from the great leader Moses and imitated his steps and stood straight before God, or like Josiah who turned his heart to God beyond all that his ancestors had done and received God's favor, not just for himself, but for his entire nation. Today God wants to continue using young people who are willing to obey him.

Review / Application: Ask the students to identify throughout the Bible people who said yes to ministry as a way of life.

- He was born in Tarsus; he was a persecutor of the church; he preached to the Gentiles. (Apostle Paul)
- Man full of the Holy Spirit, faith and wisdom who was martyred for his faith in Jesus. (Stephen)
- Young pastor, of good testimony, disciple of Paul. (Timothy)
- He was one of Paul's companions in whom he placed a lot of trust, he was gentle. (Titus)
- Hebrew leader, called by God to liberate his people. (Moses)
- A native of Bethsaida, his name was Simeon and also Simon, son of Jonah; Andrew's brother, he was a fisherman, he denied his Master three times. (Peter)
- He spoke of the Kingdom of God, he performed many miracles, he was born in a manger, he is the son of God. (Jesus)
- He was the second king of Israel; youngest son of Jesse; he was a shepherd of Bethlehem; he acquired fame for his musical abilities and for his bravery in his confrontation against the giant Philistine Goliath. (David)

Challenge: Look closely at those involved in the ministry of the local church and ask them some of the following questions:

- How did they decide to devote their time and talents to the work of God?
- How did they know that they should get involved in this specific ministry?
- Were they challenged by other people to take on this task?

Share your answers with the rest of the class during our next class session.

We Are Witnesses

Attention!
Start by giving students time to share about their interviews of ministry leaders.
Accept

Objective: That students recognize that the call to fulfill the Great Commission is for all Christians.

Memory Verse: *«Therefore go and make disciples of all nations, baptizing them in the name of the Father and of the Son and of the Holy Spirit,...»* Matthew 28:19

Connect | Navigate

Introductory Activity (12 - 17 years).

- Materials: Pencils, blank sheets of paper, a watch, three chocolates and a mailbox (this can be a wrapped cardboard box).

- Instructions: Distribute a blank piece of paper and a pencil to each participant and ask each one to write as many names and surnames of their friends as they can. They can be friends from their school, neighborhood, etc. Give half a minute, and once the time has passed, ask them to add up the names, and then put their paper, with their own name at the top, in the mailbox. The three participants who have written the longest list of friends will win.

Ask: Have you shared the gospel with these people? How have you been able to express the message of Jesus to each of them?

Introductory Activity (18 - 23 years).

- Materials: Box with objects: a Bible, a letter, devotionals, a light bulb, paper, radio, cell phone, etc. Markers and a blackboard.

- Instructions: Ask them to divide into two groups and each group to organize itself into pairs. Then each pair must stand back to back, so that player "A" faces the group and player "B" faces the board, with a marker in hand. The one who runs the game must give player "A" an object from the box. He should describe it to the partner Player B without telling him what it is. Player "B" will have to draw it without seeing it. Keep track of the time it takes each pair to describe the object and draw it. Couples who do it in less time will win their group.

How quick are we to share the gospel and be witnesses to his Word? The world needs light, each drawn object expresses a message.

Connect | Navigate

The book of Acts tells the story of the first church. The Holy Spirit is the author of all the events in each of the stories.

The first church was founded by the apostles, by people who through the years took on the responsibility to be witnesses of Christ. This story is a narration of events, of miracles, of changed lives. Jesus asks us to be his witnesses so that through his story we present his message and bring salvation (Matthew 28:19).

1. A witness who waits for the promise and receives it

The disciples had enjoyed many experiences with Jesus, but the time had come when they would have to go on alone. Jesus had fulfilled his purposes and was physically leaving earth and going to heaven. He had many plans for his disciples and a special calling for their lives; he wanted them to be his witnesses. The disciples took on a great challenge to achieve the plans that Jesus had for them.

The disciples had to learn to "wait." Jesus had promised them that they would have the guidance of the Holy Spirit, and that in the plans they undertook and projects they assumed and being his witnesses, the Holy Spirit would be there to help and comfort them in everything. Waiting is hard, as is trusting, but if we learn to wait upon the Lord, Jesus will use us and make us part of his great projects.

It's time to be disciples of Christ. We don't want to get carried away by our own conscience or by our own decisions, but rather we want to learn to consult God on each of our decisions, and much more in terms of service to God. Let's follow the example of the disciples (Acts 1:13-14) who learned to wait by being all together praying to the Lord.

2. A witness who assumes his role and bears fruit

"Making disciples" wasn't an easy task; it was a great challenge and the disciples had to take it up with great commitment on their part. Their task was key; they had to be witnesses (Acts 1:8), they had to share the story of Jesus, the story of salvation. But "making disciples" wasn't only talking about the gospel, it also included sharing the teachings of Jesus to the point where people publicly declared that they belonged to Christ through baptism.

We must recognize that this great challenge of "disciple-making" wasn't just in the past. It's a commitment that wasn't only given to the disciples in the time of Jesus, but it's a task that we who consider ourselves children of God, who are committed to the message of Jesus Christ, must consider and apply to our lives now.

We must be witnesses, taking on the role of disciplers, carrying the name Christ on high, sharing his Word, working more seriously so that people accept Jesus, learn from him and seek to be baptized. Also, we must motivate them so that they are encouraged to continue sharing this great challenge with others and forming new disciples.

3. A witness summoned and who plays his best game

Being summoned to be part of a team, assuming the role assigned to us there, identifying with the team and sharing the same purpose, leads us to have a sense of belonging and motivates us to achieve goals and challenges.

The disciples were from Jesus' team and they knew they made a great team. When Jesus left and came back risen to summon them, they believed in Him and were encouraged to go to the place where Jesus ordered them: "Then the eleven disciples went to Galilee, to the mountain where Jesus had told them to go" (Matthew 28:16). But not all of them went to the gathering; one of the twelve was missing for he was no more (Acts 1:16-19).

In the secular world, the largest number of teams are driven by sport. Being a player called up to belong to a national team is a great privilege. But not all players are willing to give their all, not all assume their role, not all give the best of themselves during the game. Only the best team brings home the trophy of winner, best, or one of the best.

Jesus summons us to give our best; we need to assume the role of witness. Jesus knows how talented we are and is confident that we can play the best game. It's interesting that in Matthew 28:17, it says that "When they saw him, they worshiped him...", but it's also sad to read "but some doubted."

Jesus trusts us and has hope in us. Let's not doubt the great things he can do with us; Let's accept and play the best game. Let's respond with confidence to the command that He left us: "...go and make disciples of all nations,..."

Let's remember that walking with Jesus is learning more about him every day; it's experiencing his grace, enjoying his goodness. Becoming his witness is helping others live the same experience, having the great opportunity to see lives transformed by his message, and giving blessings to each person who meets him.

Review/Application: Ask your students to look up the following scriptures and find the names of Christ's witnesses who were his disciples:

Acts 2:14 (Peter)   Acts 3:1 (Peter and John)

Acts 6:8 (Stephen)   Acts 8:26 (Philip)

Acts 9:36 (Tabitha)   Acts 16:1 (Timothy)

Acts 17:10 (Paul and Silas)   Colossians 4:12 (Epaphras)

Ephesians 6:21 (Tychicus)

Challenge: How can you express that you're a witness for Jesus? Think of creative ways to be a witness for Christ. Share your ideas with the class next week when we next meet.

New People

Objective: That students understand that we're God's people, chosen out of love, and therefore it's our responsibility to keep his commandments.

Memory Verse: *"The Lord your God has chosen you out of all the peoples on the face of the earth to be his people, his treasured possession. Therefore, take care to follow the commands, decrees and laws I give you today."* Deuteronomy 7:6,11

Attention!

Don't forget to ask for testimonials from last week's Challenge. Ask: "In what way were you a witness during the week?"

Accept

Connect | Navigate

Introductory Activity (12 - 17 years).

- Materials: A sheet of paper and a pencil for each student.

- Instructions: Design on the sheet of paper, a chart with several boxes and in each box write things that your students may have in common, (name, age, height, weight, shoe size, month of birth, gender, number of siblings, etc.). Inside each box leave a space for them to fill in and another for their colleagues to sign. When your students arrive to class, give them the sheet and a pencil to fill in the boxes. Then tell them that you'll give them a set time and they are to ask each other and find the person who matches what is written in the box and ask them to sign. At the end ask, How many of you knew those who had similar characteristics to yours, without asking? There are many things that you have in common and that perhaps you didn't know because you don't know each other in depth or because you never talked about it. But yes, there is something that all of us in this place have in common. Then start the lesson.

Introductory Activity (18 - 23 years).

- Materials: A Bible, large clothes, i.e., pants and a T-shirt into which two people can fit into at the same time, a small table, a chair, something to drink, a glass, a plate, something to eat; It can be a sandwich, or a cake, or a dessert, or just a packet of cookies. They'll also need silverware and napkins.

- Instructions: Ask for three volunteers who want to help you and have them come to the front. Ask two of them to dress in the set of clothes you brought, with the arm of one person in one shirt sleeve and the other person's arm in the other sleeve, and one person in one leg of the pants and the other person in the other leg. Explain that they'll be "the body" and the third person will be "the head" of this body. The "head" will position himself in the middle by standing behind the body and putting his head between the two people of the body. Move the table and chair forward with all the items. The "head" must give the "body" instructions and the "body" must perform them. Example: "The head will say: "I'm very tired, I want to sit down. I'm thirsty, I want a drink., I'm hungry, I want something to eat. I wonder what today's devotional says?" (Deuteronomy 7:6-11). "The body" must try to sit in the chair, figure out how to eat and drink and look up the Bible verse so that "the head" can read it aloud. After the activity is complete, ask your students what lessons they learned from what they observed. Then start the lesson.

Connect | Navigate

Ask: Have you stopped for a moment to think how important and special you're to God? The Bible tells us in Genesis 1:26-27 that we were created in his image and likeness and he made us rule over all the earth. He also tells us in his Word that he made us little less than the angels and that he crowned us with glory and honor (Psalm 8:5-8).

When we accepted him in our hearts, he gave us a very privileged place and even made us his beloved children, we're part of his family and his special people.

You may wonder, how is it that we're so important to God? Why? For what? God gave us that great honor and place, with a great purpose; let's see what his Word says.

1. We are part of His people

Let's read Deuteronomy 7:6-11 and 1 Peter 2:9. In these verses, we find a word that's common in both passages; the word that's emphasized is "people."

In the Old Testament, the concept of "the people of God" was born. Its origin was with Abraham, patriarch of the people of Israel. God called him to leave his land and everything there and go to an unknown place, and it's there that God gave him the promise (Genesis 12:2). God chose Israel as his people to keep his law, his commandments, and be an instrument of redemption, so that through them the nations would know God.

God wanted Israel to be a beacon to the nations, just as He mentioned in Isaiah 42:6-8. But we all know how history continued. The people that God chose was unfaithful on repeated occasions. They disobeyed his law, worshiped other gods, and little by little they turned their backs on God and forgot the purpose to which God called them.

In time, God raised up prophets, judges, and kings to guide his people, but time after time they fell into sin and turned away from God.

However, when the right time came, God, who's merciful and whose great love is incomparable, sent Jesus Christ to save the world (Luke 19:10). Before Jesus came, it might have been thought that God didn't care any more about Israel. However, in Jesus Christ, the full love of God for the entire human race was demonstrated.

Jesus Christ didn't come only to redeem or save Israel, but all mankind, just as it says in John 3:16.

The only way to become part of God's people is by placing our faith in Jesus Christ, who through his sacrifice on the cross made it possible to be reconciled to God. Sin separated us from God; we were slaves of the devil, yet he looked at us with love and forgave us.

Thanks to his blood shed on the cross, we can become part of the people of God, not of a nation, nor of the Jews, but of the people of God.

2. The privileges God has granted us

Deut. 7:6-11 clearly shows God's love for his people, and today his words are extended to us who are part of that chosen people. Allow your students to explain in their own words each phrase of the text. If necessary, clarify some of the concepts that they don't understand: we're a holy people, we're chosen to be a special people, we were insignificant, he loved us and rescued us from servitude so that we may keep his commandments.

In 1 Peter 2:9, we find four characteristics or privileges that God gave to his children, to those who believe in him as their Savior and Lord.

a. A chosen people: You belong to a family, you're an offspring, that is, we're God's offspring (Gen. 12:1-9).

b. Royal priesthood: According to some scholars, it may indicate that you "belong to or serve the King, God." Or it can also mean "a royal house", or "a royal residence." That is, Peter expressed to his readers that they are a house or a palace where God the King resides. Just as the Old Testament priesthood should be free from contamination, they should be holy people, consecrated for this service. God calls us to live holy lives so that we too can be a holy priesthood.

c. Holy nation: Denotes that we're part of a nation, and not just any nation, but one that's specially dedicated or consecrated to God, since He has separated us from the world for his honor and glory.

d. God's special possession: It means that we belong exclusively to God. He bought us with the price of the blood of his son Jesus. We were nobody, we didn't deserve his love and mercy. However, he chose us as his people. This means that he gave us an identity; we're now his children, and in return for what God did for us, our lives are at his complete service.

Review/Application: Allow time for your students to write in their own words what 1 Peter 2:9 means.

Challenge: It would be great if you could organize yourselves to plan a day or afternoon in a specific place in your neighborhood or near church to put evangelism into practice. (I'm glad to help) Maybe you haven't had the chance yet; there are many ways to share the gospel: through a booklet, a play, a dance, etc. Don't miss this opportunity to share what God has done for you!!

A Missionary Heart

Objective: That students feel part of a church with a missionary call, willing to commit to God to fulfill the Great Commission given by Jesus Christ.

Memory Verse: *"How, then, can they call on the one they haven't believed in? And how can they believe in the one of whom they haven't heard? And how can they hear without someone preaching to them?"* Romans 10:14

Connect — Navigate

Introductory Activity (12 - 17 years).

- Materials: Clippings from newspapers, magazines or pamphlets of national or foreign tourist places, one for every 4 or 5 students; one or two sheets of paper and pencils.

- Instructions: Show your students the clippings, and let them choose the place they would like to visit. Gather them in groups according to the place chosen, provide them with paper and pencil to make an approximate budget of expenses, including passport cost if it's abroad, visa procedures, unforeseen events, etc. Then do an analysis, together with the students, of the obstacles to going on a trip like the one that was budgeted. Make a list and save it for the end of the class.

Introductory Activity (18 - 23 years).

- Instructions: In advance, prepare two young people (may be from the class) to act out an experience of a mission trip. Ask one of them to share all the difficulties they witnessed (including personal costs for the trip) and the other to mention achievements. Then take stock with the group. (Encourage the role-players to agree to make the trip worthwhile.) If someone in the church had an experience of a mission trip or activity, invite them to share it and not do the role play. Finally, you can plan an extra classroom activity with the students, it could be to a hospital, nursing home, etc. to take something to share.

Connect — Navigate

Without a doubt, the results of a recreational trip aren't always entirely satisfactory, despite the fact that it had been a rest activity. The bustle of the trip and unforeseen events (illness, accidents, theft, etc.) may overshadow the restful actions and result in tiredness. However, there remains the satisfaction of having done activities different from the routine. Possibly, the economic factor ends up in a difficult situation due to having taken out a loan, or if the expenses were paid with a credit card, and more than expected was spent. It happens in some cases that travelers return beaten or ill due to climate changes and food, which involve more expenses and discomfort. At other times, it may be that none of this happens and everything turns out excellent.

Who would be willing to invest the same time and money in a trip to non-tourist places and without rest and relaxation? For example, a trip to evangelize without the comforts of hotels with comfortable beds, toilets, showers, restaurants, easy transportation, recreational games, etc. Ask: Would you be willing to invest the cost of a trip to serve? Rather than sharing time with family or friends, would you be willing to share your time and energies with people with very low resources, sleeping on the floor, using latrines, eating differently, being rejected by some people in the community?

The meaning of the word "gospel" is nothing more than "good news." When we share that Good News with others, we're sharing what Jesus Christ did to give us salvation; we're presenting the gospel to others; we're preaching his Word, fulfilling "the Great Commission" entrusted to those of us who are Jesus' disciples.

1. The Great Commission

The Lord Jesus told his disciples to make more disciples, and if we're his disciples, we must obey his command (Mark 16:15-18). This reading corresponds to what is called "the Great Commission," because it's what Jesus Christ left for us to fulfill. The church is made up of all of us who believe that Jesus was born as a man yet was God. He was crucified and died to give salvation to humanity. He rose again on the third day, and ascended to heaven, where he is our intercessor. The church must continue sharing the message of salvation to all who don't yet know it and are walking in darkness.

2. A Missional church

The church that fulfills the task entrusted is a missional church. When the Lord Jesus was finishing his mission on earth in physical form, he promised not to leave his disciples alone. He made the promise to send the Holy Spirit, who as part of the Trinity would fill the void that he would leave. The presence of God through his Spirit provides comfort, peace, strength, authority and everything necessary to fulfill the Great Commission. He is the one who distributes the gifts for the edification of the body of Christ. In 1 Corinthians 12, Paul referred to gifts and their functions, and specifically in verse 11 he mentioned that it's the Holy Spirit who distributes what He wants to whom He wants. Each one has a specific function within the body, therefore, it's in unity that the mission of the church is carried out.

3. Steps to Follow

In the same way that the diversity of gifts is needed for the body to function, there must be a procedure. To achieve success in the mission, it's important to take into account the following steps:

A. PRAY. It's the key that opens doors. This is part of the armor that a Christian should wear (Ephesians 6:10-18). Paul also mentions praying at all times in all circumstances, in good times and in bad (Philippians 4:6).

Ask: Are there different kinds of prayers? Yes, we can mention the prayer of gratitude, intercessory prayer, the asking prayer, to name some. To be successful in prayer, it must be done with "thanksgiving," that is, with gratitude, giving thanks to God in every situation. It must also be done with faith, believing that what is asked for will be received (Matthew 21:22), and as the apostle Paul did, with joy, (Philippians 1:4). Whoever joins the mission of sharing the Word cannot put prayer aside. Through prayer, we have communication with our God, we can talk to Him, tell him everything we feel and ask for what we need.

B. LEARN: Learning is one of the elements needed to go to the battlefield. It's essential to know the strategies that are going to be used and learn to handle the weapons that we have at our disposal to fight the enemy (Ephesians 6:10-18).

C. TEACH: The knowledge acquired is to be used for personal benefit and for the church. We must not forget the Great Commission and make more disciples. What is learned is shared with others, so that the gospel continues to spread, as established by the Lord Jesus.

D. GIVE, SHARE: it's the strategy that Jesus used to give the message of the good news. He used his power to restore physical health through miracles of healing, feeding the crowds and his disciples, and bringing peace to those deceived by the devil. The works we do are the result of our faith in Jesus Christ (James 2:14-16). The Bible teaches us to be generous. Paul also taught this principle (Acts 20:35). Jesus was so generous that he gave up his own life as a sacrifice to save everyone who believed in him.

You can contribute to missions by giving economic resources in money or in kind, remembering that what you contribute is the best (Colossians 3:23). Many may not be able to physically go on missions, but they can give to sustain the missionaries.

It's urgent that youth also get involved in missions. The Lord Jesus was concerned (and undoubtedly still is) when he expressed to his disciples that "...The harvest is plentiful, but the workers are few" (Luke 10:2). The workers are increasingly scarce, and many people die without having heard the message of salvation. Today, many youth are training in various professions and trades, but only for personal gain. Some are content to simply go to church and listen to the sermons, but they don't want to commit to sharing the Good News.

God gave Ezekiel a very harsh word (Ezekiel 3:18-19) and even the Apostle Paul took it into account (Acts 20:26). We must not turn a deaf ear to the Word of the Lord; we must put into practice all his commandments so that we can do well. Nobody said it would be easy; however, one keeps going while there is hope, one seeks God while he can be found in earthly life. Let's use all our resources to go to the battlefield and bring the news of the gospel to those who don't yet know it. Our mission is to share, not to convince because that's the task of the Holy Spirit. We must be challenged to use our strength, vitality, enthusiasm and desire to serve to bring the lost to God.

Review/Application: Allow time for your students to answer True or False to the following comments.

1. The workers to preach are very few. (T)
2. Only pastors should be missionaries. (F)
3. Works don't need faith. (F)
4. Generosity is also necessary in work. (T)
5. I can dedicate myself to teaching without having learned. (F)
6. Prayer is a key to open doors. (T)
7. Jesus doesn't care much about lost souls. (F)
8. We can all get involved in missions. (T)
9. Only by traveling can one be involved in missions. (F)
10. You have to preach only to Christians. (F)

Have you students complete the following scripture: Ezekiel 3:11

"Go now to your people in exile and speak to them. Say to them, 'This is what the Sovereign Lord says,' _____."

Challenge: There are currently 195 officially recognized countries in the world: 54 countries are in Africa; 48 in Asia; 44 in Europe; 33 in Latin America and the Caribbean; 14 in Oceania; 2 in Northern America. (https://www.worldometers.info/geography/how-many-countries-are-there-in-the-world/#:~:text=There%20are%20195%20countries%20in,and%20the%20State%20of%20Palestine.)

Encourage your students to make a prayer chain so that during the week everyone can take turns praying for the countries that our church hasn't yet reached.

Am I a Sheep?

Objective: That students will see the church as the flock of Jesus that depends on His care and direction.

Memory Verse: *"I am the good shepherd; I know my sheep and my sheep know me."* John 10:14

Attention!
After praying, remind them of last week's challenge and discuss how the prayer chain went.
Accept

Connect | Navigate

Introductory Activity (12 - 17 years).

• Matériel: Large piece of paper and markers or blackboard and chalk. You can also use cutouts from magazines or photos of sheep, rams, pastures, sheep dogs, shepherds, pens, and other items related to shepherds.

• Instructions: Form two teams. Ask the students if they know or have seen any shepherds and their flock. Most likely they have at least seen them in movies or photos. On the paper or chalkboard, have them draw or paste pictures of the animals and people involved in shepherding. It may include the sheep, the shepherd with his staff, the sheepdogs, and perhaps even the wolves that attack the lambs. Then give each group time to describe what each character does and the picture they put on the board. The group that gives the most complete description will be the winner.

Ask if they know of famous shepherds that appear in the Bible.

Introductory Activity (18 - 23 years).

• Materials: Large paper and markers or blackboard and chalk, dictionaries and/or any other reference materials.

• Instructions: Let's get acquainted with some important concepts from the lesson. Ask students to find the meaning of the words in the list below. Also try to explain what each thing, animal or person listed does. If reference materials aren't available, encourage young people to express the meanings in their own words. In any case, it's important that the teacher prepares to give an explanation of each word.

Write this list on the board:

• Sheep	• Pasture
• Shepherd	• Go astray
• Rod	• Thief
• Crook	• Gate
• Fold	• Graze
• Flock	• Path

Connect | Navigate

What is the church? The church is the group of people who believe in Christ and come together to worship him. But what else is the church? Jesus, and later the apostles Paul and Peter, used metaphorical figures, or examples, to explain about the church, the relationship between its members, and Jesus' position in it. Sometimes they call it a body, other times a people, and even a building. But the best known is the figure of the flock and the good shepherd.

Without a doubt, the metaphor of the church as a flock is the one most used today, and many times without realizing it. For example, we call the men and women God placed to lead and teach the church "shepherds".

As we'll see in the following paragraphs, this concept was born in the Old Testament. But Jesus himself used it to describe believers and to teach what our relationship with Him should be like. Read the Gospel of John 10:7-21 together; surely they'll enjoy listening to another version then they are used to. What is the flock of Christians like? Who is the true shepherd of that flock?

1. The Church: God's Flock

Practically every Christian knows Psalm 23 by heart, which speaks of Jehovah as a shepherd who cares for his sheep and provides them with food (recite it together). And since we're in the Psalms, Psalm 100:3 says in The Living Bible: "Try to realize what this means—the Lord is God! He made us—we are his people, the sheep of his pasture." Also in the writings of the prophets we can see God's people described as a flock: Ezekiel 34 and Micah 7:14.

In the New Testament, in the passage from John 10:7-21, Jesus presented the parable of the flock; in verse 14b he says, "I know my sheep and my sheep know me." In other words, the sheep that know Jesus belong to his fold, or pen. Verse 4 of John 10 says that the sheep follow the shepherd because they recognize his voice. This means that not everyone belongs to the church of Jesus, or to his fold, but only those people who know Christ so well, so intimately, that they can recognize his voice and follow him.

Sheep also distinguish voices that aren't from their shepherd. This is how John 10:8 expresses it: "All who have come before me are thieves and robbers, but the sheep haven't listened to them." In other words, the Christian flock follows only and exclusively the good shepherd, who is the Son of God. Furthermore, in Him we have eternal and full life in every way. We don't have to wait until we're in heaven, but right now here on earth we can enjoy the rich blessings that God gives us (v. 10).

John 10:16 says that there are some sheep that don't belong to his fold, that are lost, but Jesus will go look for them to bring them back. So this is good news! Those who don't know Jesus Christ as their shepherd, when they hear his voice and come to him, they'll be part of his flock.

2. Jesus, The Good Shepherd

Jesus presented himself as the shepherd who calls the sheep by name and they listen to him (John 10:3).

Ask: What does a shepherd do for his sheep? Let's look at Psalm 23:

a. ***He provides food and sustenance*** (v. 2). The Lord supplies physical and spiritual food (the Word), which helps us to mature and grow in faith, and quenches our thirst with the water of life, (John 4:13-14).

b. ***He guides us on the right path*** (v. 3). Jesus said "I am the way…" (John 14:6). If we follow him, we won't get lost.

c. ***He rescues us and protects us*** (v. 4). The shepherd's crook is a long stick curved at one end, like a hook. This was used to pull sheep that move away or fall into holes and get trapped. It also served to defend sheep from wild animals. Jesus rescues us when we're in trouble and difficulty, but he also pulls us back into the flock if we're straying. He also defends us from the enemy's attacks.

d. ***He encourages us and gives us strength*** (vs. 3-4). Christ cares for us and we shouldn't be afraid. He helps us to be confident and gives us encouragement to keep going. In any situation, we can be sure that Jesus is by our side.

It's beautiful to know that our shepherd gave his life for us (John 10:11). There's no greater act of love than the one Jesus did for us! He gave his life in payment for our sins, and now we can have eternal life. He watches over us and protects us from deceivers (John 10:1-2) who are thieves: "Dearly loved friends, don't always believe everything you hear just because someone says it's a message from God; test it first to see if it really is. For there are many false teachers around…" (1 John 4:1 TLB)

3. A Flock and a Shepherd

Today, each local church has its own shepherd/pastor. Our pastors pray every day and seek God to follow the example of Jesus. They provide us with the nourishment of the Word of God and lead us to draw closer to Him. If we drift away, or we're in trouble, they care about us and try to help us; they encourage us to follow the Christian life.

If someone wants to hurt us or teach something that isn't right, they are wise to distinguish it and protect their sheep. These men and women of God have given their lives to serve the Lord and his church. And although there are many pastors in the world, there is a pastor who is older than them, who is perfect and who guides them in their work, Jesus, the good shepherd.

In the same way, although there are many local churches throughout the world, and each one is different from the others, all Christians belong to a single flock. In this flock are those who know Jesus and follow him only; when we hear his voice and obey him, we have salvation and eternal life. We are his sheep, and we're completely dependent on Jesus Christ. But also those who aren't yet of the flock can come to belong to Him. They only have to listen to the voice of the good shepherd who calls them to follow him.

Review/Application: Allow time for your students to match the word in the first column with the correct match in the second column: in the first column appear the concepts that we studied in class and in the second what they represent.

A. Flock	(B)	Physical food and the Word of God to grow and mature in faith
B. Food & Sustenance	(F)	They are the ones who neither listen nor follow Jesus.
C. Rod & Staff	(E)	The Holy Spirit guides us to follow Jesus.
D. Gate	(A)	Group of people who know Jesus, believe in him, listen to his voice and follow him.
E. Path	(G)	Jesus died on the cross to pay for our sins and give us eternal life.
F. Lost Sheep	(D)	Jesus is the only door to salvation.
G. Give Life	(C)	The good shepherd rescues us from danger and protects us from the enemy.

- Now that you know that the church is described as a flock, how should you change your attitude towards other brothers and sisters who are members of the same flock with you?

- Do you think sheep can take care of themselves?

Challenge: Is God calling you to be one of the shepherds of his flock? Or does he want you to be the voice that calls out to the lost sheep? In flocks, the more experienced sheep also help guide others. Do you help the little ones in the faith within your congregation? You may have thought that God's work is almost finished, but there is still much to do. If you haven't already done so, put yourself at the service of your church, whether it's to help, teach, accompany, or advise others. And remember the model of Jesus.

Not of This World

Attention!
Take some time to discuss the Challenge from last week.
Accept

Objective: That students understand that as a child of God, they are in the world but not of the world.

Memory Verse: *"But you're a chosen people, a royal priesthood, a holy nation, God's special possession, that you may declare the praises of him who called you out of darkness into his wonderful light"* 1 Peter 2:9

Connect | Navigate

Introductory Activity (12 - 17 years).

- Instructions: Once everyone is in the class room, dramatically choose just a few young people. Separate them from the rest of the group and tell them something secretly or give them a treat and congratulate them. Let the rest of the group complain about the special treatment that the "chosen" received. Then regroup them and ask them how the "chosen" felt about having received special treatment. Ask others how they felt about not being chosen.

  The Bible tells us that we're God's chosen people. (Give everyone else a treat.)

Introductory Activity (18 - 23 years).

- Materials: Blackboard and chalk or equivalent.
- Instructions: Ask students to list things they are careful about when making choices (examples: party clothes, shoes, boyfriends). Write the results on the board. Then ask them to rank each item by giving a number from 1 to 5. The 5 means that they are extremely careful when choosing that item. The 1 means they aren't so careful.

  In life we have to choose between many things. God chose a very special people and gave them a unique task.

Connect | Navigate

God, in His perfect plan, chose a very special people, the Israelites. They were taken out of slavery and separated from other peoples. God asked them not to do anything they saw in Egypt, or what they saw in the other pagan nations that would be around them (Leviticus 18:1-5). Ask: Why did God ask His people to turn away from others? Why did God want to keep them in the midst of the culture of that time, but make them different? God asked this so that the people would stay under his direction and commandments and not turn away after other false gods and beliefs.

We can learn a lot from the people of Israel. As Christians, we have to live in the midst of this world and its cultures. Ask: What should our attitude be about this? How should we behave? Should we assimilate/adapt to the current culture or should we be different? Wouldn't it be easier if we completely separated ourselves from this world and form a completely "Christian" community?

As God's people, we've been called to live in this world, but not to be part of this world. 1 Peter 2: 9 helps us understand: "But you're a chosen race, a royal priesthood, a holy nation, a people for God's own possession, so that you may proclaim the excellencies of Him who has called you out of darkness into His marvelous light" (NASB1995).

Let's see how this verse, 1 Peter 2:9, applies to our lives.

1. Chosen People

People: "a group of persons related by common descent or heredity; a group of tribes or peoples forming an ethnic lineage;" (https://www.dictionary.com/browse/race?s=t).

Ask students to talk about their ancestors. As a teacher, tell a story (yours or someone you know) that's striking about a grandparent or great-great-grandparent and share it with the group.

Ask students to think about how wonderful it would be to be the descendant of a hero or famous person. Ask: What historical person would you like as one of your ancestors? What if we find out that we're descendants of royalty?

Although Christians come from different ancestors and countries, our spiritual race is the same. Through Jesus we've been adopted into the family of faith (Ephesians 1:5 and Galatians 4:4-5). We are now part of a "chosen people", our behavior and conduct must honor our faith family. In our daily walk, at school, at work or in the market, we must represent our faith family well with our attitudes and actions. There are times that this is difficult since what prevails in this world are rudeness, insolence, bad words and double meaning jokes. But we must remember that God called us to be different. We are a people and a chosen race. We cannot act down to the standards of this world. We have to be different. By doing this, we'll be living according to our faith family, planting seeds of love, hope and faith in this world. Ask: What things are cultural and affect us?

2. Royal Priesthood

Royal Priesthood: The world in which we live tells us, through culture and media, that our purpose in life is self-preservation. It all comes down to how we can get pleasure and satisfy the big "me." The actions of humans are based on a totally selfish concept.

But the Scriptures point us to something different. In Revelation 1:5b-6, we read that as believers, we're priests, but not in the way of the Old Testament priest, whose function was to offer sacrifices for the forgiveness of sins. Jesus Christ came to this world to be the High Priest and bear our sins once and for all, thereby opening direct access to God for us (Hebrews 10:19-22). In 1 Peter 2:4-5, we're told that our priestly role is to offer spiritual sacrifices. Ask: How is this? Our primary role as spiritual priests is to live lives that honor God and serve our God and thereby bringing others closer to God. Our service to God extends to our attitude towards other people.

So, as Christians and part of God's people, we need to understand that our purpose for being on this earth doesn't conform to the definition of this world. Our function in this world isn't for self-righteousness and self-preservation. Christians, the people of God, are a royal priesthood..

3. Holy Nation

Holy Nation: God is looking for a holy people (Exodus 19:5-6). Leviticus 11:45 says "I am the Lord, who brought you up out of Egypt to be your God; therefore be holy, because I am holy." God is holy and wants his people to be holy. The life of holiness is completely opposite to what this world demands. You're seeing more and more how the world flatters the sinful life, but condemns the life of holiness. Athletes who decide to "come out of the closet" and go public with their homosexual life are flattered and encouraged, while athletes who put their faith in God on a public platform are marginalized.

Still, God asks us to be a holy people. Our holiness has an effect on this world. When God's people go against the current of the world and walk in the holiness of God, creation is liberated. Sin and evil lose their hold on people and salvation is inevitable. Romans 8:19-22 tells us that creation itself is waiting for its freedom. People of God, let's begin to walk in holiness!

Ask: How can we live a life of holiness in this world? Is it possible? What type of oppositions will we have? How can we overcome those obstacles?

4. A People chosen by God

God not only chose us as his people, He paid a great price for us. John 3:16 tells us that God gave his most special treasure for us, his son Jesus Christ. He redeemed us from our sins (Ephesians 1:7), saved us, and gave us eternal life. We can ask ourselves, like the psalmist: "What is mankind...?" (Psalm 8:4) Why us? Why does God put so much energy and effort into mere human beings?

In his infinite grace, God chose us to pour out his love on us. Our response to this love should be one of gratitude and proclamation. Our desire should be to share this good news with everyone.

As young Christians, you need to understand that we live in this world, but aren't of this world. God chose us as his people; he adopted us and made part of his family. We're of a royal priesthood, a holy nation and a people chosen by God... For what? Simply to "proclaim the excellencies of Him who has called you out of darkness into His marvelous light'' (1 Peter 2:9).

God doesn't want us to seclude ourselves in a holy community, physically cut off from the world. God wants us to reflect him to this world, to practice the royal priesthood in spiritual sacrifices to our neighbor, to be a holy nation that impacts creation, and finally, because of God's great love with which he chose us as his people, to proclaim to the whole world the great virtues of God.

God is looking for a people to stay holy and clean in the midst of this world. But, he also wants a people that impacts the world through holiness. Young people ... you are challenged to be God's people... to be in this world ... but not of this world.

Review/Application: Allow time for your students to respond to the following:

1. What things do you still do that belong to the world?

2. What things of the world have you stopped doing?

Challenge: It's important that we apply what we've learned. As priests, we've been called to offer spiritual sacrifices. Make a list of ways you can offer spiritual sacrifices to God. Pick something from the list that you'll focus on next week. Find a classmate and pray with him or her to ask God for help in this spiritual sacrifice that you're going to offer God. When you meet them in the next class, you should be prepared to share your experiences.

Live and Grow

Objective: That students understand that the church is the community of believers who recognize Jesus Christ as their Savior.

Memory Verse: *"...you also, like living stones, are being built into a spiritual house to be a holy priesthood, ..."* 1 Peter 2:5a

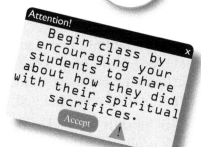

Attention!
Begin class by encouraging your students to share about how they did with their spiritual sacrifices.

Accept

Connect | Navigate

Introductory Activity (12 - 17 years).

- Materials: Paper and pencils.
- Instructions: Write the word "CHURCH" on the board in large letters. Put the paper on a table for them to grab one. Then have each student write their definition of church on their piece of paper and post it on the board. Read the definitions, and at the end, explain that in the lesson they'll have more biblical insight about the Church than what they had written down.

Introductory Activity (18 - 23 years).

- Materials: Blackboard, tape, paper and pencil.
- Instructions: Form and assign each group a letter of the word "CHURCH" and have them write a phrase referring to the activity that God asks of us as a church. Then highlight the fact that by working together, we can see progress in our spiritual life, just as together you did this project. In this lesson, we'll see some parameters that show the privilege of being part of the family that's the church.

Connect | Navigate

From the beginning in God's mind was the desire to have fellowship with humanity, but sadly, sin thwarted that initial plan. Then, God sought a way to restore communion with mankind; for that he sent an intercessor. Today, thanks to Christ, we have the privilege of being able to belong to the family of God.

Ephesus was a city of the Roman Empire; today it's located in western Turkey. The apostle Paul visited that city in passing at the end of his second missionary journey (Acts 18:19). However, he planned to stay there for a time during his third missionary trip (Acts 19).

When he arrived in Ephesus, it wasn't easy for him to preach the Gospel in that port city. He ended up staying there for about three years until he managed to plant and organize the church. It's very likely that he stayed in Ephesus longer than in other place. Then he left young Timothy as the pastor.

After a few years, the apostle sent a letter to the church in Ephesus (Ephesians 2:11-22). In it, he outlined in various sections the role of the church of Christ. He began by describing who makes it up and what its purpose is. The church of Christ is all of us who have recognized Christ as our personal savior. To explain how to become part of Christ's church, Paul first taught what the church is not, then what the church is, and then what its dynamics are.

1. What the church is not

According to the Old Testament, the only people of God was the people of Israel because of their history and covenants. However in this letter Paul, implied the universality of the Gospel by affirming that everyone who received Christ in their life automatically and by grace became part of the people of God, the spiritual Israel that is the church (v. 19).

The city of Ephesus wasn't located politically within the Israelite nation, and they always looked like foreigners, but Paul bluntly told the church that they were no longer foreigners. The new covenant written in the blood of Jesus made it possible for everyone to be part of God's people. With this, Paul made them remove the mentality of foreigners from their heads; now they were part of the people of God.

To substantiate this teaching, he wrote them a letter (Ephesians 2:11-13). The term "uncircumcised" denoted, as he later told them, how "remote" and "alien" they were before, for the Jews in the Old Testament were those of the circumcision. But Paul explained to them that by the blood of Christ, their situation had now changed; They were no longer foreigners or estranged from God.

An "upstart" is said to be someone unknown, someone who doesn't correspond to a certain position or doesn't meet the appropriate conditions to be in a certain place. According to Dictionary.com an "upstart" is: "a person who has risen suddenly from a humble position to wealth, power, or a position of consequence." Paul not only wrote that the blood of Christ allowed them to be God's people, but also that this blood has the power to position us as heirs of his Kingdom, "...brought near by the blood of Christ" (v. 13).

2. What the church is

In the face of the affirmations that we aren't foreigners, now comes the positive part of who we are:

Paul's intention to help us understand goes beyond simply believing in physical citizenship; He leads us to understand that our citizenship is spiritual and makes us partakers of the homeland of the saints (Ephesians 2:11-14). The apostle leads us through the privileges of a child of God, expressing that we belong to a heavenly nation because we're fellow citizens with the saints (v. 19).

But we're not only fellow citizens with the saints, but also members of the family of God. What a privilege! You and I are part of God's family. This is the greatest of all privileges, the greatest that we find in the Word. Before, we were dead (2:1), far away (2:13,17) and we were strangers, without hope and without God (2:12). The Lord took us from there and made us members of his family. It was by his grace that he adopted us as his children (1:5), blessed us with every spiritual blessing (1:3), made us accepted through his beloved son (1:6), made us heirs (1:11), and sealed us with his Holy Spirit (1:13).

Perhaps in our past we were beaten, abused, mistreated or ignored and we've seen ourselves as worthless, without the love of those closest to us. Today we have the good news that we're very special to God. We've earned that privilege through our Lord Jesus Christ; "For it's by grace you have been saved, through faith—and this isn't from yourselves, it's the gift of God..." (Ephesians 2:8).

3. The dynamics of who we are

In Ephesians 2:19-22 we find three special purposes that we must take into account within the dynamic as God's people.

A. A building dynamic

Just as in a carpentry workshop, the carpenter uses all the tools to make a beautiful piece of furniture from a piece of wood; or also as a chef to cook a delicious stew, you have at your disposal all the necessary utensils for your art. We would say the same of the body of Christ, where we need all the members to build one another spiritually on the biblical foundation (v. 20).

We build ourselves:

- Through the talents, gifts and ministries that God has given us. Paul mentions five ministries that serve to edify us: Apostles, Prophets, Evangelists, Pastors, and Teachers (Ephesians 4:11-12).
- Through love (Ephesians 4:16).

- Through wise encouraging words (Ephesians 4:29).
- Through the teachings inherited from the prophets and apostles and that are in the Word (Ephesians 2:20).

Like all the buildings in a city that are build on large rocks or strong foundations, likewise, the church, which is us, has only one foundation, which is Christ (Ephesians 2:20), the immovable Rock. In addition, the apostles and prophets are the columns that support the church. The prophets played a prominent role in the Old Testament and the apostles in the New Testament. By this, the apostle Paul meant that the Bible is our foundation for building the church.

B. A dynamic of coordination

This has to do with the attitudes of unity that must exist among us as a church. When a bricklayer wants to build a wall, he doesn't put brick on brick only; this would be illogical. He uses the mortar or cement paste. In chapter 4 of Ephesians, Paul teaches us about unity and gives us four essential attitudes to keep us together as the mortar on the bricks: Humility, meekness, tolerance and patience, and all this must be grounded in the love of God. (v. 2). These four essences of unity are opposed to pride, bitterness, inflexibility and nervousness that do much damage to interpersonal relationships.

C. A growth dynamic

Unity not only keeps us together, it gives us spiritual growth. The Christian life isn't about monotony, but about well-structured growth (Ephesians 4:15).

The church is called to grow in number and quality, but above all it must be concerned with its spiritual quality growth. The outstanding characteristic of its growth is in the love that it practices. Our growth in quality will enable us to grow in number. Paul exhorted the Ephesians to be "...rooted and established in love, may have power, together with all the Lord's holy people, to grasp how wide and long and high and deep is the love of Christ,..." (Ephesians 3:17-18) . Years later, the Lord Jesus said about that same church that they no longer grew in that love; for this he demanded that they repent (Revelation 2:4-5).

Review/Application: Ask you students to answer the following questions:

1. Where was Ephesus located and where is it now? (It was located in the southwestern part of the Galatia region, which is now the country of Turkey.)

2. What do the terms "foreigner" and "upstart" mean within the biblical context? (A foreigner was someone who wasn't part of God's people. An upstart was a stranger, with no position in the kingdom of God, who tried to be more than people thought he should be.)

3. What is the church built on? (On the foundation of Jesus Christ, the rock, with the pillars established by the Bible written by the prophets and apostles.)

4. According to Ephesians 4:2, what are the four basic attitudes to keep us united and coordinated? (Humility, meekness, tolerance and patience)

Challenge: It would be nice to ask yourself where or what you are? Do you feel like a stranger and upstart? I implore you to be part of the privileged who sit at the Lord's table as family members. If you're already a part of this family, share that this week with someone you think moved away from the family a while ago.

What Are We?

Objective: That students understand the figure of the priesthood and the responsibility of the church to exercise the priestly function.

Memory Verse: *"For we don't have a high priest who is unable to empathize with our weaknesses, but we have one who has been tempted in every way, just as we are—yet he didn't sin."* Hebrews 4:15

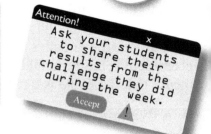
Attention!
Ask your students to share their results from the challenge they did during the week.
Accept

Connect | Navigate

Introductory Activity (12 - 17 years).

- Instructions: Divide the class into two or more groups and have each one write a list of characteristics that they have observed in a Catholic priest. Some students may not have seen a Catholic priest; in this case, have them make a list of the characteristics they have observed in their pastor. Afterwards, they'll share what they wrote with the whole group. Give them time to ask questions, which will give you the opportunity to answer some and then announce the title of the lesson, telling them that the other questions will be answered in the course of the lesson.

Introductory Activity (18 - 23 years).

- Materials: Sheets of paper and pencils.

- Instructions: Perform a drama of the moment. Provide yourself with a priestly tunic and collar; a tie and a basket. Ask the class to choose who will dress up as a priest and another as a pastor. Have them put on the clothes and then distribute sheets of paper to everyone else. Have them write something for the priest or pastor. Receive the papers in the basket. Once everyone has deposited their papers, take them out one by one and give them to the "priest" and the "pastor", who will then read them to the whole class. It will surely generate discussion and questions, an ideal time to announce the title of the lesson and then develop it.

Connect | Navigate

There are different nations in the world. On many occasions, there are wars between two or more nations. When the situation permits, mediators or a mediator are used. Generally, the UN secretary general, the presidents of the most powerful nations, the pope or other famous people are mediators.

In some countries, there are Conciliation offices, which are centers for the solution of family and neighborhood conflicts, etc. Many human conflicts are resolved with mediators or conciliators.

1. The Human Priests

There are priests in all religions. In Old Testament times in Israel, the separation between human beings and God required mediators; these were called priests (Hebrews 5:1-4).

A. What were the priests of Israel like?

Read Hebrews 5:1-4 and list characteristics of Jewish priests.

Verse One:

1. They were to act on behalf of men and women.

2. Their relationship with God was special.

3. They presented offerings and sacrifices for the sins of the people.

Verse Two:

1. They were patient, especially with the ignorant and lost.
2. They recognized that they (the priests) were human beings with weaknesses.

Verse Three:

1. They had to offer sacrifices for their own sins.
2. They had to offer sacrifices for the sins of the people.

Verse Four:

1. In the Jewish people, a priest was called by God. Exodus 28:1 says that it was God who ordained Aaron and his sons to be his priests for the people of Israel.

B. Other characteristics of the Israelite priesthood

The Old Testament offers a lot of teaching about priests. Let's see:

1. God chose Aaron and his sons to be mediators between God and the people of Israel (Ex. 28:1). After the Babylonian captivity, this choice focused on the descendants of the priest Zadok (Ezekiel 44:15-16).
2. By offering sacrifices and holy offerings to the Lord, they had to live holy lives, without being contaminated by anything, especially by corpses, except those of an unmarried sister or his parents (Leviticus 21:1-4).
3. They should avoid hairstyles and tattoos that threaten the integrity and purity of their bodies (Leviticus 21.5).
4. They were to only marry a virgin woman (Leviticus 21:13) or a priest's widow (Ezekiel 44:22).
5. They had to teach the people to differentiate between good and bad, holy and profane, and clean and unclean (Ezekiel 44:23-24).
6. They wisely taught the law of the Lord (the first five books of the Old Testament, called the Pentateuch), considering themselves God's messengers to his people (Malachi 2:7).
7. They were never women, always men. Thank God, in Christianity, both women and men have the privilege of ministering to the Lord (Acts 2:18).
8. They were supported by the people through offerings, tithes, firstfruits and other rights that God himself established (Numbers 18:8-32).

2. Christ: the perfect high Priest

The priesthood that descended from Aaron (Exodus 29: 9), Moses' brother, (Exodus 4:14) was imperfect and temporary, culminating in the sacrifice of Christ on the cross. Jesus Christ was the High Priest who replaced the Israelite priesthood (Hebrews 4:14-16; 7:22-28). Let's look at some of the characteristics of Jesus as High Priest:

A. Christ can serve us perfectly

Through Christ, we're cared for (Hebrews 4:14-16):

1. Because he is the Son of God, divine and human at the same time (v. 14). He knows our human weakness and the closeness of God; hence he can lead us to please God (v. 15a).
2. He went through all human experiences, especially temptations (v. 15b). The hardest and most difficult temptations were endured by our Lord as a man. That's why he can understand us and help us so that we can overcome temptations.

B. He is the guarantor or guarantor of a better pact than that of the law (Hebrews 7:22-28).

1. Jesus Christ is unique, he is eternal; the Aaronic priests were many, because they were not eternal (vv. 22-24).
2. The redemption he offers is eternal (v. 25).

3. He permanently intercedes for us (v. 25).

4. He is holy, innocent, without blemish, and set apart from sinners. We summarize the above in the expression: "...one who is holy, blameless, pure,..." (vv. 26,28).

5. He doesn't need to offer sacrifices for sins every day because he has already offered a perfect and eternal sacrifice (v. 27).

In short, the Aaronic priesthood was imperfect, it was a precursor of the priesthood of Christ. This priesthood was necessary until the sacrifice of Christ, but when Christ died, rose again, and ascended to heaven, he became our perfect, permanent and faithful High Priest who intercedes permanently for us.

3. Christians are priests too

In 1 Peter 2:4-9, we find the following.

A. Our condition as Christians

We are living stones by receiving life from the living stone that's Jesus Christ (v. 4-5a) and called to build the house of God (us), and at the same time, we're holy priests for our God (v. 5). As Christians we believe in God and in Jesus Christ. For us, He is THE MAXIMUM ("precious"), the most beautiful and expensive jewel (v. 7). Also, in our condition as believers in Christ, God declares us as a chosen lineage, a royal priesthood, a holy nation and a people chosen by God (vs. 9-10).

B. Our Christian priesthood

Basically the priest is a mediator and intercessor. We have already seen that the Aaronic priests mediated between the people and God; but this ministry lost its validity when Christ died as the perfect sacrifice for the sins of all mankind. Since then, Christ is our High Priest. He is our permanent mediator and intercessor (1 Timothy 2:5).

The Bible affirms that we, the believers in Christ, are also priests:

1. We are priests because we offer daily offerings and sacrifices of praise and adoration to the Lord, either personally or in community in the church (Hebrews 13:15).

2. Because we intercede before the Lord through prayer. We intercede for our family, the sick, etc., but especially for sinners, because we love them and want them to repent (Philippians 1:4; Colossians 4:12).

3. Because we're called to dedicate our total life to God and live in holiness. An Aaronic priest had to be holy. Christ our High Priest was and is perfectly holy; that's why we have to be holy, totally consecrated to the Lord (1 Peter 1:15-16).

C. The purpose of our priesthood

We are to serve God every day of our life, in all aspects, with everything we have, without losing heart in our faith or imitating the world.

Christ calls us to serve him daily in holiness and righteousness, to be intercessors for unbelievers so that they believe and are saved.

Review/Application: Have your students answer the following questions:
- What was the priesthood like in Old Testament times according to Hebrews 5:1-4?
- What truths about the priesthood of Christ do you find in Hebrews 7:22-28?
- How do you feel knowing that you are a priest?

Challenge: Through Facebook, text, WhatsApp, or other social media, send your friends a great gift: 1 Peter 2:5, 9,10. Try to send it to at least ten friends. Do it Monday and Tuesday. And then on Thursday and Friday invite them to your youth group.

New Challenges

Objective: Encourage your students to think about the privilege and responsibility of being members of the church.

Memory Verse: *"Now to each one the manifestation of the Spirit is given for the common good."* 1 Corinthians 12:27

Attention!
Ask some of your students to share about what they posted on social media and how their friends responded.
Accept

Connect | Navigate

Introductory Activity (12 - 17 years).

- Materials: Small pictures of the human body with the names of the parts (you can find them in a human biology book, at a bookstore, or online), newspaper, permanent markers.

- Instructions: Organize your students into three groups, give them a sheet of newspaper and a marker. Have them appoint a coordinator and a secretary. Ask them to draw a human body without naming the parts, and then lead them in answering the following questions:

  1. According to the teaching of the apostle Paul, what does this body symbolize?

  2. How many members is the body made up of?

  3. How important is the unity of the body?

  4. Can we Christians say that we don't need other members of the body? Why?

  5. Use biblical or church terminology and name the body parts you drew according to the different ministries they have in the church (Example: leader, deacon, etc.).

Introductory Activity (18 - 23 years).

- Materials: Paper with the following verses printed on them.

- Instructions: Organize your students into two groups. Direct each group to choose a moderator and a secretary. Have them read the printed Bible verses and complete the following:

- Matthew 16:18.
  The founder of the church is _____.

- 1 Corinthians 12:12.
  The body is _____, the body has many _____ all the parts form one _____

- Ephesians 1:22.
  The head of the church is _____.

- Ephesians 5:24.
  The church is subject to _____.

- Ephesians 5:27.
  The church is _____.

- Colossians 1:18.
  Paul uses the figure of _____ to refer to the church.

- 1 Timothy 3:15
  Paul also uses another figure, the_____, to refer to the church.

Connect | Navigate

The Christian church is the living organism that Jesus Christ founded and is made up of all the people who have surrendered their lives to the Lord. "The church of God is made up of all spiritually regenerated people, whose names are written in heaven" (Manual of the Church of the Nazarene. 2009-2013, CNP, USA: 2010, p. 35). So, it's of capital importance to know it and to know that as members of it we have functions to perform.

Belonging to the church of Jesus Christ is a powerful experience in each person's life. To feel part of it's to be sure that God reached us by his grace and granted us salvation through his blessed son Jesus Christ. The book of the Acts of the Apostles tells us that "And the Lord added to their number daily those who were being saved." (Acts 2:47). So we're in the Lord's church, not by chance or by human will but by the sovereign action of God. He called us, and when we heeded his call, he forgave us and incorporated us into the glorious body of Christ.

1. Being a member of the church is a privilege

Privilege is the grace or prerogative granted by a superior to a person. In the one that concerns us, we refer to that great blessing that God gives us of belonging to his church.

There are people who don't know God, or who, having known him, have departed from him; they are men or women who despise the church, don't consider it important, nor do they see the need to be part of it or work with it in the fulfillment of its mission.

Many live indifferent to the faith and aren't at all interested in what happens in the church. However for its members, it's a great joy to belong to the glorious church that Jesus Christ bought with his blood. For them, it's not just anything to be members of the church because they know that Christ loves her and gave himself up for her; they know and believe what the Word says about it (Ephesians 5:25-27).

"The church is the body of Christ. He is the head and all who believe in Him are His members. The church is glorious as a result of the radiance of the majesty of its head. It's also glorious for the beautiful harmony of its members." (The Glorious Body of Christ. R.B.Kuiper, Wm.B. Eerdman. Den Dulk Foundation, USA: 1985, p. 90).

So as members, we must be happy, motivated and grateful to belong to the most important and impactful organization in the world.

One of the most exciting and blessed moments that pastors have is when they welcome new members into the church and say to them: "The privileges and blessings we enjoy by joining the church of Jesus Christ are very sacred and precious. In it is a communion so holy that it cannot be experienced in any other way." Only in the church is found the help of fraternal care and counseling.

"In it the pious care of the pastors is given, with the teachings of the Word and the beneficial inspiration of congregational worship. The church fosters cooperation in the service of others, doing what cannot be done otherwise" (Manual of the Church of the Nazarene. 2009-2013, CNP, USA: 2010, p. 212). We can create an environment of tolerance in the church regardless of our way of thinking..

2. Being a member of the church implies responsibility

To speak of responsibilities is to speak of the duties that the members of the church must fulfill. A duty is: "the fulfillment of an obligation in general". It is "subordination". (Dictionary of Political and Social Legal Sciences. Osorio, Manuel. Heliasta, Buenos Aires: 1997, p. 274).

We're going to study four responsibilities, duties, or commitments that church members have.

A. Contribute to the unity of the church

It's imperative for all members of the church to live and work harmoniously. Schisms and divisions within the church aren't God's will and have always damaged the church's witness to a divided world (Ephesians 4:2-3).

There was a strong division in the Corinthian church. Four parties had been formed: the followers of Paul, the followers of Apollos, the followers of Cephas (Peter), and the followers of Christ (1 Corinthians 1:12).

Faced with such a dire situation, the great apostle was forced to make an energetic appeal to the Corinthians, and by extension, to all of us today. It was a call to unity (1 Corinthians 1:10). So, we're called to foster unity and fellowship within the Lord's church. In 1 Corinthians 12:12-27 we have a teaching and illustration about the unity of the church and the various functions, activities, and gifts that members have.

B. Building the church

Building is "the act, business, occupation, or art of building houses, boats, etc" (Dictionary.com).

In a strict and absolute sense, Jesus Christ is the one who builds his church. He declared to Peter and the rest of the apostles: "I will build my church" (Matthew 16:18). He continues to build his church. But in a relative and secondary sense, each member of the church contributes to its edification with their good testimony, work and use of their gifts and talents. The following are apostolic teachings related to the importance of building up the church: "love builds up." (1 Corinthians 8: 1b); "...not everything is beneficial" (1 Corinthians 10:23); "...build each other up" (1 Thessalonians 5:11); "...being built into a spiritual house..." (1 Peter 2:5); "...building yourselves up in your most holy faith..." (Jude 20). Let's do our best to build up others and not harm the Lord's church.

C. Value and not belittle other members of the body

This leads us to be supportive, to have a compassionate, merciful and understanding attitude towards other members of the church. Paul took a further step forward when he told the Philippian brethren to regard others as superior to themselves (Philippians 2:3-4). We find that same line of thought in his first letter to the Corinthians when he wrote about the members of the body that need each other. It teaches that no member should be despised (1 Corinthians 12:21). Solidarity, unity, fellowship, and mutual considerations among members of the church are expressed in 1 Corinthians 12:26.

D. Sustain the ministry

God's method of sustaining His work on this earth is through tithes and offerings. Church members should tithe and give generously as God prospers them (Malachi 3:10; 2 Corinthians 9:7).

3. Being a member of the church is having opportunities to serve

The highest vocation, and at the same time the most humble that all members of the church have, is that of service. It is about the action of serving God and neighbor.

For this, we have the paradigm, the model to follow: the Lord, who lived here serving the Father and also the people (Luke 22:27; Matthew 20:28).

So as members of the church, we must take advantage of the opportunities it gives us to serve.

Review/Application: Organize your students into two groups. Ask them to read the Bible verses and match the teaching with the correct verse.

Bible Verse	Teaching
1. 1 Corinthians 12:12	Not looking to our own interests, but the interests of others. (7)
2. 1 Corinthians 12:14	God has placed the parts in the body, just as he wants them to be. (3)
3. 1 Corinthians 12:18	Members (parts) have equal concern for each other. (4)
4. 1 Corinthians 12:25	The body has many parts (members). (2)
5. 1 Corinthians 12:26	We are the body of Christ and each one is a part (member) of it. (6)
6. 1 Corinthians 12:27	The many parts (members) form one body. (1)
7. Philippians 2:4	If one member (part) suffers or rejoices, they all suffer or rejoice. (5)

Challenge: If you're a member of the church, make sure you know your privileges and responsibilities. If you're not already a member of the church, talk to your pastor about the steps to take. Mention the names of those who missed class today and plan to visit them during the week to find out the reasons they didn't come to church; Pray for them and encourage them to continue serving the Lord.

A Faithful Friend

Attention!
After praying ask your students if they've thought about becoming a member of the church if they aren't already and if they called or spoke to anyone who wasn't in class last week.
Accept

Objective: That students understand the kind of love God wants us to love our friends with.

Memory Verse: *"...but there is a friend who sticks closer than a brother."* Proverbs 18:24

Connect ▸ | Navigate

Introductory Activity (12 - 17 years).

- Materials: Blackboard and chalk (or equivalent), masking tape, newspaper or magazine clippings, colored markers to write on the paper.

- Instructions: Write the following on the board or on a large piece of paper: At the top, "best friend"; in the middle, "good friend"; and at the bottom, "bad friend." Then hand out the magazines or newspapers to the students and ask them what things make a person your best friend. Give them some ideas like these: They might like soccer or video games, watch movies or read, laugh or be serious. Afterwards, ask each one of them to find a clipping and paste it near a phrase on the board or paper if they consider that the illustration corresponds to a bad, good or best friend. After everyone has pasted at least one thing, invite students to put themselves in their friends' shoes with this question: "If your friends had to rate you, would they think you were a good friend?"

Introductory Activity (18 - 23 years).

- Materials: Blackboard and chalk or large sheets of paper (one per team) and colored markers.

- Instructions: Divide the class into teams; If there aren't many students, pair up or do the activity in a group. Then ask: If there was a recipe for making friends, what would it be? Next, using the input of each member of their teams, they should write and present a five-step recipe that allows anyone to make friends.

Connect | Navigate ▸

We all like to have friends, and the more friends we have the better. The Bible gives us the key to having friends.

Ask: Imagine for a moment that you could make a single wish and it was granted. What would you wish for? Surely, something that you have longed for all your life and that you want to last forever. Jesus had such a wish before he was handed over and crucified: He prayed to the Father, asking that his disciples, including us, would unite with one another in love (John 17:20-21).

To see Jesus' wish fulfilled, there are only two options: The first is that we wait for others to come to us to offer us their friendship; but we would have to wait a long time for this to happen. The other option is that each of us is the one who takes the initiative to reach out to others to be their friend. If all of us take this attitude, unity will be a reality. Jesus gave us the key to achieve it; read it in John 15:12-13. If anyone has another version, give them a chance to read it

1. A new commandment

On one occasion, a teacher of the law approached Jesus to ask what he had to do to inherit eternal life (Luke 10:26-28). Doesn't it seem strange to you that Jesus' command was that we love one another? It could be considered contradictory that God tells us to love others; isn't love supposed to be a free choice? However, this teaches us that it's our Father's will that we choose to love ourselves and others.

For God, it's important that we not only love Him, but that we also love our neighbors, and that includes those who are our friends and those who aren't. Jesus himself wanted to teach this very important principle in the kingdom of God. Thus, during his Last Supper, the Lord gave his disciples a command, a new commandment (John 15:12).

A very important reason for obeying this commandment is that by doing so, we're Jesus' friends (John 15:14). We could find many other reasons, but what we're interested in understanding is that God asks us to love each other. Ask: What is a commandment? Can you choose to obey it or not? What consequences would there be in both cases?

As true Christians who seek to please God, we must obey him and love others.

2. The best example of love

Christ lived his life as the best example of love for one's friends. When Jesus gave the command to His disciples, He said to love each other in the same way that He had loved them (John 15:12b). Perhaps we've thought that the way we show love to our friends is the best way; maybe because it's the most natural thing in our life or the most comfortable thing, or we imitate the way they showed love to us. So, we call our friends by phone, we send them e-mails, we invite them to our house, we go out with them, and we do many other things to prove that we're interested in their thoughts, their plans, their activities, their life, etc. . When we do so, we're surely being very honest with them. However, God's will is much better than ours, and He asks us to love as Jesus Christ did. Here are five principles of his love.

a. The Lord loved us first (1 John 4:19). This teaches us that we're the ones who should begin to love our others regardless of whether or not they show interest in loving us.

b. He came to serve (Matthew 20:28). Among the wrong reasons to befriend someone is to take advantage of the friendship. Jesus taught us that instead of seeking to use our friends, we're the ones who must be available to them and offer ourselves for their benefit.

c. He made himself equal to us (Philippians 2:7). We must put ourselves in the shoes of our friends, feel what they feel, know what interests them, rejoice for what makes them happy.

d. He forgave us (Luke 23:34a). We may feel that unforgivable things have been done to us, but if anyone had every right to not forgive, it was Christ. In this way, the Lord teaches us to forgive wholeheartedly; Regardless of the offense, we must give forgiveness to those who have harmed us. Jesus also taught us to pray to God to help us do so.

e. He brought us closer to God (Ephesians 2:13). Thanks to Christ, we can draw closer to God. In the same way, we must help our friends come closer to God. And beyond just helping, we are to encourage and invite them with our testimony and way of loving them.

It doesn't look easy at all, does it? However, when God asks us to love others, He promises to be with us to guide us and help us do the things we cannot. At first it will cost us work, and frankly, we can never love as perfectly as Christ. But little by little, with the help of the Holy Spirit, we'll learn and mature in our friendship relationships.

Actions such as visiting our friends, spending time with them, and others that have been mentioned are secondary signs of love that are also necessary. But without these five principles of God's love, such actions would be useless. When our love for friends resembles that of Jesus, the actions will arise naturally.

3. Show yourself friend

What a great privilege we have! Loving our friends in the same way that Jesus loved us is a great joy. But it also requires that we strive to achieve it. Ask: Do you remember anything very meaningful that a friend did for you? How did you feel at that moment? Would you like your friends to feel this way?

One of the principles of Jesus' love is initiative; This means that we have the opportunity to show this kind of love to our friends before they do. We must remember that we can sincerely love them, but it's always better to show them with actions that we really do. And there are many ways to express our friendship: Inviting our friends to church activities, seeking common interests, spending time with them, forgiving them when they offend us, hanging out with them, and so much more.

There's a phrase that goes like this: "Friends are the family you choose." This refers to the fact that we come to love our friends so much that we consider them an important part of our lives. The Bible itself has a similar phrase ... Do you remember the memory verse? It says that there are friends who are closer than some siblings; In other words, with our friends we share more things than our DNA. This doesn't mean that we love our siblings less, on the contrary; it means that we can look for our blood brothers to be our friends too.

Loving our friends is something relatively easy because they are people we like. However, Jesus said that anyone can love those who love him, but only God's children can love their enemies. What do you think of what Matthew 5:38-48 says? Having friends is very important in your development as adolescents and youth. And it's also important to God, because He teaches us to love our neighbor regardless of whether we like them or if they hurt us. The Lord wants us to love each other so much that he gave us the example of his Son as our role model. Just as Jesus did, we can take the first step in showing love to our friends, or in reaching out to those who don't seem to love us. In this way, we'll live as true children of God.

Review/Application: Allow time for your students to answer the following questions, and then share their answers with the class.

◊ When it comes to making friends, what is the hardest thing for you to do?

◊ What is difficult for you in establishing a new friendship relationship?

◊ How could you change or improve that?

Challenge: Unity in love is extremely important for the spiritual growth of the church. Think of a classmate of yours or someone you know who goes to church but you haven't considered them in your circle of friends. Take the initiative and approach them to become their friend. Follow Jesus' example and show them that you want to reflect God's love in you life.

Patience!

Objective: That students understand that as followers of Christ, we must learn to tolerate one another and not be quick to get angry.

Memory Verse: *"My dear brothers and sisters, take note of this: Everyone should be quick to listen, slow to speak and slow to become angry."* James 1:19

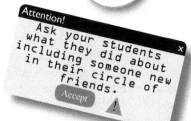

Attention!
Ask your students what they did about including someone new in their circle of friends.
Accept

Connect | Navigate

Introductory Activity (12 - 17 years).

- Materials: Sheets of paper and pencils.
- Instructions: Give a sheet of paper and a pencil to each student. Then, ask them to make a table with three columns, and tell them that in each column they are to write down the following titles respectively: Things I couldn't forgive; Types of people that I don't tolerate; things that make me angry.

This is an awareness-raising activity that sets the frame for the class and helps the teacher introduce the topic of tolerance.

Introductory Activity (18 - 23 years).

- Materials: Sheets of paper and pencils.
- Instructions: Give a sheet of paper and a pencil to each student. Then ask your students to answer the following questions with the first thing that comes to mind.

1. What has been done to you that you consider impossible to forgive?
2. What kind of people is it difficult for you to be around, and why?
3. When a person who has offended you tries to apologize, what attitude do you have?
4. Have you apologized to someone for something you have said or done? How did that person respond?

Allow about five minutes for your students to respond and another five for them to share their responses. It's suggested that no corrections be made while students share their responses. With the development of the lesson, students will expand their answers.

This activity is about making a starting diagnosis on the issue of tolerance to others. It's not about seeking deep answers, but only about sensitizing students. If the teacher thinks it wise, you can ask other questions to contextualize your class.

Connect | Navigate

Tolerance is basic for human coexistence. But cultural, ideological, social, political, gender and creed differences lead us to have frictions that, when not treated with love and respect, tend to end in arguments, divisions and anger.

Ask: What does the Bible recommend for resolving conflicts? How can we cope with the differences between us? The Bible gives us some clues in this regard that we'll analyze in this lesson.

1. Key #1: listen before you speak

James reminds us that we must be ready to listen and slow to speak (James 1:19). When a conflict arises, people often express their version of events and take for granted that "their" version is "the" official version. Few consider asking the other first what happened. Few really want to know the motives behind the actions that sparked the argument. The figure of the conflict mediator arises as a necessity to try to settle disputes between two parties, trying to make them heard and reach an agreement. According to the Association of Mediators for the Elderly and their Environment (AMNE), a mediator seeks effective communication between the two parties, understand the needs and interests of the other, and clarify situations that may have been overlooked, among other points (Consulted June 28, 2014 from http://amme-mediacion.org/funciones-del-mediador/).

To achieve this, it's essential to know how to listen. The other person also has a version and wants to be heard. Probably in the problem in question, there are circumstances that we don't know. It could be that the conflict happened because of cultural or social differences or misunderstandings. In this regard, the recommendation of James in 1:19 is clear: Listen before you speak. This implies being willing to let the other speak first. But, what happens when "the offended" is so angry that they don't want to listen to the other, or even see them?

2. Key #2: Beware of Anger

"...human anger doesn't produce the righteousness that God desires" says James 1:20. There's a popular phrase that says: "He who gets angry loses." When people get angry, they get confused and say and do things that they later regret. Unfortunately, some of those actions or words have irreversible consequences. Acting while angry can lead to outbursts that end in offenses, physical assaults, or immoral acts.

Ask: Are there any groups of people who are especially difficult for you to deal with? (They can go back to the questions at the beginning of the class.) Why is it so difficult for you to put up with that group of people? How much do you know about them? Do you know their history, their problems, the reasons that lead them to act, dress, speak in that way?

Is there an attitude that you don't tolerate? Can you think of any legitimate reason for that attitude that you dislike?

A common way of explaining this is "putting yourself in someone else's shoes", but when people are angry they are unable to do so. Therefore, before letting anger cloud our understanding, we must seek to understand the reasons that lead others to act as they do.

Colossians 3:8 says: "But now you must also rid yourselves of all such things as these: anger, rage, malice, slander, and filthy language..." If we act angry, we'll most likely act irrationally, and far from fixing the problem, we'll add fuel to the fire. So when we feel so angry that we cannot control the situation, it's time to ask the Holy Spirit to help us and fill us with love.

3. Key #3: clothe yourself in love

Colossians 3:12-14 says: "Therefore, as God's chosen people, holy and dearly loved, clothe yourselves with compassion, kindness, humility, gentleness and patience. Bear with each other and forgive one another if any of you has a grievance against someone. Forgive as the Lord forgave you. And over all these virtues put on love, which binds them all together in perfect unity."

It's impossible to tolerate your neighbor if there is no love. The apostle Paul knew that differences between people cause great divisions. Therefore, he recommended that the Colossians love each other, be kind to each other, and be patient. Those recommendations are still valid today. Thus, in order to cope despite our differences, we must above all clothe ourselves with love. And when the love of God fills us, we're able to forgive offenses, to be patient and listen before we speak.

Of course, it's not about allowing ourselves to be disrespected or hurt, but rather about allowing ourselves to be filled by the Spirit of God and allowing him to work in us to respond with love and patience to difficult situations. The last part of verse 13 puts the finger on the wound: "Forgive as the Lord forgave you." Ouch!

"Live such good lives among the pagans that, though they accuse you of doing wrong, they may see your good deeds and glorify God on the day he visits us" (1 Peter 2:12). When God's people clothe themselves in love, God is glorified.

Review/Application: According to the Bible verses used in class, answer the following:

1. What should you do among unbelievers? (1 Peter 2:12). (Live so well that even if you are accused of doing evil, they will observe your good works and glorify God.)

2. What should everyone be ready for? (James 1:19). (To listen.)

3. Why should they clothe themselves with compassion and of kindness, humility, kindness and patience? (Colossians 3:12-13). (So that they tolerate each other and forgive each other if one has a complaint against another.)

4. What does anger not produce? (James 1:20). (The righteous life that God wants.)

5. What is the perfect bond? (Colossians 3:14). (Love.)

Challenge: During the week, think about some people who are difficult to tolerate or with whom you have had a conflict. Pray this week for those people or that situation and ask God to give you love to approach them and/ or give them the opportunity to explain what happened. Your youth leader or another adult may need to mediate.

Oops, Conflicts!!

Eduardo Velázquez • Argentina

Lesson 34

Objective: That students learn to wisely face conflicts with friends.

Memory Verse: *"If it's possible, as far as it depends on you, live at peace with everyone."* Romans 12:18

Attention! Start by asking your class about the person they have conflict with and what they did about it. Accept

Connect | Navigate

Introductory Activity (12 - 17 years).

- Materials: Pictures of piranha fish on paper, tape or something else to make the sides of the river, materials to transport of various sizes and weights, ropes to cross the river with

- Instructions: Divide the class into two groups. Explain that they have to cross a river full of flesh-eating piranhas and transport certain merchandise from one shore to the other, but the only way to do it is by crossing the river (which will be shown with the tape) on the ropes. Remind them to keep their balance on the way over while transporting the material to the other shore, and on the way back when they return to look for new materials (always staying on the rope). There may be several paths to cross (place multiple ropes), but the only rule for doing so is that they must not take their feet off the rope while crossing the river. Everyone has to get to the opposite shore carrying material. Each member of the group will transport their chosen material and place it where indicated. If the place where they meet is large, both groups can do it simultaneously, or one group at a time.

This dynamic will end when everyone has passed over the river, or if there are few students, when each group has transported everything assigned to the other shore.

When finished, ask: Which materials were the easiest to transport? Did you help others get across? Did you feel anger or frustration at any time? If you did it again, would you do it the same way?

Introductory Activity (18 - 23 years).

- Materials: A list of 10 materials necessary to be rescued on the moon, and which must be hidden somewhere in the enclosure.

- Instructions: Divide the class into two groups. Tell one of the groups that they should read the list of materials lost on the moon, first individually, and then as a group. Then they must make a list and decide which of the five materials will be rescued.

Tell the second group that they'll observe the following characteristics of the group that's playing:

◊ People in the group who lead the meeting.

◊ People whose comments are ignored.

◊ How the group makes decisions.

◊ Observe the atmosphere of the meeting (positive atmosphere, possible verbal aggressions, etc.). The second group in general must observe the difficulties that the group has in reaching an agreement.

At the end of the dynamic, with the whole group together, reflect on the results obtained and observed. This dynamic is a technique to see how the group works together, the interaction that occurs, how conflict is detected and dealt with, roles, etc.

Connect | Navigate

Conflicts between people are frequent and are part of our daily reality. Going through conflicts with friends, schoolmates or perhaps with the family, can be a frustrating experience and can sometimes be emotionally destabilizing because we don't know how to deal with them.

In this lesson, we're going to deal with the issue of conflicts and how to direct them towards a healthy experience that allows us to grow in the relationships of our Christian life.

1. What is conflict?

The Bible shows us many accounts of Old and New Testament believers who had interpersonal conflicts. Ask: How could children of God of great faith and communion with God go through this type of situation?

The explanation is that conflicts are a part of life itself. Thus, we have conflicts with ourselves, with others, and the greatest conflict is the one we have with God. This human reality is a consequence of the separation of the human being from God due to the disobedience of Adam and Eve in Eden.

Conflict occurs when two or more values, perspectives or opinions are contradictory by nature or cannot be reconciled; or it also occurs when the pursuit of objectives are incompatible by different people or groups.

So conflict can occur when our values and perspectives are threatened.

It also occurs in violent or non-violent processes of social change when there are different positions in groups that try to work together, but find themselves unable to reach an agreement between the parties that are debating an issue, and finally try to impose their criteria over another or others. We all know where this situation ends.

Ask for examples of conflicts that do or could arise in their lives.

2. Facing conflicts wisely

Ask: How does God want us to deal with conflict? Let's see some guidelines below.

One of the first things to consider in times of conflict is establishing a relationship of love and trust with God as your primary relationship (James 4:1-10). What does this have to do with getting along with other people? A lot! The Bible constantly emphasizes that the key to success in relationships with other people is a successful relationship with God. Therefore, failure in relationship with others is a symptom of an absent or deficient relationship with God (vs. 6-10).

How does this work? The God of the Bible is the only one who can meet our needs for security, direction, purpose, forgiveness, etc. He is both loving and sovereign. He is absolutely committed to my well-being and is able to work toward that goal in every situation, and he also expects us to reflect this same well-being towards the lives of our neighbors (Romans 15:1-2; Galatians 5:13-16; Ephesians 4:22-26).

There are conflicts that arise out of selfishness because we want to be right and we seek our own benefit without caring about others. Only as we put our lives under the lordship of God can we relate to others in healthy ways.

Another aspect of this is that we need to recognize if our attitude towards other people is correct. A good exercise is to examine ourselves and see if in the middle of a conflict, we have the right motivation and are putting our neighbor before ourselves. If that isn't the case, make the necessary changes.

It's also useful and important to recognize and ask for forgiveness for attitudes and actions that hurt or have caused harm to others in daily dealings.

Something very important is how we love others instead of how they love us (James 3:17-18).

It's vital to focus not on what cannot be controlled (how others treat us), but on what can be controlled (how we treat others). As we do this, God's Spirit guarantees us his peace, hope, and joy, even if others don't respond the same way.

3. Growing up in conflict

In 1 Peter 3:8-9, the Apostle Peter presented five key aspects that we can learn to develop in any conflict: (1) Harmony, by seeking the same goals; (2) Compassion, responding to the needs of others; (3) Love, by seeing and treating others as brothers and sisters; (4) Mercy, by being sensitive in our affection and interest; and (5) Humility, by seeking to encourage others and rejoice in the triumphs of others. These five qualities are of great help so that believers can maintain good and healthy relationships and reduce conflicts.

Peter had to work compassion and humility into his life. In his early days with Christ, these attitudes didn't come naturally to his life (Mark 8: 31-38 and John 13:6-9 to get an idea of what Peter was like).

But the Holy Spirit transformed him, making his impetuous personality available to God, teaching him what compassion and humility are.

Another area that we must develop is prayer. Commonly in our daily relationships, we verbally hurt people or are hurt by them, then we turn our backs on them or take our greeting away from them. Peter, recalling Jesus' teachings to turn the other cheek (Matthew 5:39), encouraged believers to respond with prayer on behalf of those who offend them. In the kingdom of God, revenge is unacceptable behavior, as is insulting a person regardless of whether it was done with intent or not. To avoid conflict, we must resist the tendency to hurt those who hurt us. Instead of reacting angrily, let's pray for those people.

Review/Application:

Ask students to make a list of situations where they may be in conflict with friends. Then ask them to write down what they can do about it. For a better understanding, see the table below that presents two examples.

CONFLICTS	WHAT CAN I DO?
Jealousy	Pray and trust the other person.
Jokes that other people don't like	Ask for forgiveness and don't tell those jokes again.

Challenge: Think about the attitudes or personality traits that cause conflict with your friends. Make the decision to change and pray to God in the days to come for help. Then share your progress in our next class.

Conquest!

Objective: That students understand the importance of bringing our friends to Christ.

Memory Verse: *"We have found the one Moses wrote about in the Law, and about whom the prophets also wrote—Jesus ..."* John 1:45

Attention!

Talk about the Challenge from the last lesson.

Accept

Connect | Navigate

Introductory Activity (12 - 17 years).

- Materials: Index cards with the Bible verses from the instructions section below printed on them.

- Instructions: Organize your students into small groups of three, and give them the index cards with the Bible verses on them (Job 2:11; Proverbs 17:17; Proverbs 18:24; Proverbs 27:10; Matthew 19:19; John 15:13; John 15:14). Ask them to read the verses and then write on their paper what they see about friendship. Then have each group share what they found with the class.

Introductory Activity (18 - 23 years).

- Materials: Index cards and pencils; Blackboard and chalk or large sheet of paper and markers.

- Instructions: Ask your students to sit in a semicircle. Then distribute the index cards and pencils. Ask them to write the meaning of the word "friend". When they are finished, ask them to share what they wrote. Then write on the board (or large sheet of paper) the definitions that you consider most relevant. Give your students time to discuss and give their opinions.

Connect | Navigate

Generally, we talk about everything with our friends, and sometimes we share about work, celebrations, concerns and we seek together some solutions to certain problems. However, we also have the opportunity to speak with them about Jesus Christ and his blessed Word. At times, we may be hesitant or perhaps afraid to tell them about Jesus because we don't know how they'll react; but despite everything, it's our duty to do so. Today we'll see this topic in the light of John 1:35-51.

1. Jesus Christ loves our friends

Our friends are part of the human race whom the Lord Jesus loves and wants to reach with his saving power. All people are included in his love and grace, for God loves them and wants to transform them.

If our friends don't know Jesus, they are slaves of sin and need to be free (John 8:34). No matter what condition they are in (vices, theft, sexual debauchery, wickedness), the Lord loves them just as they are and has all the power to set them free.

The weight of sin that Jesus bore on his body and his Spirit while hanging on the cross was also for them. There was our blessed Redeemer, bathing the tree of Golgotha with his blood, thus providing the effective remedy for the sins of all.

The apostle John in his first letter says it like this: "He is the atoning sacrifice for our sins, and not only for ours but also for the sins of the whole world." (1 John 2:2).

The Lord knows that if your friends continue on their current path, they are heading for eternal damnation. Without Jesus Christ, there is no way to obtain salvation (Romans 3:23-24).

2. Our friends should seek and follow Jesus Christ

A. They need to hear about Him

John, an apostle of the Lord, recorded John the Baptist's powerful statement about Jesus (John 1:36). Two of his disciples heard the powerful words, and as a result they decided to follow Jesus (v. 37). Ask: What does it mean to follow Jesus? It means denying yourself and allowing the Lord to occupy the first place in your life; it's being willing to suffer for Him and abandon everything in order to continuously offer Him love and faithfulness. Ask: What does it mean for me today to deny myself? We have to love other people, material goods, money, fame, pleasures, delights, and even life itself less than we love God (Luke 14:26-27).

B. They need to do an honest search

Our friends need to be aware and convinced of their need for God and to undertake their search sincerely and urgently. They also need to know that if they seek him, they'll find him, for the Holy Spirit will help them. This is part of the ministry that He performs (John 16:8).

When Jesus saw that the two disciples of John the Baptist were following him (John 1:35-42), he asked them: "What do you want?" (v. 38). With this question, He opened the door for them to establish a sincere and timely dialogue, conversation and exchange with Him.

Today we may ask ourselves the following: What were they really looking for? What motives and purposes did they have? This was very important to Jesus because their answers would show that they were not looking for things, but for a person. The two disciples wanted to know Jesus and be with Him. They weren't looking for something for themselves, for their search wasn't motivated by selfish and petty interests. In other words, they didn't come to gain an advantage and personal gain; it wasn't an eagerness to satisfy their own appetites; they didn't want easy cheap discipleship, without repentance and lacking in commitment.

"Rabbi,… where are you staying?" (The term rabbi occurs frequently in the Gospel according to John.) With this expression, they affirmed their true interest. Jesus knew that the two disciples were sincere in their search; He saw them as well intentioned and surely thirsty to be with Him, the Lamb of God who takes away the sin of the world and the was fulfillment of biblical prophecies. Therefore, the Lord extended a cordial invitation to go with Him, an invitation accompanied by an imperative: "Come … and you'll see." (v. 39). This was an opportunity that they joyfully seized. Thus, the Bible tells us the following: "They went" and then they realized reality, because it wasn't simple curiosity that moved them; they went and "...spent that day with him." (John 1:39).

C. You need to share it with others

The Gospel according to John mentions one of the men who heard John the Baptist and later became a disciple of Jesus, and later became an apostle. This indicates that the work of John the Baptist wasn't in vain. He prepared the man to follow Jesus. This is an example of productive discipleship.

Andrew began his ministry of sharing Jesus with others. He started in his own home with one of his closest relatives. We know that in our homes, there are people who don't know Christ and need him. This is fertile ground to sow the Word in their hearts.

Andrew shared his find with his brother, Simon (John 1:41). His testimony was clear and compelling. The long awaited Messiah, announced by the prophets as God's promise, had finally arrived! He was already identified. There wasn't the slightest doubt in his words. It was true.

Andrew gave the message to his brother, but also, "he brought him to Jesus." This was a bold decision that led him to the Savior. The Lord looked at him with love and changed his name to Cephas, that is, Peter (v. 42). The Lord saw not only who he was, but who he could become by the transforming power of God.

The transformation of Simon Peter is an example of what God is capable of in the life of anyone who responds with sincerity, humility and submission before Him.

Was Simon Peter some great powerful man? No. He was a humble fisherman, lost in his crimes and sins, but sought and found by his brother Andrew and transformed by Jesus.

3. Our friends need our help

In the development of his ministry, Jesus met Philip and invited him to follow him (John 1:43). This invitation from Jesus, as well as Philip's willingness, made him a disciple. Next step, Philip proceeded to share his faith. Nathanael was the person with whom He spoke and communicated the good news. The person He was talking about was exactly the one the Scriptures were talking about (v. 45).

Moses and the prophets, divinely inspired by the Holy Spirit, announced the coming of the Messiah who would come to "inaugurate" a new stage in God's relationship with human beings. Philip identified the Messiah in Jesus of Nazareth, and that's what he communicated to his friend. The task of sharing Jesus isn't always easy, but persistence pays off (Galatians 6:9).

Philip had to deal hard with the skepticism of Nathanael who wasn't easily convinced. "Nazareth! Can anything good come from there?" Asked this man (v. 46). And that's the skeptical person; doubt and insecurity rule their mind. So, we ask ourselves today the following: What would Nathanael's concept of the Messiah have been?

Philip wasn't discouraged; he invited his friend to come see for himself. For this reason, he said: "Come and see...". In this way, Philip invited Nathanael to act and observe with great attention.

When Nathanael approached the Lord Jesus (John 1:47), Jesus made a statement that surprised and shocked him as well. We see this in his reply to the Messiah: "How do you know me?" Jesus declared that before Philip called him, when he was still under the fig tree, he saw him (John 1:48). This was enough for Nathanael. In fact, it clearly showed Jesus' omniscience in recognizing him, and therefore, Nathanael decided to become his disciple (John 1:49).

True friends always want to treat us well and are ready to do things to help us. They don't wish us ill, but are willing to defend us against those people who try to harm us. Certainly, we can trust our friends because they'll never betray us to our detractors. So, the greatest and best good we can do for our friends is to share Christ with them.

Review/Application: Organize your students into small groups and have them read the following scriptures: Job 2:11; Proverbs 17:17, 18:24, 27:10; John 15: 13,14. Then have them write the scriptures they were given in the left column; and in the right column, the teaching given by each of the passages.

BIBLE VERSE	TEACHING
Job 2:11	Friends arrive to console and comfort.
Proverbs 17:17	A friend loves at all times.
Proverbs 18:24	He who has friends must be a friend himself.
Proverbs 27:10	We must not leave our friends.
John 15:13	Laying down your life for a friend is the greatest love.
John 15:14	Jesus considers us his friends if we do what he tells us to do.

Challenge: Find friends and form a visiting group from your local church and go visit your friends, tell them about Christ, and invite them to receive him into their hearts as Savior and Lord. Or you can also write down your ideas on ways to share Jesus with your friends. Tell them to your classmates and start practicing them.

Forgive...?

Objective: That students understand that forgiveness is a commandment, not an option.

Memory Verse: *"... if you forgive other people when they sin against you, your heavenly Father will also forgive you. But if you don't forgive others their sins, your Father won't forgive your sins."* Matthew 6:14-15

Attention! Start a dialogue with your students before class begins. Talk about how you share Christ with your friends. Accept

Connect | Navigate

Introductory Activity (12 - 17 years).

- Materials: Papers, markers, and sticky paper tape.

- Instructions: Write opposite words on the paper, but only one word per paper (for example: Love-Hate, Cold-Hot, Refrigerator-Oven, etc.). Then draw a dividing line in the middle of the room and place the papers on a table, mixing them beforehand. Also, with sticky paper tape, make a diagram on the floor like the picture below, and divide the students into two groups. Each group must line up behind the center line (red or blue depending on the team). Then point out that on the count of three, the first person in line for each group should run to the north pole and grab a piece of paper, and immediately afterward, run to the south pole and find the corresponding opposite word (for example, the distribution of words in each pole can be the following: Love, Cold and Refrigerator must go in the north pole. Hate, Hot and Oven must go in the south pole). The first group to find all the opposite words will win.

Introductory Activity (18 - 23 years).

- Materials: A device to play music (radio, Ipod, phone, etc.), soft instrumental music, sheets of paper, and pencils.

- Instructions: Prepare the room with a very solemn atmosphere. Then ask students to enter the room silently. When everyone is seated, ask them to reflect on their lives. Ask them if they have ever been hurt or disappointed by another person (be it a boyfriend, a parent, a family member, etc.). Hand out sheets of paper and pencils, and ask them to write down the names of the people who hurt them in a very personal way, and also to write how they felt at the moment of disappointment and how they feel about that person now. Assure them that they'll keep those papers and that they'll not be read in public.

At the end of class, ask your students to pray to God and forgive these people. Then tell them to put away or tear up the papers as they see fit.

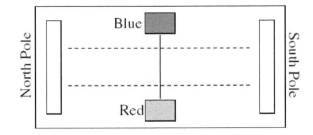

On October 2, 2006, 32-year-old Charles Carl Roberts entered and abducted students from West Nickels Mines School from a quiet Amish community (they are an Anabaptist Christian ethnoreligious group, known primarily for their simple lifestyle). Later, Roberts shot ten of the kidnapped girls before committing suicide. Five of the girls died from their injuries. "One day after the massacre, the grandfather of one of the victims was heard warning younger relatives not to hate the murderer, saying, 'We must not think badly of this man'. Another father said, 'He had a mother and a wife and a soul and now he stands before a just God.'" Jack Meyer explained, "I don't think there is anyone here who wants to do anything less than forgive and not only help or reach out to those who have suffered a loss in this way, but also to the family of the man who committed this act." (http://en.wikipedia.org/wiki/Amish_school_shooting).

1. Background to Joseph's story

Joseph's parents were Jacob and Rachel (Genesis 37-44). Joseph was his dad's favorite. Ten of his half brothers sold him to a caravan of Ishmaelites, and he was taken as a slave to Egypt. There he suffered loneliness as he was forced to spend a long time away from his family. He was also the victim of slander and lies, and was imprisoned without cause. Finally, under God's faithfulness, Joseph's life took a turn for the better. Pharaoh had a dream, and Joseph, with God's guidance, interpreted it, and that's how he became the "second-in-command" of all of Egypt. God blessed Joseph, so everything he touched was prosperous. In the seven years of well-being, Joseph helped the people use and save for times of famine and need. When the time of famine came, Joseph led Egypt to be one of the most powerful countries of those times and became someone of renown. But even though Joseph had accomplished much, his heart was still affected by the injuries his brothers had inflicted upon him. Joseph had to face his feelings of bitterness, desires for revenge, and unforgiveness in order to be able to achieve the fullness of all that God had prepared for him and his descendants.

Like Joseph, many of us have faced difficult times. We've been struck by blows of life, many of them coming from loved ones. Ask: Do you identify with Joseph? Is there something in your life that negatively affects you that you don't want to remember?

2. Forgiveness, a commandment

In the story of Joseph, forgiveness was a noteworthy thing (Genesis 45:1-8). If we look at Genesis 44:18-33, we can see evidence of the true repentance of Joseph's brothers. Unlike when they sold Joseph, when they met again they took into account the feelings of their father, Jacob. They had learned their lesson. In Genesis 45:1, we see that Joseph noticed this genuine repentance. For this reason, he couldn't contain himself and asked all those present (except his brothers) to go out. Seeing the fruits of his brothers' repentance, Joseph was able to show his forgiveness.

Genesis 45:1-2 reveals a powerful truth to us. Joseph didn't want to divulge the sin of his brothers in public, but at the same time, he didn't mind showing his emotions to the Egyptians. Joseph wept and screamed so loud that even Pharaoh's house heard him. Joseph wanted to privately deal with the offense and offer forgiveness between the family. When we're hurt by others, we have to take this reaction very seriously. In these times, it's easy to air the "dirty laundry" of the "brothers and sisters" through social media.

Joseph realized that his brothers were scared when he revealed who he was, and instead of "putting his finger on their sore" and emphasizing the pain and hurt, Joseph asked them to come closer to him (vs. 4-6). It's interesting to note that by revealing himself to his brothers, Joseph was able to go beyond reproach or judgment (v. 5). He reassured them by saying: "... don't be distressed." Here we can see the fruit of a heart that was truly free from bitterness and resentment. It's evident that Joseph had indeed forgiven his brothers.

In Genesis 45:7-8, we see that Joseph decided to set his sights on God's purpose rather than on his pain or feelings of vengeance. He focused his energies on discovering what God's plan and purpose was in the midst of all his suffering. So, God gave Joseph the strength to forgive his brothers.

Joseph's blameless life in the midst of adversity brought about the fulfillment of God's plan. When the time came to reunite with his family and save them from hunger, Joseph forgave his brothers and made room for God's plan to continue to be fulfilled in the formation and preservation of the people of Israel.

3. How do I offer forgiveness?

We find the Lord's Prayer in Matthew 6:9-15, and something very interesting about this prayer is the insistence on forgiveness. Verses 12 through 15 focus on the need to forgive. But the most interesting thing about these verses is that they are reciprocal. As our debts are forgiven, so we must forgive our debtors.

Usually when we talk about hurts or wrongs that have been done to us, our focus is on the other person. But… what about us? We too have offended. We are also guilty of offenses. Jesus was the only one who didn't offend, the only one who never hurt anyone. When he was offended, he was able to forgive (Romans 5:8). Therefore, our first step in offering forgiveness should be to take our eyes off the person who hurt us and turn our eyes to Jesus, the greatest example of forgiveness (Ephesians 4:31-32).

Next, we must pray for ourselves and for the one who hurt us, understanding that only God can give us the strength to forgive. If you keep thinking about the offense, this will bring you more pain and bitterness. This resentment will give you desires for revenge that won't leave you alone until you take an action. Fattening bitterness is like a snowball rolling down the side of a mountain; it starts out small, but ends up as a big ball that explodes when it reaches its destination. Continuing to relive the offense will tie you to the past and won't let you live and enjoy the present or move into the future.

When thoughts of offense come to you, take them to God. Rest in Him. Choose forgiveness, happiness, and freedom; the choice is yours. Let's understand that forgiving doesn't mean that what the person did was right or that we'll forget it. To forgive is to put the situation in the hands of God, not berate, and let God take control.

Ask: What if the person who offended me isn't interested in forgiveness? Remember that you're not forgiving for the other person's welfare only, you're forgiving because it's God's commandment and because it's necessary for your happiness and spiritual and emotional freedom. Forgiveness is a commandment from God that will bring freedom into your life.

Review/Application: Give your students some time to look up the following verses and write what they say about forgiveness.

1 John 1:9 (Forgiveness comes from God.)

Ephesians 1:3,7 (Forgiveness comes from God.)

Matthew 18:21-22 (We must forgive.)

Mark 11:25; Ephesians 4:32; Colossians 3:13 (We must forgive as God forgave us.)

Challenge: Read the Lord's Prayer three times (Matthew 6:9-15). Think about the people who have hurt you. Make a list of the ways you can offer forgiveness.

Now make a list of the people you've hurt. List some things you can do to teach them about repentance.

My Best Friend!

Objective: That students understand that in Jesus Christ they'll find their best friend.

Memory Verse: *"I am the vine; you are the branches. If you remain in me and I in you, you will bear much fruit; apart from me you can do nothing."* John 15:5

Attention!

Start by asking how last week's Challenge went.

Accept

Connect | Navigate

Introductory Activity (12 - 17 years).

• Materials: Newspapers.

• Instructions: Place pages of newspaper on the floor. When the students arrive, instruct them to imagine that they are on a ship that has begun to sink and that the newspaper represents boats at sea that can save them. But they have to follow the orders they are given. When they hear "The boats can save 4", they must stand on the sheets of paper in groups of 4; the people who don't find a "place in the boats" will "drown." The number that can be "saved" will vary according to the order given by the one who runs the game ("the boats can save" 3 or 6 or 2... etc).

When you finish the activity, have your students comment on how they felt when they didn't find a place in the "boat," or how they felt when they were unable to "save" their friends.

Introductory Activity (18 - 23 years).

• Materials: Music player.

• Instructions: Invite the students to form two circles (one inside the other) with the same number of people, and ask them to look at each other. Then put on background music. Next, ask them to wave at the person they are facing, say their name, what they like to do, and what they like to eat. Then give the signal for them to turn the circles each in the opposite direction, and then stop. In this way, they will be in front of another person. Then ask them to hug each other and answer the same questions that they answered earlier to the other person. Then have the circles move again, and ask them to greet each other with their feet, then answer the questions. Move circles again, then great with their elbows, shoulders, etc. In the end, they must give their own applications and conclusions.

Connect | Navigate

Question: How many times do you say, when referring to someone, that he or she is your best friend? Or how many times have you said to someone directly: "You're my best friend?" Surely numerous times. Having friends is wonderful; it's something special. We share with them and they share with us; we walk together, we exchange ideas; and many times we have things in common. But we must bear in mind that possibly at some point, they may fail us, just as we may fail them. We are and will be human, and therefore, we tend to fail. Some people say that "man's best friend is the dog." Ask: What do you think? (Allow your students to discuss this.) Today in this lesson, we'll talk about someone who is a friend whom we can certainly call "my best friend." Once we have Jesus in our hearts and he becomes our best friend, we'll need to take into account the following aspects that we'll study below.

1. We'll abide in Him

In John 15:1-17, we see the result of that close relationship, and this is the production of abundant fruit that satisfies the expectation of the Father. Let's see what John 15:5 tells us. Jesus clarifies who He is by saying: "I am the vine," but he also points out who we are: "you're the branches." The idea is that we, understanding that we're the branches, do the following:

A. We will abide in Him and He in us

It is said that on one occasion, when missionary Hudson Taylor spent the night at a friend's house, he asked him: "Are you always conscious of abiding in Christ?" Taylor replied, "Last night while I was sleeping, did I stop staying at your house because I wasn't aware of it? In the same way, we should never think that we don't remain in him because we aren't aware of him" (Mundo Hispano Biblical Commentary, Juan. Volume 17, Mundo Hispano, USA: 2005, p. 321). Abiding in Christ is that vital union that exists between Christians and Jesus Christ. The word "remain" basically means "stay." Every Christian is inseparably linked to Christ in all areas of their life. So, obey his Word (it instructs you on how to live); offer him your deep adoration and praise; and submit to his authority. Abiding in Christ is evidence of genuine salvation. People who remain in Christ have genuine faith; they are the ones who will stay, won't withdraw, won't deny or abandon Christ. The true disciples of Jesus are those who continue to live what the Word commands (John 8:31).

B. We will bear much fruit

By abiding in Him, we'll bear much fruit and recognize that without Him we can do nothing of real importance (John 15:5). The desire of Jesus Christ, as our best friend, is that we never separate from Him; that we share with Him, that we learn from Him and, above all, that we know Him.

Just like the branch, we're attached to the vine to bear fruit. Ask: What fruit will be seen in us? Just as the vine has many grapes that reproduce, so will our life be if we remain in Him: We can be disciples who form other disciples. These fruit will allow us to speak about Him with freedom and security. If we abide in him and his words abide in us, by asking whatever we want it will be done (John 15:7); of course, as long as what we ask is according to his will.

In this passage from John 15, Jesus mentions the verb "remain" 10 times. This word describes the relationship of Jesus with the Father, the relationship of Jesus with his disciples, and vice versa.

2. We'll be loved by Him

Christ has a model of love, and that model of love is his Father. As his Father loves him, he loves us (John 17:23-26) and invites us to abide in his love (John 15:9-11). If we abide in Him, His joy will be in us.

When Christ talks about these very special things, can we doubt that he is our best friend? Or rather, are you going to doubt that he can be your best friend? Of course not! Jesus Christ wants our total well-being. No friend wishes the worst for someone; on the contrary, he must always wish the best, and if not, I can tell you that he isn't your friend. John 15:13 says: "Greater love has no one than this: to lay down one's life for one's friends." It's impressive how Jesus shows, as a faithful friend, his love for us.

3. His love is universal

As humanity's best friend, Christ invites us to love one another, as He has loved us (John 15:12).

This expression: "Love each other," translates a verb in the present tense, describing a constant, enduring attitude and action. Jesus not only commands us to love each other, but also specifies the quality of love that must exist between us: "...as I have loved you."

Christ wants to be humanity's best friend. He teaches us that the joy of fellowship among believers is one of God's great gifts. No matter where we are, we can be a family when we're with brothers and sisters in the faith. In John 15:17, we find the eleventh commandment; there we're told that the most important thing for Christ is that his disciples love each other. Christ showed his love for us, even when we were sinners: "But God demonstrates his own love for us in this: While we were still sinners, Christ died for us." (Romans 5:8); and "This is love: not that we loved God, but that he loved us..." (1 John 4:10).

If our best friend loves humanity, then we must love it too. We love people because we've known the greatest thing: God's love. So, we must share Christ, our best friend. That's love!

Make Christ your best friend. He loves you and has shown it by going to the cross for you and for the whole world. I invite you to say today with certainty: "Jesus Christ is faithful to me; he gives me his power. Jesus Christ is my solace, my perfect peace."

Review/Application: Ask your students to answer the following questions:

1. Who is a friend? (A friend, a term that we use widely in our language, is that individual with whom one maintains friendship.)
2. What type of friend has been introduced to you in this lesson? (The best friend.)
3. How should friends be? (United.)
4. What is a vine? (A plant whose fruit is the grape.)
5. What are the branches? (Green, tender and thin shoots of the vine.)
6. Mention the qualities of Jesus as your best friend. (This question can be answered in their own words.) He is a sincere friend, who listens, tender, good, discreet, generous, etc.

Challenge: During the week, reflect on the type of relationship you have with Jesus, if he really is your best friend and if you stick with him. Likewise, I suggest that we plan a visit to someone this week and share our best friend Jesus with them. God wants to use you for the good of others who need to know him.

Objective: That students learn that the Holy Spirit is the third person of the Trinity and that he fulfills the mission entrusted by the Father to build the church.

Memory Verse: *"Greater love has no one than this: to lay down one's life for one's friends."* John 15:13

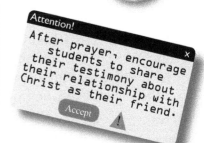

Attention!

After prayer, encourage students to share their testimony about their relationship with Christ as their friend.

Accept

Connect | Navigate

Introductory Activity (12 - 17 years).

• Instructions: Begin by asking the youth how many friends they have on FaceBook. Then ask the following questions:

Of all your friends on FaceBook . . .

* How many do you talk to regularly?

* How many of them have you seen more than once?

* Who would you go to rescue if their car ran out of gas on the freeway?

* How many would you donate a kidney to?

* Would you give your life for some of your FaceBook friends?

* The word "friend" is used very loosely in our times. We often don't have a real awareness of what it means to be a true friend.

Introductory Activity (18 - 23 years).

• Materials: Paper and pencils.

• Instructions: Distribute a pencil and paper to each student. Then ask each young person to write two truths and a lie about themself on the paper. For example: Truths: I was born in Puerto Rico; I grew up in the United States. Lie: I lived in Mexico. When everyone has written them down on their papers, ask each student to read their three sentences. The other students will try to say which of the three sentences isn't true.

Connect | **Navigate**

In our time, we have the tendency to call someone a "friend" when in reality they are "acquaintances" of whom we know very little. Today, we don't take the time to make ourselves known and plant deep friendships.

However, there are well-known phrases about friendship, such as:

• "Friends are the family you choose."

• "A friend is one who knows all your faults, and loves you despite them."

1. A Friend

The word "friend" is used very loosely in our times. With the popularity of social media, we tend to classify anyone we know as our "friend." We don't stop to analyze in depth the meaning of that word.

Ask: What does the Bible say about friendship? Does the Word of God provide us with an example of true friendship without limits?

In 1 Samuel 18:1, we find the account of two young men, Jonathan and David. They were from two very different "worlds" and they met under unusual circumstances.

Jonathan was born a prince of Israel. His father was King Saul. He was raised in the palace and was exposed to the best teachings and training in the country. As the eldest son, Jonathan was the first in line to inherit the kingship of Israel.

On the other hand, David's life was very different from Jonathan's. David was born in the town of Bethlehem. He was the youngest of eight siblings. He was "dark and handsome, with beautiful eyes" (1 Samuel 16:12 NLT). Likewise, David was the shepherd of his father's sheep. When his brothers went to battle, David had to stay home tending the sheep. But David's humble background didn't prevent him from having great qualities. He had a right heart before God and was a courageous boy who wasn't afraid to face those who threatened his sheep (1 Samuel 17:34-36).

It was this courage that caused these two very different boys to meet. It happened that one day, David went to take food to his brothers who were in the battle against the Philistines. There, he learned about the threat of Goliath. As we all know, David killed Goliath and won the victory for Israel. 1 Samuel 17:57 tells us that David was still clutching Goliath's head when he appeared before King Saul. That's when Jonathan and David met. It was such an impressive gathering that their souls were linked from that moment on (1 Samuel 18:1).

From this story, we can learn several things: 1) Friends can come from different backgrounds. 2) There are common qualities that unite friends. 3) Friendship goes beyond being a mere acquaintance. 4) To have a genuine friendship, there has to be a depth of soul and heart.

At this point in the lesson, encourage your students to talk about one of their special friends. Ask: What are their differences? What similarities do they have? How did you meet them? How did you cultivate your friendship?.

2. Characteristics of a friendship without limits

The account of the friendship between Jonathan and David was detailed in seven chapters of the Bible (1 Samuel 19-24). Encourage your students to read all seven chapters over the next week.

In these chapters we find five exemplary characteristics of a true friendship, a friendship without limits.

LOVE: Love was the basis of the friendship between Jonathan and David. Between these two young men there was neither envy nor jealousy. From the beginning, the two of them let love reign between them (1 Samuel 20:17).

So strong was Jonathan's love for David that even he risked his life by interceding for David's with his father (1 Samuel 20:32). The argument between Jonathan and Saul was so bad that Saul not only insulted him, but also tried to kill Jonathan, his own son. However, this didn't stop Jonathan's love as he continued to support David. Even as his own father was chasing David in the wilderness, Jonathan sought out David for encouragement (1 Samuel 23:16). This was the last time David and Jonathan saw each other; shortly after, Jonathan died.

We can learn a lot from this virtuous love. Jonathan never clung to his position as prince or tried to manipulate David. Nor did he humiliate him or try to impose himself on him. Rather, Jonathan used the biblical principle of love to maintain his friendship with David. Ask: Is love something that's said or reflected in actions?

COMMITMENT: Jonathan and David were men of their word. At various points in history, we see how they made covenants with each other (1 Samuel 18:3, 20:16, 23:18). Jonathan and David were committed to their friendship. They didn't allow circumstances or other people to intervene in their relationship. They even constantly renewed that commitment they had to one another.

There are often many conflicts among the friendships of young people. Today they can be friends, but not tomorrow. It's important that you understand the necessity and blessing of having a friendship that has depth and commitment between two people.

RESPECT: From the beginning, Jonathan recognized God's call on David's life (1 Samuel 18:4). This may be difficult to understand. Jonathan's action was very symbolic. He was giving up his future kingship, his claim as prince to the throne, and he was acknowledging and respecting God's call on David's life as future king. The Bible goes further to clarify this point (1 Samuel 23:17).

In a friendship, respect is paramount, especially when there are changes in growth. As young people grow, changes will occur in their lives. One may be accepted to a better university, while the other friend is left behind. It may be that one of the friends has the opportunity to travel to other places, while the other does not. It's important that young people can learn to respect each other rather than envy each other because of changes in their lives.

Ask: Have you ever experienced this kind of respect in a friendship?

CONFIDENCE: Jonathan and David lived through very difficult times. They suffered persecution, deception (1 Samuel 18:19), slander (1 Samuel 18:24), attempts against their lives, etc. Those were very tense and emotional times, but the friendship of those two young men was so deep that they weren't afraid to trust each other. Their confidence was so strong that they could show their emotions openly (1 Samuel 20:41).

It's imperative that you understand that in a true friendship, it's important to trust each other. Friends don't need to be afraid of being totally open with each other. But to be able to receive trust, you have to give it.

Can someone here tell us about a time when a friend disappointed you? How bad it feels! But how good it feels to have someone who can be trusted, someone who doesn't let us down, someone with whom we can be completely open. I encourage you to reap trust in your friends.

LOYALTY: The friendship between Jonathan and David had a tragic end. Jonathan was killed next to his father. David suffered greatly for the deaths of both (2 Samuel 2:11-12). Although Jonathan was no longer at David's side, the commitment of their friendship didn't diminish. On several occasions, Jonathan had asked David to take care of his family if something happened to him (1 Samuel 20:15). David never forgot this promise; he was loyal to their friendship.

The Bible tells us in 2 Samuel 9 that one of the first things David did as king was to seek out Jonathan's offspring. Upon finding his son, Mephibosheth, David not only gave him back all the lands that had belonged to Saul (his grandfather), but also extended an invitation to him to always be part of the king's table (v. 7) . Because of his loyalty to Jonathan, David extended mercy and kindness.

Review/Application: Acrostic - Allow time for your students to assign a quality of a friend to each letter of the word friend. Example:

F - Faithful

R - Respectful

I - Intentional

E - Enduring

N - Never-ending

D - Devoted

Challenge: It's time to examine ourselves. Today we explored the different characteristics that come with true friendship without limits. Consider your life and the friendships you make. Take some time to write down some of the characteristics you should be working on.

I'm A Foreigner

Attention! Allow a few volunteers to give testimony of what their relationship with their friends is like.
Accept

Objective: That students understand the causes of migration and become aware of the social problems experienced by migrants.

Memory Verse: *"Do not mistreat or oppress a foreigner, for you were foreigners in Egypt."* Exodus 22:21

Connect | Navigate

Introductory Activity (12 - 17 years).

- Materials: Paper and pencils.

- Instructions: Instruct students to divide their paper into 3 columns. Title the first column "What I Know", the second column "What I Hope to Learn" and the third column "What I Learned". Instruct students to fill out the first two columns before starting the lesson. Then start the lesson. Keep in mind that students will initially work on only the first two columns; and at the end of the class, they'll finish the third column.

Introductory Activity (18 - 23 years).

- Materials: Paper and pencils.

- Instructions: Ask your students to answer the following questions with the first thing that comes to mind: What does migration mean? Why do people migrate? What is globalization? What do you think is the relationship between globalization and migration, if there is one?

Allow about five minutes for them to respond and another five for them to share their responses.

With this dynamic, it's not about seeking deep answers, but about making a baseline diagnosis on the issue of migration. Therefore, don't make any corrections. With the development of the lesson, the students will expand their answers. At the end of the lesson, they'll be able to fill out the worksheet and review their answers from the beginning.

Connect | Navigate

Ask: How many of you know people who have left their places of origin to go to work or seek a better life elsewhere? Allow time for students to share some responses. This is part of the migration phenomenon. Most likely at school, at work, among neighbors and / or brothers or sisters of the church or the students themselves, there are people who for various reasons have left their places of origin and have settled here; or perhaps we ourselves are migrants or children of migrants. Today's lesson is about migration, how globalization has fostered its development, and what the mission of the church is in the face of this phenomenon.

1. Migratory movements

Migratory movements can occur within the same country, or from one country to another. In general, they are due to economic, political, ideological, or security reasons, among others. If we go back to the book of Genesis, we have some examples in Terah (Genesis 11:31), Abraham (Genesis 12:1), and Jacob and his family (Genesis 29:1, 46:1-34).

Technically, the scholars on the subject differentiate between emigration, immigration, remigration and transmigration. *Emigration* is leaving the place of origin to settle in another. *Immigration* is arriving in a country or region from elsewhere. Sociologists also use the terms *remigration* (returning to the place of origin after having emigrated) and *transmigration* (changing residence so frequently that it becomes part of everyday life). (International migration in times of globalization. Pries, L. Nueva Sociedad, 1999, p. 163).

It's also important to note that there's a difference between migration and forced displacement. The destruction of Israel (and its capital Samaria) at the hands of the Assyrians (2 Kings 18:9-12) and that of Judah (and its capital Jerusalem) at the hands of the Babylonians (2 Kings 25:1-12; 2 Chronicles 36:17-21) with their subsequent deportation, rather than a migration, is considered a forced displacement, since the people were forced to leave Palestine as a result of an armed conflict. According to the International Organization for Migration (IOM), a displacement occurs among those people who "have been forced to flee or leave their home or place of habitual residence, in particular as a result of, or in order to avoid effects of, armed conflict, situations of generalized violence, human rights violations, or natural or man-made disasters" (Migration and Displacement, IOM, http://www.crmsv.org/documentos/IOM_EMM_Es/v2/V2S09_CM .pdf accessed: December 16, 2013).

Migration, on the other hand, although it has in most cases economic deterioration and the consequent need to improve living conditions, is considered a voluntary act in which people decide to leave their place of origin. Current living conditions encourage people from all sectors of society from different nations and ethnic groups to decide to opt for migration as a way to help their families move forward.

Thus, migration gave rise to nations such as the United States, Canada, Australia, and was an important part of the cultural melting pot in places such as Argentina, Brazil, and Chile, among others.

2. Globalization and migratory movements

International migrations increased after the Industrial Revolution when a large sector of European society became impoverished and it was necessary to seek a better economic future in other lands. It was then that a multifactorial process known as globalization took place. Usually associated with economic and market issues, the term globalization encompasses other areas of human endeavor. For the purposes of this lesson, this term will be defined as the harmony between nations and their economic, technological, cultural and social interdependence. Thus, globalization has contributed to people changing their residence seeking to improve their living conditions.

Consequently, people of different nations, languages and cultures (or subcultures) come into direct contact when they coincide in the same region. This causes people to modify part of their traditions and customs in the new environment that surrounds them and incorporate cultural elements typical of their new place of residence.

The changes include such simple matters as modifying diet, or changing the way of dressing, and even modifying language and redefining cultural and linguistic identity. Thus, it's not uncommon to meet children of migrants who don't speak the language of their parents, or who aren't familiar with the traditions of their parents. Also, many of them have strong internal conflicts when trying to define their identity; while others see in their own cultural and linguistic diversity an advantage to adapt to new migratory situations.

God's people in the Old Testament faced these identity crises (2 Kings 17:24-41). Thus we see that the Northern Kingdom assimilated the customs of the Assyrians, forgot the commandments given to their parents (Exodus 20), and incorporated new behaviors into their daily lives. Likewise, when the people of Judah were taken captive to Babylon, they also assimilated part of the culture of that place. The Hebrew language fell into oblivion and the people incorporated Aramaic as their language of daily use.

3. The mission of the church in the face of migratory movements

As many have probably seen, there are cities, countries and regions that receive waves of migrants every year. Border points tend to witness these movements in a more tangible way. And given the World Bank's harsh economic predictions for the future (http://www.bancomundial.org/temas/remesas/. Consulted December 22, 2013), these waves of migration will hardly diminish.

Ask: What should the church do in this situation? How can the church minister to migrants? Allow a few minutes for students to share their ideas. The vast majority of migrants arrive in difficult conditions. Leaving their place of origin and the exhausting journeys that are experienced physically, emotionally and economically leave people in a vulnerable situation.

Some carry with them just enough money to settle in their new place of residence; however, most lack it. Others have had to travel on their own or be separated from their families on the trip and are alone and without acquaintances in the place where they'll reside. The most fortunate have work and others are mobilized for their jobs; but they don't have a place that makes them feel at home.

The church is called to be an instrument of God in the restoration of people by opening its doors and ministering to those in need. The church can be that place that migrants call home. There are churches that decide to establish soup kitchens for migrants, and others create collection centers to help the already established shelters. There are also congregations that have special presentations at Christmas or Easter in migrant shelters; while others specialize in migration issues to help heal the conditions of vulnerability.

Most open their doors and present the message of salvation and restoration. We can all put ourselves in the place of migrants. Let's imagine their situation and what they have had to go through, and ask ourselves: How would we like to be treated if we had to emigrate elsewhere? As the apostle Paul says in 1 Corinthians 9:19-23, if the church really wants to win everyone, it must be able to understand each person and the situation in which they arrive. After all, we ourselves (who make up the church), or our ancestors, also migrated from elsewhere and have found a place that we now call home, and one day we'll travel to our eternal home.

Review/Application: Allow time for your students to decipher the hidden word by unscrambling the letters and write the definition in their own words.

Niloboglazita: **Globalization:** (The harmony between nations and their economic, technological, cultural and social interdependence.)

Tnrasnoramtigi: **Transmigration:** (Change residence so frequently that it becomes part of everyday life.)

Ramotinimig: **Immigration:** (It is arriving to a country or region from another place.)

Tiendyti: **Identity:** (This is the name given to the set of characteristics of a person or group that differentiates them from others.)

Nasomiliatsi: **Assimilation:** (Incorporate what is learned with previous knowledge.)

Clurteu: **Culture:** (Ways of life, customs, knowledge, artistic, scientific and industrial development from a certain time, social group, place, etc.)

Notigraimer: **Remigration:** (Return to the place of origin after having emigrated.)

Challenge: During the week, develop a work plan that your church can implement on behalf of migrants. Talk to your pastor about the needs of your community and what the church can do about immigration.

What Do I See or Read?

Objective: That students know how to choose the media content that is best for them.

Memory Verse: *"Finally, brothers and sisters, whatever is true, whatever is noble, whatever is right, whatever is pure, whatever is lovely, whatever is admirable—if anything is excellent or praiseworthy—think about such things."* Philippians 4:8

Attention!

Talk about the Challenge concerning immigration from last week.

Accept

Connect | Navigate

Introductory Activity (12 - 17 years).

- Materials: Blackboard, several youth magazines, scissors, newspapers and adhesive tape.

- Instructions: Divide the class into groups of four and ask students to review magazines and newspapers and cut out the sections that stand out to them the most. Then have them post them on the board to display to the whole class, mentioning why those clippings caught their attention.

  This activity helps students identify the information they choose and learn to discriminate if it's useful or not. Ask: Do your clippings and information provide you with something necessary?

Introductory Activity (18 - 23 years).

- Materials: 10cm x 10cm colored paper and pencils.

- Instructions: Ask each student to write on a piece of colored paper the name of a radio or television program that they like to watch or listen to, or the name of a website they like to visit.

- Then, collect all the pieces of paper and randomly take one, read it, and ask the class to explain what the program is about. As you finish reading the slips, ask the class the following: Which of these programs build us up and help us to be better? And which ones harm us, or only entertain us without contributing anything good?

Connect | Navigate

The media influences the way people act and think, and can change the way they know and understand the reality around them. For example, when we analyze the most popular television programs such as animated series, dramas, reality shows, etc., we'll surely notice that several of the people we know act like those in the programs or speak with expressions from there or dress like their characters, because undoubtedly, their lives are being influenced by the content. In other words, their way of thinking or acting is being modified, and therefore, the reality they live is affected.

The media, speaking of radio and television programs, is 80% entertainment and 20% information. So, since the largest percentage is entertaining, it's logical that some programs are attractive, enjoyable and occupy a lot of our time regardless of whether they benefit us or not. Ask: How many hours do you watch television, or listen to music, or are on the Internet, every day? Does this content benefit you, does it make you a better person? How does it contribute to the growth of your life?

Adolescents and young people are exposed to the media all the time, and are a favorite point of attack since you are the largest consumers. For this reason, it's important for you to learn how to filter or choose what you see, what you hear or what you read so that your personality is properly formed and isn't harmed by the negative content of the media. To achieve this, you must apply these three tips that come from God's Word:

1. Think of the best

Not everything is bad and not everything is good. But if the media influences our thinking and modify the way we perceive reality, we must filter the content. But, how can we filter what they offer us? Well, by applying the filter of Philippians 4:8: "Finally, brothers and sisters, whatever is true, whatever is noble, whatever is right, whatever is pure, whatever is lovely, whatever is admirable—if anything is excellent or praiseworthy—think about such things."

The media can deliver many messages and diversity of content; but we must apply this rule of thought (read it 2 or 3 times).

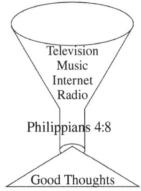

The Bible advises us to watch our thoughts. Many doctors say that people get sick more from thoughts than from other factors such as biological or dietary factors. So God was wise to say that we should be aware of our thoughts. Everything that enters our mind must be true, honest, just, pure, virtuous, worthy of praise, etc.

Analyze the type of content you're receiving from the media and see if it edifies you. If not, you should possibly change them. Remember that what doesn't do you good destroys you. If you want to be a better person, you must choose well what you let enter your mind. This advice may force you to take on a great challenge: Say yes to what makes you better, and say no to what generates bad thoughts, negative actions, destructive words, etc. in you. Everything that's unfair, dishonest, impure, deceptive, vain, selfish, bad, etc. only corrupts your mind and causes people to act in wrong and harmful ways.

Therefore, to be a better person, it's worth trying to think and choose what Philippians 4: 8 commands.

2. Retain the best

Read 1 Thessalonians 5:21-22: "...but test them all; hold on to what is good, reject every kind of evil."

Then show the class an interesting object (this could be a cube or special ornament, a rare stone, etc.). Then ask them to examine the object and say what they see, what they like, or the material that the object appears to be made of, as well as its use, etc.

Examining means discerning, discriminating, differentiating, distinguishing between good and bad. So, the Word asks us to examine everything that comes to us, a program, a song, an image, content, etc in the same way that we did with "the object." It must be examined so that we can distinguish whether it is good or not, whether it blesses us or leads us away from the truth.

The contents of mass media cannot be taken lightly, thinking that they don't affect us, because they'll always influence our life. The verse from 1 Thessalonians advises us to "hold on to what is good." In other words, not all content is worthy of holding on to. This doesn't mean that we must disconnect from the world, but we must act with an examining mind that will be able to keep what is beneficial and discard what is useless.

Although the truth from the aforementioned verse may seem obvious: "Reject every kind of evil," it's necessary to meditate on it because abstaining implies a voluntary action of applying a "no" to something that I'm possibly wishing for or liking. You have to make sure you reject, discard, eliminate what leads to error, and that the Bible calls "every kind of evil." So what are we going to do with horror movies, violent series, lyrics that induce debauchery, sensual or pornographic images, etc. We must seriously think about abstaining from them.

3. Do the best

Colossians 4:5 says: "Be wise in the way you act toward outsiders; make the most of every opportunity." The Bible advises us here that our way of living must be wise, not only when we're alone, but also when we're in the presence of others. We have a great responsibility to be an example and a good witness at all times. Sometimes people who approach or seek Christ do so more by seeing the lives of believers than by hearing their words.

Set up the following situation: "John and all his classmates meet in a house to watch movies. Suddenly, someone puts on a bad movie without consulting others. Most want to watch it, and some know that John is a follower of Jesus." Ask: What would you do in John's place? Present the following options:

a). You would be quiet and continue watching the movie.

b). You would say that you don't agree, but you would stay so as not to lose your friends.

c). You would explain your disagreement and leave the place.

Which of these would indicate a wise attitude that takes care of your mind and uses your time well?

Definitely the third. Doing so is quite a challenge, even for the brave, but it will glorify Christ and everyone will know that you care more about what God thinks of you than what people say. This is an attitude of true rebellion that changes the world for the better.

The media can be used for our benefit; but we must always examine and select well the content we choose. In this way, our mind will remain healthy and our behavior will be good thanks to it. Let's not forget that our choices can have an impact and be a testimony to others.

Review/Application: Ask your students to answer the following questions in their own words:

1. What does God want us to think about? (Whatever is true, noble, right, pure, lovely, admirable, excellent or praiseworthy.)

2. Of all the content in the memory verse, what am I doing well and what do I need to improve?

   True:

   Noble:

   Right:

   Pure:

   Lovely:

   Admirable:

   Excellent/Praiseworthy:

3. How should I spend my time?

Challenge: Our challenge this week is to analyze the programs we watch, the music we listen to, the pages we browse, and get rid of the content that's useless. What do you think, can we do that?

Making a Difference

Objective: That the students understand how their Christian identity separates them from the world.

Memory Verse: *"...so that you may become blameless and pure, 'children of God without fault in a warped and crooked generation.' Then you'll shine among them like stars in the sky."* Philippians 2:15

Attention! Before class, ask your students how they did with the analysis of the programs they watch, the music they listen to, and the pages they navigate.

Accept

Connect | Navigate

Introductory Activity (12 - 17 years).

- Materials: A considerable amount of candles (could be the ones used for a birthday cake) and matches, battery-operated lanterns / flashlights.

- Instructions: Have the items turned on/lit, as well as the electric or natural light in your classroom, before your students arrive. After welcoming them, let them know that you want to do an experiment and turn off the light switch. Divide the class into two groups and ask one group to role-play a situation where a Christian is light and another group role-plays a situation where a Christian isn't light.

Introductory Activity (18 - 23 years).

- Materials: Blackboard and chalk or large paper and pencil.

- Instructions: Ask your students to help you come up with a description or definition for the word "identity". To do this, have this definition according to the Cambridge Dictionary (https://dictionary.cambridge.org/dictionary/english/identity) as a reference: "who a person is, or the qualities of a person or group that make them different from others." Then ask them about how God influences the development of our human identity.

Connect | Navigate

The word "luminaries" has the connotation of being something that has the ability to shine or give light. Generally, this word is used in reference to the stars that we see in our sky. In an astronomy class, it's taught that stars don't really have their own light, but rather strongly reflect sunlight. During the day, when sunlight is very bright, we cannot see any stars in the sky, but at dusk and in full darkness, the stars can be seen with a glance, and their light is bright and remarkable in the midst of all the night darkness.

In Philippians 2:15, Paul called the Christians living in Philippi "lights" because their love was something that shone amid the wickedness and hatred of those around them. In this lesson, we'll study more about that light, and how we too can be lights!

In the dictionary, the word "identity" is defined as the set of characteristics of a person that makes them different from other people. Identity includes physical characteristics, such as fingerprints that are unique to each person, as well as emotional, psychological, and intellectual characteristics. In the same way, there are spiritual and moral characteristics that separate and mark a person as a son or daughter of God, and the absence of such characteristics indicates otherwise. In today's lesson, we'll see that our lives must bear the marks of a Christian identity, and that this will be the only way to make a difference in a world where these characteristics are sometimes difficult to find. In doing so, our lives will point the way to Jesus.

1. An identity that gives us freedom

In our Galatians 5:1-5 study passage, we see that Paul wrote about a very special freedom, and compared it to the sad condition of slavery. In his message, he reminded the Galatians that life without Jesus is a life of slavery to sin.

In our days, we see that despite the fact that many people struggle to win freedom, and that generally in the world, slavery is prohibited by human rights, we see that many people still suffer from slavery that's even more difficult to abolish, and that's slavery to sin. Thus, there are people who suffer the consequences of a vice (pornography or gambling), the consequences of a substance addiction (drugs or alcohol), the consequences of crime (time in prison), the consequences of impulsive decisions (an unplanned pregnancy), etc. To this list of consequences, it's necessary to add the emotional consequences that a person may suffer, such as depression, anxiety, suicidal thoughts, irritability, and other conflicts that can affect personality and interpersonal relationships.

The apostle used the word "slavery" appropriately, because the person is ultimately unable to stop doing the actions they do despite the terrible consequences; that is, the enemy tempts and traps them again and again.

That's why the apostle Paul made it clear to the Christians in Galatia that they, as children of God, had all the power of God at their disposal so that they no longer had to obey the desires of evil. They could be truly free to choose their actions.

As young people, you must recognize that you also face and will face situations that can easily trap you and leave you slaves for a long time; perhaps with greater consequences than you can imagine. A preacher said: "Sin pays, and pays bad." This is a teaching about the great lie that the devil tells us: "Do it, no one is going to get hurt" or "Nothing will happen, no one will find out." The reality is that they are lies that we must recognize and ignore. Rather, we must remember that Jesus died to set us free from all the tricks of evil, and that we have every freedom to reject sin.

An important characteristic of Christian identity is that of true freedom to choose the best for our lives.

2. An identity that gives us security

In today's second study passage (1 John 2:18-28), we read that the Apostle John wrote to Christians about the importance of recognizing Jesus as the one sent by God to provide salvation. However, despite the great example that Jesus gave us during his life here on earth, and all the miracles and signs that he did by the power of God, there are many people who didn't recognize him as the Messiah.

Sadly, that same situation continues to repeat itself in our day since many groups of people deny Jesus' place in salvation. These groups include other religions such as Eastern religions, Islam, and Jehovah's Witnesses, to name a few.

In the midst of a world where insecurity abounds and affects the lives of many young people, the young Christian can make a difference. Today, insecurity leads young people who suffer from it to make decisions based on fear. For example, there are young people who participate in smoking marijuana or drinking alcohol who are driven mainly by the fear that if they don't participate, they won't be part of the group of friends.

In the same way, insecurity leads young people to participate in having sex for fear of losing a dating relationship and feeling alone. In contrast to the above, Christian identity gives us wonderful security in God's active and eternal love!

3. An identity that makes us different

The apostle Paul wrote to the Christians who lived in Philippi and gave them a recommendation which is found in Philippians 2:15. He wrote about the role they played in the society in which they lived, and encouraged them to make a difference. He wrote that the children of God are to be people of whom there should be nothing bad to say about them, nothing to claim, because they do things without evil or "without fault" (Philippians 2:15). These qualities are in complete contrast to those of most other people who continually make decisions that are bad and hurtful to others. Our life, characterized by righteousness, justice, and love, becomes a light that illuminates the injustice and hatred of society.

We must consider that it's not always easy to be a star in the midst of a generation "warped and crooked" (Philippians 2:15). As a young person, you may have experienced situations of ridicule for some of the decisions you've made because of your Christian beliefs, for example, not accepting invitations to parties where alcohol is served, not participating in listening to certain kinds of music or smoking, obeying your parents or respecting your teachers, etc. Many times, non-Christian youth will feel envy, jealousy, or even hatred toward Christian youth who work to do things according to God's plan, and those feelings will lead them to harass the Christian youth or influence him to change. However, it's very important to remember that God understands what we're going through and wants to help us.

Jesus himself suffered great consequences in doing the will of God, including being killed on a cross. But we see that Jesus, even in those moments, showed love for others and great security in the love that God had for Him. God wants to help you so that your life can be a star that shines more and more in the darkness of the world. Christian identity is an identity that makes an undeniable difference. Don't let your light stop shining!

Review/Application: Ask your students to think of practical ways they can make a difference in their daily lives.

SITUATION	YOUR DIFFERENT RESPONSE
HOME/FAMILY	Example: Respond with respect/Be helpful
SCHOOL	Example: Work to get good grades.
JOB/WITH FRIENDS	Example: Don't participate in negative activities.

Challenge: Remember that you can make a big difference in the way you live your life. How can God help you do this? God has big plans for your life (Jeremiah 29:11), and He wants to give you all the power you need so you can make it happen. The important thing is that you depend on him every day and that you obey him in everything. Stay tuned this week for circumstances in which you can make a difference and share with the class the next time we meet together. God won't leave you alone.

Christian Counterculture

Objective: That the students recognize that the Christian message is, on many occasions, contrary to cultural practices.

Memory Verse: *"For the Spirit God gave us doesn't make us timid, but gives us power, love and self-discipline."* 2 Timothy 1:7

Attention! Start class by asking your students how they made a difference during the week.

Connect · Navigate

Introductory Activity (12 - 17 years).

• Materials: Pencils, colors, erasers and white sheets of paper.

• Instructions: Ask your students to draw a picture of Jesus as they imagine Him to be, mostly based on their readings about Him.

The idea is that they see a Jesus much more "human" than the one we've seen in the films.

As they finish the activity, show them a drawing previously found by you showing Jesus sweaty (because he walked all the time), somewhat dirty (he always walked on the dusty streets), skinny (from fasting), haggard (from prayers), disheveled and with his hair and skin tanned by the sun (they can be figures of different people with those characteristics; and if you cannot get drawings, put up posters that say the characteristics mentioned).

Introductory Activity (18 - 23 years).

• Materials: Blackboard and chalk.

• Instructions: Ask your students to come to the board and write the characteristics that should identify a Christian.

Remind them that many of the characteristics aren't physical, but ethical. Christians make a difference in the midst of a society that promotes anti-Christian values.

Connect · Navigate

Jesus Christ, the only Lord we follow, isn't someone most people of our day are comfortable with. His sayings, for example, aren't funny phrases to copy and paste on a wall; his parables aren't children's stories that call us to recreation ... Our Lord is, in addition to many things, a master of the counterculture. His life and his teachings reflect that: He challenged established traditions, religious habits, he didn't conform to custom and thus confronts our way of living today.

1. Different people

Unlike other teachers of the time, Jesus didn't choose the best students of the Mosaic Law. Rather, he searched the streets and squares for whom He wanted to call. These people didn't have good social references or were wonderful role models, but He called them anyway.

It's funny, because in the Bible we read that God used all his children to do different things: Paul preached the gospel to the Gentiles (Acts 9:15); Peter changed his racial prejudices (Acts 11:15-18); a former prostitute became part of God's people (Joshua 2:12-14); Jacob's name was changed (Genesis 35:9-11); And, among many other things, the early Christians didn't aspire to material things, but gave part of what they had to help each other (Acts 2:42-47).

They are values that don't conform to the cultural norm, but rather represent a cultural contradiction called counterculture. The common or normal thing would have been for Paul to preach the gospel just to the Hebrews; for Peter to be involved in reforming Judaism and nothing more; that the prostitute Rahab would have remained exercising her trade in another place or had even died with her people; that God would have dispensed with the trickster Jacob and that, finally, the first Christians would have decided to do business to get more, rather than give what they had. But that's not what happened.

Let's look around and ask ourselves: Are Christian people today living according to cultural values, or are we different people (like so many biblical characters) who send a different message to common practices?

2. In favor of a different culture

The criticism that many Christian authors have made of today's church of Christ is that we're just a little "subculture"; that's to say, a small cultural note in the middle of the great cultural context that we're surrounded by. We are thus a religious expression of the same culture. The reason for this criticism is that we don't make any difference with respect to the practices that many people do that offend God, who already told us his will in his written Word.

So non Christians steal money from companies, many Christians also steal money; so people miss their classes at school, many Christians also do so; yes, young people lie about things, but many young Christians do so as well; yes, people fight, but many Christians fight too; So many people are irresponsible at work, but many Christians are also. We don't make a difference! We're doing the same things.

It's fashionable to wear a certain hairstyle, so that's how Christians comb their hair! The phrases, habits and appearance that the world promotes are in the church of Christ and dwell there without anyone questioning this.

A Christian subculture, which is like saying that being Christian only has to do with certain religious habits and identifying with Christ, but it doesn't permeate our entire daily life. We aren't making a difference!

When fashions come out, many Christians adopt that fashion; half the world talks and acts like a certain television character, and many Christians speak and act exactly the same; Many people are involved in gangs, and sadly many Christians don't see this as an offense to God, even imitating signs and gestures like those used by various criminal associations to identify themselves.

Why, if God has given us a different Spirit to his children, do we keep trying to imitate the world?

Paul told his spiritual son that the Spirit of God "gives us power, love and self-discipline." (2 Timothy 1:7). And if it's God who has done this, then surely we can live differently than other people do.

Attention! It's not about being fanatics and opposing everything they tell us; but rather to affirm the values of the kingdom of God in the midst of cultural issues that offend God.

3. A Christian culture

Christian people can distinguish ourselves from the rest of the world by what we do in the midst of this culture that we have to live in (to paraphrase the Sermon on the Mount in Matthew 5 to 7, and the Pauline recommendations in Romans 12 and 13) saying:

- If everyone imitates the dress and speech of singers and celebrities, we Christians imitate the way in which Christ loved people.

- If everyone is late to work or school, Christians let's be on time.

- If when people disagree, the discussion ends in an argument, Christians express our point of view with love and try to understand the perspective of others.

- If some people don't fulfill their obligations at school or work, Christians are responsible for everything.
- If many people live in a home where insults reign, Christians, let's make our homes nice places, because there the peace of God reigns.
- If many get angry and hold a grudge against other people, Christians dare to ask for forgiveness and forgive.
- If people seek to fulfill only their own interests, Christians seek to help the interests of others to be realized as well.
- If people are blinded by ambition, Christians can be joyful in giving and serving others.
- If people are unfaithful, Christians, let's be faithful even with our thoughts.
- If people fail their promises, Christians keep what we promise even when it was only expressed verbally.
- If others show off their works of charity, Christians can live compassionately without the need for propaganda.
- If people seek to blame, Christians seek forgiveness.

    (Allow more ideas from your students.)

Jesus Christ calls us to be renewed every day in our thoughts and actions. Today is restoration day!

If we have allowed culture to absorb us, today we can make vows before God to be Christians, people who live and promote a life that pleases and honors God and benefits those around us.

Review/Application: Based on the example below, ask your students to list ten cultural values that the world promotes and compare them with those that God has sent us to live in the Bible.

CULTURAL VALUE	BIBLICAL PASSAGE	VALUED BY THE KINGDOM OF GOD
Ambition	Luke 6:38	Generosity
1		
2		
3		
4		
5		
6		
7		
8		
9		
10		

Challenge: This week, watch your life and make an effort to do things that honor God and benefit those around you.

Corruption?

Objective: That students clearly understand that integrity cannot go hand in hand with corruption as an ally.

Memory Verse: *"To the pure, all things are pure, but to those who are corrupted and don't believe, nothing is pure. In fact, both their minds and consciences are corrupted."* Titus 1:15

Attention! Don't miss the chance to continue challenging your students to live God-honoring lives by asking them about last week's challenge.

Accept

Connect | Navigate

Introductory Activity (12 - 17 years).

- Materials: Paper and pencils.
- Instruction: Ask your students to make a list of what they identify as corruption in the family, in the church, in society or nation, and also in themselves. After finishing the list, ask them to read it and make some comments.

Introductory Activity (18 - 23 years).

- Materials: Six sashes or signs that identify six students who will play the following characters: a policeman, a teacher, a politician, a Christian, a doctor, and a judge.
- Instructions: Each character will introduce themselves to the other students. Then the students will ask the characters about the corruption in the institution they represent. As you conclude this activity, under your direction as a teacher, make a list of the most relevant aspects of corruption seen in society today.

Connect | Navigate

There is corruption all over the world. However, it should be mentioned that the level of corruption in each country isn't the same. There are places in the world where corruption has reached practically all sectors and people, regardless of their social, economic, religious or intellectual condition. Faced with all of that, God has called his disciples to be upright. But ... how can one be whole in the midst of a corrupt world? Let's try to understand this integrity-corruption contradiction.

1. God's Purpose for Man: Integrity

The Bible affirms that God created man in his image and likeness. This means that human beings were created righteous, incorrupt, full of love and goodness, holy and pure, but sin changed everything, and now we often don't see much of God's image in mankind anymore.

A. What is integrity?

Let's see what the Cambridge dictionary says about "integrity": "the quality of being honest and having strong moral principles that you refuse to change; the quality of being whole and complete". Whole means: "a complete thing; all of something" (Cambridge Dictionary.org).

Integrity, then, has three characteristics:

1. Complete or whole. A person of integrity is someone who doesn't have cracks, wounds or something missing in their life. Applied to the spiritual sense, it means that Christ's presence is of such a nature that their life of holiness is real and is seen in their words, attitudes, deeds, and healthy relationships with others (1 Timothy 4:12). God wants us to surrender our entire lives to Him and serve Him fully.

2. Sexually pure. This isn't only in relation to girls, but to all guys as well. A Christian of integrity is one whose sexual life strictly adheres to God's command. They don't play with the opposite sex or indulge in sexual immorality (fornication, adultery), pederasty (sexual activity involving a man and a boy or youth), homosexuality, or any sexual perversion (1 Corinthians 6:9). The Lord wants us to go through the stages of life fully. A youth who starts having sexual relations without being married is rushing through the stages of his life and won't be fulfilling God's plans.

3. Honorable. The person of integrity is someone who can be trusted because they are righteous (Psalm 37:35-37). Righteousness is possible for those who have a source of righteousness in their hearts; that source is Christ. The person of integrity isn't thinking only of themself, but also about others.

B. Some Biblical Expressions About Integrity

1. Only those who are upright can be on the mountain of God, that is, in the house of God (Psalm 15:1-2).

2. God appreciates the praise of the upright (Psalm 33:1).

3. He who worships God walks in integrity in the midst of his house (Psalm 101:2).

4. In order to be whole (upright), it's necessary to learn the righteous judgments of God (Psalm 119:7).

5. Those who live with integrity can walk, travel, etc. confidently (Proverbs 10:9).

6. A father who is upright passes on happiness to his children (Proverbs 20:7).

7. A poor man of integrity is better before God than a rich man of perverse ways (Proverbs 28:6).

8. Integrity must accompany us throughout life and even death (Job 27:5).

9. Church leaders should teach with integrity and be examples of it to others (Titus 2:7).

2. A case of corruption in the first century church

Luke tells us what happened in Samaria with the man known as Simon "the magician" (Acts 8:14-25). Looking at this case, we can better understand what's happening now in our context.

A. What is corruption?

According to Dictionary.com, "corruption" is: "the act of corrupting or state of being corrupt; moral perversion; depravity; perversion of integrity; corrupt or dishonest proceedings; debasement or alteration, as of language or a text." Let's also see the meaning of "corrupting": "to destroy the integrity of; cause to be dishonest, disloyal, etc., especially by bribery; to lower morally; pervert; to corrupt youth; to alter (a language, text, etc.) for the worse; debase; to mar; spoil; to infect; taint." (https://www.dictionary.com/browse/corrupting?s=t).

In the spiritual sense, corruption alters or twists the Word of God, the commandments of God, Christian doctrine and the behavior that corresponds to a Christian.

B. Signs of corruption in Simon "the magician"

Simon "the magician" had wielded magic in Samaria for a long time and had led people to believe that "This man is rightly called the Great Power of God." Later, Philip came to Samaria preaching the gospel. Many people were converted to the Lord, Simon "the magician" being one of them. Upon hearing of these things, the apostles in Jerusalem sent Peter and John to confirm with the brothers, and then something unexpected happened. As John and Peter laid their hands on people, praying for them to receive the Holy Spirit (vs. 15,17), Simon, seeing such a wonder, wanted to buy their power with money (vs. 18,19). The reaction of the apostle Peter was angry when he told Simon that his money and he perished together; because he had no part in that matter (vs. 20,21). But at the same time, he told him to repent of his wickedness and pray to the Lord in the hope that God would forgive him for having such a thought in his heart, to which Simon seems to have repented (vs. 22-23).

Simon "the magician" corrupted and wanted to corrupt the following:

a. He corrupted decent work (Acts 8:9-11). By making use of magical arts, he earned money contrary to the will of God.

b. He corrupted people's minds (Acts 8:10). He made people believe that what he did was done by the power of God. Tremendous falsehood: Attributing the actions of the devil to God.

c. He wanted to corrupt the gospel and the giving of the Holy Spirit (vs. 18-19). Accustomed as he was to receiving money for the ancient magical arts he did, this man thought that he had discovered a more productive source to raise money.

When it comes to Simon, we don't know how he ended up, but there are historical indications that seem to indicate that he was the father of a heresy within Christianity in the first centuries. Likewise, his name has been linked forever to the practice of buying church posts. This is called "simony," a corrupt practice that has done so much damage to the Christian church, especially in the Middle Ages, but from which we still aren't free from to this day.

Living with integrity in the midst of a corrupt world is a challenge for Christians. Any area of our life can be corrupted. We must obey God and live pure, that is, rightly before the Lord and thus contribute to the transformation of humanity into the image of Christ.

Review/Application: Allow time for your students to respond. The answers are found in the lesson.

1. In what ways was Simon corrupted according to Acts 8: 9-19? _____

   Acts 8:9-11 _____   Acts 8:10 _____   Acts 8:18-19 _____

2. What do the following passages teach you about integrity?

   Psalm 15:1-2 _____   Psalm 33:1 _____   Psalm 101:2 _____

Challenge: During the week, pay attention to any instances of corruption you hear about or see around you or in the media, and think about what Bible teachings you would tell those involved. Share these at the next class.

Keyword

Objective: That students examine their behavior and form responsible character in every area of their lives.

Memory Verse: *"Whatever you do, work at it with all your heart, as working for the Lord, not for human masters."* Colossians 3:23

Attention!

Give your students time to share about last week's Challenge.

Accept

Connect | Navigate

Introductory Activity (12 - 17 years).

- Materials: Prepare two separate sets of 8cm x 6cm letters that spell the word "responsibility".

- Instructions: Form one or two groups, depending on the number of students. Then give them separate sets of letters (the letters must be in a mess) so they can form the word "responsibility".

  After about five minutes, or if they take less time better, ask the group that finished first to write a short definition of the word in question. Ask the other group to prepare an example that illustrates that word.

Introductory Activity (18 - 23 years).

- Materials: Sheets of white paper and pens.

- Instructions: Hand out individual sheets of paper and pens, and tell them that each one should write down five important things that they do during the day from when they get up to when to go to bed.

  Ask: What motivates you to do all the things you wrote down. When someone says the word "responsibility," how do you define that word.

  To conclude, mention that later everyone will write a definition of this word.

Connect | Navigate

1. The demand for responsibility: Commitment

The first ingredient in building a responsible character is commitment. And this is the serious problem in many adolescents and young people, because they don't see through their commitments, and therefore, they aren't responsible. However, many of them long for privileges. So, we wonder how they'll have privileges if they don't make and keep commitments in their lives.

Young Joshua is a practical example of commitment. Because commitment demands sacrifice, he took on every challenge with great responsibility. One of the first challenges he had to face was his appointment as prince of the tribe of Ephraim. He was chosen because of his mature character from among all of his tribe to go along with eleven other princes of the other tribes as a spy into the land of Canaan (Numbers 13). After forty days of arduous work in enemy lands and with many dangers of death, they returned and gave an account to Moses. But Joshua and Caleb were the only ones who bravely enforced his efforts.

Do you remember the meaning of responsible? We mentioned that the responsible person is that person who fulfills their obligations and pays attention to what they do or decide. Thus, the story of Joshua shows us the three decisive steps that helped him act responsibly: He left, he saw the land of Canaan, and he returned with the desire to conquer. Actually, Moses didn't send them to see whether or not they could conquer it. Joshua and Caleb understood that they went to spy on Canaan to develop a strategy of conquest. When faced with a challenge, it's easy to throw in the towel. Ask: Have you ever heard the phrase: "He who doesn't risk wins nothing"? In reality, Joshua took the risk with faith and commitment; therefore, he was later able to enter the promised land.

If we want to achieve great things in our lives, it's time for us to take responsibility. The first thing is to start each day with commitment and a fighting spirit, and faith in the mighty name of Christ. Ask: Are you studying? Do you have a job? Do you have projects? Those are commitments to which you must be accountable and faithfully abide by.

In addition to the great challenges that Joshua took, we can also see from his record that he took on his commitment with a lot of obedience. Commitment isn't simply doing things, but we must also take into account the advice and demands made on us by those who have more experience than us. Thus, Joshua always stood by Moses' side as his helper (Numbers 11:28), and in everything he obeyed by submitting to his leadership (Exodus 17:10). Many young men and women find it difficult to submit in obedience. In this regard, someone said the following: "The price of responsibility is obedience." Obedience will help you do things with great responsibility.

There are things that parents generally instill in their children, such as being responsible with their cleanliness, punctuality, order, study or work. Today, we need a generation that's capable of making a responsible commitment to these occupations.

2. The fruit of responsibility: Authority

Responsibility begins in our lives when we're very young. At every stage of our physical growth, we have to learn the habit of being responsible. Responsibility is a discipline that will pay off and pay off when we focus on practicing it.

Ask: Why did Joshua become the successor to the great Moses? What did Joshua do to become the overall leader of the entire Israelite nation? His book tells us about his leadership in command of the people of Israel. However, in the previous books (from the book of Exodus to Deuteronomy), we can see this young man in many experiences next to Moses, and so much so that God saw in him such potential and responsibility that he entrusted him with the highest authority in the entire nation of Israel.

God said to Joshua: "Moses my servant is dead. Now then, you and all these people, get ready to cross the Jordan River…" (Joshua 1:2). This command was nothing more than a ratification of what he had previously heard through Moses (Numbers 27:18,19,22-23). The people had witnessed this commission made to Joshua; furthermore, they already knew the responsible character of Joshua. Therefore, they believed that he was capable of leading them to the promised land. So much so that at Joshua's first command (Joshua 1:10-15), the people responded to his authority by saying: "Whatever you have commanded us we'll do" (Joshua 1:16-17).

Later, God ratified Joshua's authority before the people. Once they crossed the Jordan, God magnified Joshua in the eyes of the people so much that they respected him as they had respected Moses (Joshua 4:14). And he not only earned the respect of the nation, but he was also respected by many pagan kings when they learned of his conquering ability.

When we act responsibly, we'll also see privileges open to us. If you study or work responsibly, you'll also see the fruits of your effort.

3. The Foundation of Responsibility: Your Spiritual Discipline

Joshua's constant dedication, his perennial disposition and his continued worship developed in him a courageous and responsible heart. The writer of the book of Exodus tells us that Moses' "young aide Joshua son of Nun didn't leave the tent" where they met with God (Exodus 33:11b). His search for God and his consecration to God was total, and by this he understood that responsibility is a principle of the character of the child of God. So a person who claims to be a child of God must demonstrate it in their responsible character.

For the unconverted, responsibility is an interesting practice; on the other hand, Christians believe in responsibility as a commitment to please God above all else. Our memory verse encourages us to do everything with all our heart, as for the Lord.

An anonymous saying goes: "There's a big difference between interest and commitment. When you're interested in something, you do it only when circumstances allow. When you're committed to something, you don't accept excuses, only results." Those results become the goals that you'll have at the family, personal, work level, etc.

Joshua helps us understand that our commitment to God is essential to fulfilling our responsibilities. Spiritual discipline not only helps us to be responsible, it encourages us to achieve goals. For Joshua, it wasn't easy for him to fulfill the role that Moses had left him, but in his spiritual conversations with God, he always heard the following phrase: "Be strong and courageous!" This phrase is repeated four times in the first chapter of the book of Joshua (vs. 6, 7, 9, 18). Like Joshua, we also need those words of support and encouragement to accomplish the goal, and which we'll find only when we seek the Lord with all our heart. Thus, God had warned Joshua that he should never stop meditating on his Word, because in it were the steps to prosper in everything.

Let's imitate the responsible character of Joshua, and then we'll see those same ingredients forged in our lives. The crown that Joshua won for his responsibility was the acceptance of God and his example which endures in our minds and hearts through so many centuries.

Review/Application: Help your students reflect on the following personal questions:

1. What are the three ingredients of responsibility? (The demand is commitment, the fruit is authority, and its foundation is spiritual discipline.)

2. Do you think Joshua's life inspires you to increase your responsibility? Yes or no, and how?

3. Are you one of those who waits for someone to tell you what to do, or do you take initiative? Explain.

4. Have you failed at something for lack of taking responsibility? If so, do you feel challenged to fight? Explain. (It's good to encourage them to take their challenges seriously).

5. According to Joshua's life, what's the secret to building responsible character? (The secret a lot of consecration to God to be motivated and have a responsible character.)

Challenge: Andrea Jiménez says: "You don't grow up when you change your size, you grow up when you fit your responsibilities." Are you one of those who grows up but remains irresponsible? Or are you one of those who grows up according to their responsibilities? Make a decision today with the help of Christ.

Can You Read Me?

Objective: That the students understand that we must live honestly.

Memory Verse: *"For we're taking pains to do what is right, not only in the eyes of the Lord but also in the eyes of man."* 2 Corinthians 8:21

Attention!
Begin a dialogue about the Challenge from last week.
Accept

Connect | Navigate

Introductory Activity (12 - 17 years).

- Materials: Colored pencils, papers, scissors, cardboard, glue, magazines. The more diversity of materials you have for this activity, the greater the creativity.

- Instructions: Prepare the materials and divide the class into two or three groups depending on the number of students. The dynamic consists of expressing "honesty" using available materials. Encourage them to be creative.

Introductory Activity (18 - 23 years).

- Materials: A table game (uno, cards, scrabble, dominos, etc.).

- Instructions: Pick a table game that most can play and that isn't long. Before class begins, talk with a student and explain the activity. Tell him/her that everyone will start playing by the same rules, but suddenly, you'll start to change the rules on purpose to favor him/her (the student you're talking to before class). Then, during the game, he/she will cheat, some obvious and some not so much. Observe the reactions of the other students. Finish the activity before the whole group is upset; and at the end, ask them: What happened during the game? Was someone cheating? How did you feel when you saw someone cheating? Has everyone behaved honestly? Ask those who didn't cheat to raise their hands.

Through this activity, the students will be able to see how other people behave dishonorably (cheating) or honestly (not cheating).

Connect | Navigate

At school, they always gave us compulsory readings and one of them was, "El Lazarillo de Tormes" (The Guide of Tormes) (the author isn't known exactly). In this book, the life of a child is told, Lázaro of Tormes, who was born surrounded by poverty. His father died when Lázaro was a small child, and due to their situation, his mother put him in the service of a blind man. In the narration of these events, a scene occurs that caught my attention: When Lázaro and the blind man share a bunch of grapes.

The blind man and Lázaro arrived at a place, and a grape seller gave them a bunch of grapes as alms. So they agreed that they would both eat equal amounts: One would eat one and then the other would eat one, each eating only one grape at a time. So they began to eat the bunch, one grape each at a time; but in the next turn, the blind man began to take two grapes at a time. Seeing this, Lázaro did the same and even began to eat three grapes at the same time.

At the end of the bunch of grapes, the blind man said: "Lázaro:... I will swear to God that you have eaten the grapes three at a time."

"I did not," Lázaro said, "but why do you suspect that?"

The clever blind man replied: "Do you know how I know that you ate three at a time? Because I ate two at a time and you kept quiet."

In other words, Lázaro didn't complain or say anything when he saw that the blind man was taking two grapes at the same time; instead, he decided to take three grapes at a time. In this story, we can see that they both put honesty aside, and not only that, but Lázaro ended up looking out for his own good instead of doing things honestly.

In this scene, Lázaro thought that he had gotten away with it, but in truth, the blind man had realized what had happened. This can also happen to us since we can think that nobody will notice the "little things" that we do or say. But this is a lie. We're deceiving ourselves because in the end, everything is exposed: "Nothing in all creation is hidden from God's sight. Everything is uncovered and laid bare before the eyes of him to whom we must give account" (Hebrews 4:13). This verse reveals that the first to know everything we do is Christ.

In the Gospel according to Luke, we find the story of Zacchaeus (Luke 19:1-10), who was a tax collector. Tax collectors had a bad reputation since they tended to cheat or extort money from people to get more profit. For this reason, Zacchaeus wasn't the most loved man in the place, rather he was one of the most despised.

When Zacchaeus heard that Jesus was in Jericho (v. 1), he wanted to meet him, or at least see him. In the story of Zacchaeus, we can see that Christ impacted his life, and later this man sought to be honest and upright.

1. Christ impacts lives

Today, we can read the story of Zacchaeus, and we even know a few things about him. However, if there was only one book of his life, surely there would be parts of it that Zacchaeus wouldn't like to share. Now, let's think about our lives, as if they were a book. Ask: Would we be calm and happy sharing all the chapters? I'm sure that there are parts that we wish weren't there or that never happened.

Just as we said before, Zacchaeus was one of the most despised men in his city. His work didn't give him a good reputation; but it wasn't the fault of the work, but of his attitude.

When Zacchaeus knew that Jesus was in his city, he looked for a way to get closer to Him. He climbed a sycamore tree to get a better view of him. Jesus saw him and called him by his name. This fact sure impacted Zacchaeus' life. He probably asked himself: How is it possible that Jesus knows my name, and above all, told me that he would come to my house? Being a publican and having the attitude that he had, people probably didn't go to Zacchaeus' house very often. So the fact that Jesus called him by his name, without even knowing him, and also told him that he was going to his house impacted the life of this tax collector.

Ask: Do we remember the time Jesus impacted your life? Sure, none of us were tax collectors, but we've certainly done things we're not proud of. For example, we've told some lies, we haven't always obeyed our parents, we've spoken badly of our friends, we've fought with some friends, and other things. We wouldn't like these facts to appear in the book of our lives. We wouldn't like anyone to read those chapters of our lives. The truth is that when Christ tells us: "I'm going to your house", he's telling us that he wants to enter our lives, and it's at that moment when all things change (2 Corinthians 5:17).

2. Being honest and upright

Ask: In what way did old things pass away and become new in Zacchaeus' life? (Luke 19: 8). Zacchaeus knew that he had not been honest in his work; in fact, he had cheated people, extorted them to get more money. He hadn't been merciful when it came to collecting taxes. He hadn't cared about people's situation, and if he could get more money, he did. The disgraced tax collector had been doing these things. However, Jesus' arrival at his house transformed him. Zacchaeus realized all the wickedness that he had done to his neighbors.

The moment Christ comes into our life and shows us all the things we've done wrong, this should cause a change in us, just as it did to Zacchaeus. The Holy Spirit shows us a way in which we can live honestly.

A life of honesty and integrity doesn't just refer to money; but to all areas of our lives. For example, not cheating on exams, not taking pens from our partner, not speaking ill of our friends, etc. According to Dictionary.com, the word "integrity" means: "adherence to moral and ethical principles; soundness of moral character; honesty; the state of being whole, entire, or undiminished". Therefore, when seeking a life of honesty and integrity, we're talking about including all parts of our life, not just some and not others. It must be all.

The Lord knows all things, but we must also be careful about our testimony (2 Corinthians 8:21). A friend once told me: "Don't do good things that may seem bad." So if some of our attitudes don't speak well of us in front of others, then we should ask ourselves if we should change. The Lord knows all things, he knows our intentions, but people don't. We must be honest and upright both in solitude and in public.

Today we've seen the example of Zacchaeus. Jesus came into his life and changed his lifestyle. Zacchaeus went from being the deceiver, thief, and extortioner, to being an honest man who wanted to help the poor and give back all that he had stolen. As we've seen in the story of Lázaro of Tormes, we can think that nobody realizes the bad that we're doing, but the Lord knows everything, and maybe even our parents or other people too, as in the case of the blind man and Lázaro.

Review/Application: Allow students to give their own personal responses to the following questions:

Could people read you by seeing your attitudes? Would they see honesty in your life? Think of examples where you can act honestly. Example: Return change if a cashier gives me too much.

1. _____ 2. _____

3. _____ 4. _____

Challenge: Do I act honestly at my school, at home, in the store, in the supermarket, etc.?

Have I allowed Christ to be reflected in my life? If my life was a book, would I let people read today's chapter or last week's chapter? Think about the attitudes you should allow the Holy Spirit to change in your life. Each morning this week, remind yourself: "People will be reading today's chapter of my life ... what will they read?" and then at night: "What did others read in today's chapter of this day?"

Be Different

Objective: That the students learn that honesty is an indispensable characteristic to be able to please God and be a light to others.

Memory Verse: *Finally, brothers and sisters, whatever is true, whatever is noble, whatever is right, whatever is pure, whatever is lovely, whatever is admirable—if anything is excellent or praiseworthy—think about such things* Philippians 4:8

Attention!
Begin by asking if they cared if you read their entire book from last week in class.

Accept

Connect | Navigate

Introductory Activity (12 - 17 years).
- Instructions: Divide the class into two groups and ask one group to act out a situation in which an honest person acts for one minute. And ask the other group to dramatize a situation in which they see how a dishonest person acts. Then allow students to comment on what was done.

Introductory Activity (18 - 23 years).
- Materials: Blackboard and chalk.
- Instructions: Make two columns on the board and in one column write the word Honesty and in the other Dishonesty. Then ask students to tell what those words suggest to them. Write everything they say in the appropriate column. At the end, write a definition for each of the words mentioned.

Connect | **Navigate**

In a distant town, the king summoned all the young men to a private audience with him where he would give them an important message. Many young people attended and the king told them: "I am going to give each one of you a different seed, after six months they'll have to bring me the plant that has grown in a pot, and the most beautiful plant will win my daughter's hand." This was done, but there was a young man who planted his seed and it didn't germinate; meanwhile, all the other young people in the kingdom kept talking and showing the beautiful plants and flowers they had planted in their pots. Six months came and all the young people began to parade towards the castle with beautiful plants. The young man whose seed had not germinated was too sad to the point of not even wanting to go to the palace. But his mother insisted that he should go, as he was a participant and he should be there. Finally, he paraded last to the palace with his empty flowerpot. All the young people, when they saw our friend, burst out laughing and mocking. At that moment, the uproar was interrupted by the entrance of the king; then, everyone made their respective bows while the king walked among all the pots admiring the plants. After the inspection, the king also called his daughter, and he called the young man who brought his empty pot; Astonished, everyone waited for the explanation of that action. The king then said: "This is the new heir to the throne and he will marry my daughter, for all of you were given an infertile seed, and you all tried to deceive me by planting other plants; but this young man had the courage to present himself and show his empty pot, being sincere, royal and courageous, qualities that a future king must have and that my daughter deserves." (http://www.encinardemamre.com/premium/az/ h / honesty.htm # The fox and the monkey disputing over their nobility).

We are in a world full of evil and perversion, and finding honest people is increasingly difficult. By not having God in their lives, people live trying to satisfy themselves no matter how they achieve it. God, through his Word, asks his children to be honest to do his will and thus be light to the world.

1. Honesty

First, we have to understand this term well. According to dictionary.com, "honest" means the following: "honorable in principles, intentions, and actions; upright and fair:" (https://www.dictionary.com/browse/honest?s=t). And if we look for synonyms, we'll find the following terms as a result: "just, incorruptible, truthful, trustworthy, fair, straightforward, candid, pure" (https://www.dictionary.com/browse/honest?s=t).

As we've seen, being honest means being a person with many virtues. He is someone who tries to do things right, justly; He doesn't like deception and is responsible for his actions, therefore, he takes great care of his way of living.

For the Christian, honesty is an *attitude* and an *aptitude*. Ask: What's the difference between those two words? (Get your students to think a bit by asking them to give their opinions before giving them the answer.)

Attitude: a feeling or opinion about something or someone, or a way of behaving that's caused by this. (https://dictionary.cambridge.org/dictionary/english/attitude) Aptitude: a natural ability or skill. (https://dictionary.cambridge.org/dictionary/english/aptitude).

The Bible says in Philippians 2:13: "God who works in you to will and to act …" How wonderful! God has given us the attitude and the aptitude to be able to live honestly, unlike others who, because of the sin that dwells in them, don't have the capacity to do so.

2. Honesty in the Bible

Write on a board or on a large piece of paper the phrases mentioned below without the biblical quote. Designate one verse per person to be read aloud. After each has read their assigned verse, ask them to match it to the phrase that they think best fits what the verse says.

a) "I must be honest to be light to those who live in darkness" (Philippians 2:15).

We must stay true to our principles without being influenced by the world. So, we must influence them with our testimony and actions so that they see through us a living and real God.

b) "I must be honest so that my praise will be pleasing to God" (Psalms 33:1).

We need to live in integrity so that we can approach God with confidence and give Him our worship knowing that He receives it with joy.

c) "I must be honest to maintain unity within the Christian community" (Ephesians 4:25).

Honesty will make trust and unity flow to one another in the church; in this way, we'll bring joy to God.

d) "I must be honest to be a good servant of God" (1 Timothy 3:8).

We must serve the Lord with integrity. We are all servants of God, even if we don't have any title or position in the church. Every Christian is called to serve.

e) "I must be honest in everything I do and at all times" (2 Corinthians 8:21).

We must be honest at all times and in all places, because we don't do it for people, but for God, knowing that He always sees us.

f) "I must be honest to be blessed by God" (Proverbs 28:20).

God greatly blesses those who live with integrity, for he knows that it's not easy, but it's worth doing for the Lord.

3. Daniel, an example of honesty

A. Daniel's honesty in the face of temptation

Daniel was a young man who was taken from Jerusalem to Babylon (Daniel 1). There, he along with other young men was selected to serve the king. All of them were ordered to eat the king's food, but Daniel and three of his friends refused. Ask: Why would Daniel do that?

The problem wasn't the food, but rather that Daniel didn't want to sin against God since they were under Jewish law, which prohibited those foods. So he preferred to keep the law, despite being outside his homeland, because he knew that this would please God. Daniel was probably tempted to eat the king's food, but his desire to please God was greater than his desire to taste it.

We too have many temptations in our life, but God expects us to choose to do his will. Daniel didn't mind disobeying the king's orders, rather than those of his real King (God). Nor should we care what other people think or say. The only thing that should concern us is the opinion of God; that will help us a lot when making an important decision.

B. Daniel's honesty in the face of adversity

King Darius made a law that everyone had to worship him; otherwise, they would be thrown into the lions' den (Daniel 6). But this law didn't stop Daniel from continuing to seek God's presence. Daniel lived honestly his entire life; no one could accuse him of anything wrong (Daniel 6:4). But despite that, his enemies managed to capture him and throw him into the lions' den. We must be aware that despite our good testimony, the world will always look for something to accuse us of. However, that shouldn't stop us, but we must continue to live honestly. The Bible doesn't say exactly whether Daniel was afraid or not at that time; what we do know is that he trusted God. He knew that he could be victorious by being protected by God, or he would simply die, thus meeting his Lord. Either way, he would be the winner. Happily, God delivered him from death and punished those who wanted to harm him.

Today, the children of God also have trials and adversities, but God allows those things to happen so that our faith will be tested and strengthened, and in the end, his name will be exalted. Whatever happens, we must know that we'll always win with God on our side.

C. Daniel's honesty, rewarded by God

After each of the difficult episodes in Daniel's life, we see that he was always victorious. When he refused to eat the king's food, in the end, he and his friends were the best-looking (Daniel 1:15), and God made them smarter than the others and gave Daniel the ability to understand dreams and visions. Later, Daniel was placed as the head of the kingdom's rulers (Daniel 6:3), and later on we see how God delivered him from the lions. But in addition, Daniel's actions resulted in the name of God being praised by all the kingdom, and God prospered it.

Daniel was a man who lived a life of integrity and righteousness in every sense. That's because he never strayed from God. Daniel 6:10 says that Daniel prayed to God three times a day. This confirms that he was a man of prayer and consecration to God; for that reason, Daniel was able to be faithful in the most difficult moments of his life.

Review/Application: Allow time for your students to respond to the following:

* Define the word "honesty" with your own words.

* Do you think it's easy to be honest in today's world?

* Have you had experiences where people were not honest with you? Tell about one.

* Mention 2 or 3 examples of honesty and 2 or 3 of dishonesty that you've experienced recently.

Challenge: Daniel was a man who never denied who he was and who he believed in. Likewise, you must be the same person on the street as you are in church. Be courageous to stand up for your faith and stand firm, even if it seems like you're going against the grain. Don't let the world intimidate you or be seduced into living dishonestly. Show your friends, neighbors, family, etc. that you're the child of a holy God and that you live honestly, making a difference. How will this decision affect your life today? Meditate on it during the week and share with our class the next time we meet.

My Identity

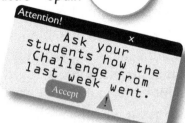

Attention!
Ask your students how the Challenge from last week went.
Accept

Objective: Remind students that part of our lives as Christians is to be humble.

Memory Verse: *"He must become greater; I must become less."* John 3:30

Connect | Navigate

Introductory Activity (12 - 17 years).
- Materials: Paper and colored pencils.
- Instructions: Distribute sheets of paper to the students and ask them to draw something that they think exemplifies "humility." Then allow each one to show their drawing and for the rest of the class to interpret it. Then each person can explain what they drew and why. Allow time for everyone to participate.

Introductory Activity (18 - 23 years).
- Materials: Sheets of white paper (one for each of your students).
- Instructions: Ask you students to make an acrostic with the word "humility" (use each letter to form a phrase or word).

Connect | **Navigate**

The stage of the adolescent and youth is characterized by overcoming, exploring their self, and also a stage in which arrogance, pride and vanity often rise up. For this reason, we find the advice of the Apostle Peter where he addresses young people to clothe themselves with humility (1 Peter 5:5).

According to dictionary.com, "humility" is: "the quality or condition of being humble; modest opinion or estimate of one's own importance, rank, etc."

The entire Bible encourages and urges us to be humble. We must build our identity on the basis of humility. To see this, we'll take the life of John the Baptist as an example.

1. John the Baptist wasn't a know-it-all

When John the Baptist began his ministry, the people of Jerusalem and all of Judea came out to ask forgiveness for their sins and to be baptized (Matthew 3:5). In the Gospel according to Luke, it's recorded that up to three times they asked him: "What should we do?" (Luke 3:10,12,14). This teaches us that for the Jewish people, John the Baptist was a sage, a person to whom people came with their concerns.

However, in his personal opinion, he didn't look at himself that way. In Matthew 11:2-3, he causes us to understand that he, humanly, had questions to resolve regarding Jesus. On one occasion, he actually sent two of his disciples to personally ask Jesus if He was the Messiah. With this, we realize that John the Baptist needed to know even more about Jesus Christ.

As we grow in the things of the Lord, we'll always need to know more about Jesus, for we can never reach the fullness of knowledge. Even though John had been very close to Jesus since they were both in the womb (Luke 1:41-44), and after having baptized him, he never believed he knew everything about Jesus.

John's humility is denoted by getting rid of the worry about what others would say when he admitted that he didn't know everything. Furthermore, John sent two of his disciples to find out what he wasn't sure about. John wanted to know more about Jesus for his spiritual growth.

Perhaps we've been instructed from a very young age in the things of God. But let's keep in mind that we have to keep asking the Lord Jesus to keep clarifying things for us as He did with John. Only the proud and boastful person believes that he knows everything and that he doesn't need to know more.

On the other hand, when John the Baptist sent the question, he wasn't showing unbelief. Rather, he was looking for a specific clarification of Jesus' redemptive purpose. After all, he was in prison for the sake of Jesus Christ.

2. Jesus referred to the humility of John

A. What did you go out to the wilderness to see?

The place where John developed his ministry was the desert (Matthew 3:1). Today, some or many preachers wouldn't choose a desert as their office for work. In a desert, there's no light at night, there's no fun, there's no easy food, there aren't any comforts. However, John the Baptist wasn't interested in a comfortable place where he would develop his ministry; what interested him was preaching in the name of God. His ministry was endorsed by God. Therefore, people even went to the desert to hear him preach the Word (Matthew 11:7).

B. A reed swayed by the wind?

With this other question, Jesus was appealing to the strong character of John the Baptist (Matthew 11:7). Just because he's humble doesn't mean that he's a reed moved by the wind. Rather, his humble character lay in his inner attitude before God and men, not in his external appearance. A reed is synonymous with flimsy, weak and delicate, and implies that such a person is easy to break, or that he is fearful or cowardly. Sometimes, we find the definition of humble as a weak, poor and fearful person. This is nothing more than a definition of a reed shaken by the wind. But not so with John the Baptist. He was strong in the exposition of his message, reliable in his testimony and stable in his call. He even paid with his own life for the consequences of his message. He renounced cowardice by not betraying his quintessential Master.

C. A man dressed in fine clothes?

With this question, Jesus wanted to show his listeners that John knew the purpose of his calling and that he was willing to live submissive to his call rather than to comfort (Matthew 11:8). He didn't make ministry his livelihood or means for carnal profit.

John the Baptist looked for a natural garment, that is, he didn't worry much about what he would wear, since it wasn't his priority (Matthew 3:4); Actually, what John was most concerned about was the garment of spiritual anointing to bear witness to Jesus Christ (John 1:6-7).

As Christians, we have to decide where to live: in the delight of our own interests and pride, or in an anonymous life for the message of the gospel, leading a simple and humble life. Today, young people are looking more for clothing brands to show their vanity. However, the humble in spirit will seek to consecrate their heart beyond what they could wear.

D. A prophet?

In the Gospel of John, we read the testimony of John the Baptist when priests and Levites asked him who he was (John 1:19-21).

For this reason, with this fourth question, Jesus wanted to make it very clear who John the Baptist really was (Matthew 11:9). We live in the middle of a religious world in which people call themselves "anointed"; However, John the Baptist teaches us that it's better to let the Master himself give his opinion about us.

John didn't recognize himself as a prophet, but Jesus said he was more than a prophet (Matthew 11:9). There is no greater privilege than receiving the approval of Christ in our office. In John the Baptist, Matthew 23:12 was fulfilled. He first humbled himself, then Jesus exalted him by stating three things: First, that he was more than a prophet (Matthew 11:9); second, that among those born of women no one greater than he had risen (v. 11); and third, he praised him saying that he was the Elijah (v. 14), comparing him to Elijah who was the highest among the prophets. Furthermore, when his birth was prophesied by the angel, the angel said of him: "...for he will be great in the sight of the Lord" (Luke 1:13-15). Perhaps he didn't realize the repercussions of his ministry; but he became the forerunner of the gospel. His only interest was to be committed to doing God's will. This led to him being the one who baptized Jesus. Not even this last act with Jesus led him to magnify himself (John 1:26-27); rather, he took his place behind the one who called him to preach. After these words, he added the most beautiful statement about Jesus (John 1:29).

Two things made John the Baptist great, and therefore, live in humility: "...he will be filled with the Holy Spirit..." (Luke 1:15) and "...the Lord's hand was with him" (Luke 1:66). Let's look for these ingredients to live in humility. The words of John the Baptist stir our being when we hear him: "He must become greater; I must become less" (John 3:30).

Review/Application: Based on today's study, ask the students to answer the following questions:

1. What has to decrease for me to be humble? (My ego.)
2. What did the people see John the Baptist to be like? (Like a teacher and the Elijah.)
3. Why did John the Baptist send his disciples to ask Jesus a question? (Because he wanted to clarify Jesus' redemptive purpose.)
4. What were the four questions Jesus asked about John the Baptist according to Matthew 11:7-9? ("What did you go out into the wilderness to see? A reed swayed by the wind? ... A man dressed in fine clothes? ... A prophet?")
5. What did Jesus declare in exalting John the Baptist for his humility (Matthew 11:9,11,14)? (First, that he was "more than a prophet"; second, that "among those born of women there has not risen anyone greater than John the Baptist"; and third, he praised him saying that "he is the Elijah who was to come" - comparing him to Elijah who was the highest among the prophets.)
6. What were the two revelations that made John the Baptist great, according to Luke 1:15,66? (First, "...he will be filled with the Holy Spirit..." and second, "...the Lord's hand was with him.".)

Challenge: Try to have deep conversations with God in personal prayer. During the week, ponder what we've talked about and identify areas of your life that you haven't completely surrendered to God, and confess any sins you have committed. In a spirit of prayer, ask God to purify your heart and sanctify you completely. If you think this is right for you, go see a spiritually mature person to help you in prayer for this reason.

Unforgettable Gift

Objective: That the students understand that it's necessary to serve the Lord while we have the opportunity.

Memory Verse: *"Truly I tell you, wherever this gospel is preached throughout the world, what she has done will also be told, in memory of her."* Matthew 26:13

Connect | Navigate

Introductory Activity (12 - 17 years).

- Materials: A ball or a stuffed animal and music.

- Instructions: The object must pass from one person to another to the rhythm of the music, the sound of a tambourine, or clapping. When the sound stops, whoever has the object must tell about the most important gift they have been given and who gave it to them.

  Reflect on how generous people can be when giving a gift. Special emphasis will be placed on the best things that we've done or given for God.

Introductory Activity (18 - 23 years).

- Materials: A teddy bear or doll.

- Instructions: The teacher will tell a story. Example: "When I came today I met "Teddy" (name of the bear or the doll). He was sad and lonely, and he needs a lot of love. I told him that this group could give him a lot of love." Ask each young person to show their love for Teddy with a gesture, such as a kiss, a hug, an affectionate phrase (I love you Teddy), etc. Once everyone has shown their love for Teddy, say: "Teddy is very happy because you all love him, but now he wants to ask you one more favor. Teddy wants to give you a gift of his love, so, he wants you to repeat the gesture you made to Teddy to the person next to you."

Connect | Navigate

Ask: What would you do if you knew that your loved one has only a few days left to live?

In life, there are opportunities that won't be repeated. If we let them pass, we may later regret not having taken advantage of them (ex. giving a hug, a smile, timely advice, a kind word, etc.). At funerals, people often share a regret at not having done some things that they can never do again because their loved one is gone.

Read Matthew 26:1-13. Divide the class into two groups to dramatize the Bible story. In point 1, one group will role-play the religious leaders' plan and in point 2, the other group will role-play how Jesus was anointed with perfume. Then they can do an analysis of the attitudes of the main characters.

1. A sinister reunion

The annual celebration of Passover (Matthew 26:2), the feast in which the Jewish people commemorated their liberation from slavery in Egypt and salvation from the death of the firstborn, through the blood of a lamb smeared on the doorposts of every Hebrew family, was close. It was a party where they could thank God for his amazing deliverance.

The Lord Jesus showed one of his divine attributes, omniscience (the full knowledge of all things past, present and future) when he let his disciples know what would happen to him during the Passover (v. 2). But they didn't give much importance to what he said, or they didn't take it seriously, or perhaps they didn't understand what he said. How they must have regretted their indifference when everything happened as he said it would! There would be no going back.

The leaders of the meeting: The religious leaders came together to devise schemes to trap Jesus with deceptions and then kill him (vs. 3-4). They were very clever because they knew that Jesus had blessed many people with his miracles and they feared that by arresting him in the middle of the Passover feast, the people would be upset. They weren't concerned with justice, but with the disorder that the cruelty of the Roman army might attract.

Principal Priests: In the courtyard of the high priest's residence, there was a meeting of the principal priests, who were the authority on religious matters. They were respected, recognized, influential people who had been called to be intermediaries of the people before God. However, from scripture we find that "These people ... honor me with their lips, but their hearts are far from me" (Isaiah 29:13). Those religious leaders were far from pleasing God with their actions. How is it possible that those who should guide people's hearts to God were the enemies of the Son of God.

Elders of the town: There was also this group called the Sanhedrin, who were representatives of the main families, and together with the high priest, they could judge civil and religious matters. They were those who represented integrity and righteousness, the promoters of justice.

It's incredible how much those religious leaders could violate all morals and ethics to suit their personal interests. The Lord had prophesied it through David (Psalm 2:1-3). That corruption has been repeated over and over again in human history, like a plague that refuses to go away. It happens in many of our countries and in some churches that biblical principles are ignored, some sins are tolerated, and certain decisions are twisted or actions justified to favor a relative or an influential member. But we must not forget that he who has more light, more responsibility will be demanded.

The high civil and religious hierarchy wasn't immune to wickedness and sin. Scripture rightly says: "...if you think you're standing firm, be careful that you don't fall!" (1 Corinthians 10:12).

Before beginning this point, invite the second group to role-play this passage.

2. Tribute in Bethany

A. Friends in Bethany

Bethany was a village located a short distance from Jerusalem, and the Gospels show that Jesus had some friends there (Lazarus, his sisters, and Simon the leper) whom he visited when he was in that region. Influential leaders were his enemies, while Jesus found hearts willing to meet their Savior among the simple people.

B. An unforgettable gift

Ask: What are you willing to face to please a loved one? Many times, people make unusual efforts to please those they love. In other cases, people select the gifts they'll give according to the honoree's social position or the degree of appreciation they have for him. So the gift can be simple or lavish.

According to Matthew, Jesus was in the house of Simon the leper, sharing with his disciples, when a woman arrived with an alabaster bottle of very expensive pure tuberose perfume, and poured it on Jesus' head.

Although Jesus' social status wasn't prominent like that of the priests or the Sanhedrin, the woman mentioned by Matthew 26 had enough esteem, respect, and gratitude for him to spend a significant sum on the perfume she poured on the Lord. That woman had to overcome many barriers to offer Jesus that gift, such as prejudices about the approach of a woman to a man in public. In addition to the criticism of those attending that dinner, Mark adds that Jesus' disciples scolded her severely (vs. 8-9).

Despite the backbiting, scorn, and scolding from those present, the woman was obedient to God's direction and did the right thing at the right time. The Lord accepted that gift with pleasure, and once again prophesied his death, saying that she had prepared him for his burial (vs. 10-12). She paid him a tribute in her lifetime. We often pay tribute to people who have already passed away and therefore, the honor comes very late.

The Lord wasn't indifferent to the gift, and even less to the criticism, since he defended her against her aggressors and exposed their false concern for the poor. She didn't miss the opportunity to please the Lord, even without knowing that such opportunity wouldn't present itself again. The Lord once again prophesied that wherever the gospel was preached, what she did would be talked about (v. 13). Our service to God may go unnoticed by people and they may criticize it, but it won't go unnoticed by the Lord.

There are things we should do for the kingdom of God, but we let opportunities go by believing that we still have a lot of time, such as visiting a sick person, helping someone in need, being kind to someone, giving a smile, etc., which usually don't require money or great sacrifice. However, that woman's gift cost the salary of almost a year of work.

Right now we must reflect on what things we've stopped doing for the Lord, knowing that we must do them. It's necessary to get to work, as the woman from Bethany did, because if we wait, it may become too late and we'll spend the rest of our lives regretting what we didn't do. Certainly God has done great things in our lives that deserve our thanks. If we know that God asks something of us, we shouldn't delay in doing it.

Review/Application: Ask your students to answer the following questions:

a). What did Jesus announce would happen at Passover? (That he would be handed over to be crucified.)

b). What sign of his divinity was seen when Jesus announced what would happen during Passover? (His omniscience.)

c). What does it mean to you that respectable people in society plotted the death of Jesus? (That they were respectable only in appearance, but deep down they were corrupt and unfair.)

d). When Jesus received the perfume offering, what was the reason for his disciples' anger? (They got angry because they considered money more important than people.)

e). What motivated the woman to give Jesus such an expensive perfume? (She was very grateful because he had forgiven her sins, also she had a lot of esteem and respect for him.)

f). Why do many people refuse to serve the Lord with their time or material possessions? (Because they don't love him or they don't have gratitude towards him.)

Challenge: Write something you know you must do to please God:

Now make a resolution to do it this week. Don't wait! You don't know if you'll have another opportunity.

Farewell

Objective: That the students will review the events of Jesus' ascension and reflect on its significance.

Memory Verse: *"While he was blessing them, he left them and was taken up into heaven."* Luke 24:51

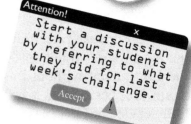

Attention! Start a discussion with your students by referring to what they did for last week's challenge.

Connect | Navigate

Introductory Activity (12 - 17 years).

- Instructions: Ask if any of the students were able to be with someone at their time of death and, if they wish, ask them to tell what that moment of farewell was like. If not, you can ask if they have had to say goodbye some someone or participated in a farewell event. Allow them to relate details of those moments. You can take an example of yours or remember a farewell that was done in church. Associate it with Jesus' farewell to his disciples and begin the lesson.

Introductory Activity (18 - 23 years).

- Materials: Blackboard and chalk, or large paper and marker(s).
- Instructions: On the board write in large letters the title: "The Ascension of Jesus" and ask your students to write (taking turns on the board) questions that non-believers may have about this event in Jesus' life. Reflect together on the doubts and questions that this event can cause us, as well as the assurance and promises that this event means for the followers of Christ.

Connect | Navigate

The authors Luke and Mark relate that after Jesus spoke with the disciples and gave his last instructions, his physical body was raised from the earth and taken to heaven until it was no longer seen by the eyes of the disciples.

During his three years of ministry here on earth, Jesus performed many miracles. However, in the last minutes of his time here, his human and physical body literally "...was taken up before their very eyes, and a cloud hid him from their sight" (Acts 1:9) and the disciples stood watching from the ground.

1. The meaning of the ascension for Jesus

The history of the Gospels tells us that Jesus became a man "made of flesh and blood," just like any other human being on planet earth. He needed to sleep (Mark 4:38) and eat (Mark 14:22); he also felt sadness and wept (John 11:35); he was angry (Mark 11:15) and suffered (Luke 22:44). That same human Jesus was the one who lived among his disciples as one of the people of Nazareth. However, we see that after being crucified and dying, Jesus wasn't like other people, but rose and appeared before his disciples, demonstrating the power of God, the power that conquers even death.

In the days between his resurrection and ascension to heaven, Jesus appeared to the disciples in the place where they were gathered (Luke 24:36-49) and showed them the marks of the nails in his hands and feet, and asked them to eat with him. These evidences are one more example of the human body of Jesus. The Gospel of Luke also tells us that Jesus appeared with two of his followers who were traveling to the city of Emmaus (Luke 24:13-35), and spoke with them in a clear and understandable way. This same Jesus was later received into heaven.

It's interesting to note that Jesus led a normal, human life in the days before his ascension to heaven. He also continued teaching his disciples the way to follow God faithfully.

It's interesting to note that this supernatural event of the ascension was experienced by Jesus with complete calm and naturalness (Luke 24:50-53; Mark 16:19-20). It's probable that Jesus was calm because He knew what was happening when He began to ascend to heaven. In John 16:16, Jesus had warned his disciples what would happen.

We know that after being raised to heaven, Jesus was received by his Father into his heavenly abode; and this was because Jesus had completed his ministerial task here on earth. For Jesus, the ascension meant that he would go to enjoy the presence of his Father again, and would no longer be separated from the Father (Mark 16:19).

2. The meaning of ascension today

In Romans 8:34, we read that Jesus, after ascending to heaven, is still working for our benefit, interceding with the Father for us, so that he sustains us and forgives us. Jesus' ascension into heaven reminds us that we now have constant access to the Father through Him. We can trust the fact that Jesus knows very well what life is like here on earth, since He experienced it himself. This also helps us trust that Jesus has mercy on us and that's why he doesn't stop interceding with God the Father for us.

In the legal processes of our modern society, defendants always seek to have a good lawyer who helps them before the Court and can speak to the judge for them, asking for mercy in the sentence. In the same way, we can compare Jesus to the figure of "our perfect lawyer" who loves us and intercedes with God for us when we fail and need mercy. Thanks to Jesus who does for us what we cannot do for ourselves!

In John 16:7-8, we see that Jesus told the disciples that his going to heaven meant that the Holy Spirit would come to be with them to help them continue the saving mission: "But the fact of the matter is that it's best for you that I go away, for if I don't, the Comforter won't come. If I do, he will—for I will send him to you" (John 16:7 TLB). It's very comforting to understand that God had prepared the Holy Spirit to continue accompanying Christians after Jesus' physical departure. We see that God is a loving God who has everything under his perfect control. We can have an attitude of gratitude for Jesus' ascension since it marks a new stage in God's plan in which we can enjoy his presence in a personal way in our hearts through the Holy Spirit.

In John 14:1-4, we see that Jesus was preparing his disciples for his departure. He encouraged them to trust and have peace, and also to retain hope of future life in the presence of God. Jesus, once again, made it clear to the disciples that his ascension was part of God's wonderful and perfect plan.

We see that Jesus' ascension to heaven has a very special meaning for us regarding our own future. Jesus' going to heaven is a guarantee of us Christians going to heaven to be in the presence of God, together with Jesus Christ. It's an unbeatable promise.

Finally, we must remember that for us as Christians, Jesus' ascension into heaven also has a deep spiritual significance, as it did for Jesus. It continues to establish our path of access to the Father for our benefit and forgiveness with Jesus as our "intercessor." It allows us to enjoy the presence of the Holy Spirit in the present, and guarantees our own heavenly presence with Jesus in the future in "My Father's house..." (John 14:2). These promises are unique and faithful, and thanks to the work of Jesus, we can fully trust that they'll be fulfilled. Amen.

Review/Application: Ask you students to complete the following chart.

PROMISES OF JESUS	MY RESPONSE
"Christ Jesus who died...and is also interceding for us." (Romans 8:34)	I can trust that Jesus wants to forgive me when I fail and sin.
"...for if I don't, the Comforter won't come. If I do, ... I will send him to you" (John 16:7 TLB)	I can trust the Holy Spirit to be with me even when circumstances are difficult.
"... I will come back and take you to be with me that you also may be where I am". (John 14:3)	I can hope that my future, after death, will be good with Jesus.

Challenge: What is your perspective on Jesus going to heaven? What did you hear? Have you ever had questions about this event? Don't forget that God is always ready to help and guide you. By praying and reading the Bible, you'll find answers and advice. Above all, remember that God has a perfect plan for your life, just as He did for Jesus. Don't hesitate to share your doubts and questions with me or other mature Christians.

Expected Surprise

Objective: That the students recognize the importance of the coming of the Holy Spirit and its repercussion on the history of the church.

Memory Verse: *"But you'll receive power when the Holy Spirit comes on you; and you'll be my witnesses in Jerusalem, and in all Judea and Samaria, and to the ends of the earth."* Acts 1:8

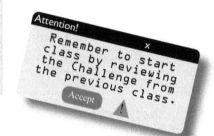

Attention! Remember to start class by reviewing the Challenge from the previous class.
Accept

Connect | Navigate

Introductory Activity (12 - 17 years).
- Materials: The Bible, markers of various colors and sheets of paper.
- Instructions: Divide the class into three groups and assign them one of the following verses: Acts 2:2, 3, or 4. Ask them to imagine what their verse describes and try to express it through a drawing. Have each group present their drawing and explain the ideas expressed in it.

Introductory Activity (18 - 23 years).
- Materials: Small sheets of paper that each contain the phrase "Jesus is risen" in a different language:
  1. Portuguese: Jesus ressuscitou
  2. Zulu: UJesu uvukile
  3. Spanish: Jesús ha resucitado
  4. German: Jesus ist auferstanden
  5. Italian: Gesú é risorto
  6. French: Jésus est ressuscité
- Instructions: Give each student a piece of paper with the indicated phrase in a different language. When instructed, they should all read their respective assigned phrase aloud several times at the same time, repeating it for several minutes.

  Explain that something similar happened on the day of Pentecost, with the difference being that the people gathered spoke different languages and each understood the message expressed by the disciples.

Connect | Navigate

On the day of Pentecost, something similar to our Christmas and New Years feast occurred: the bustle of many people gathered with great joy to celebrate the end of one season and start another.

The disciples who gathered in the place called the upper room were celebrating something very significant. But they also expected that something extraordinary would happen to them: The arrival of the promised Holy Spirit (Acts 2:1-13).

In reality, they had no idea what would happen or when, but each day they faithfully awaited the fulfillment of the promise made by Jesus.

And the fulfillment of the promise came and indeed, that day the Holy Spirit made a spectacular entrance into the hearts and life of the church. That day, it literally marked a "before" and an "after" for the church. Nothing would be the same again, not for them, not for us!

Pentecost was the disciples' passage into a deep relationship with God. The presence of the Holy Spirit produced a more intimate level in the experience of their personal faith. This transformation resulted in consecration and witness. Beginning with Pentecost, the gospel message was spread throughout the world.

1. Pentecost: a great feast of gratitude

"When the day of Pentecost came, they were all together in one place." (v. 1). Ask: What was celebrated on the day of Pentecost? What did it mean?

First of all, we must know that Pentecost was a great feast. Holidays are important, depending on what we celebrate in them. We have birthday parties, wedding engagements, wedding anniversaries, graduations, etc. Also, each country celebrates national holidays where important events in its history are remembered. Christians celebrate the birth of Jesus, his death, his resurrection, and Pentecost.

Jews celebrated various religious holidays throughout the year that commemorated significant events. Pentecost was one of the three most important (along with the Passover and the Feast of Tabernacles). During this feast, gratitude was given to God especially for the fruit of the earth and the work of each person.

The Greek word from which is translated "Pentecost" means "fifty" because it was held the day after seven weeks after the first sheaves of wheat were harvested. Since it was the day after seven Saturdays, it fell on a Sunday, or the first day of the week. That's why it was also called "the feast of the weeks" and "the day of the first fruits."

On this special day, all work was suspended and the people gathered with much joy and gratitude. The purpose was to have a meaningful approach to the presence of God. It was customary to share it with everyone (Deuteronomy 16:11-12). Surely the first Christians participated in a collective meal during this celebration, something similar to a Thanksgiving meal.

God chose the feast of Pentecost to fulfill his promise made by Jesus in Acts 1:8, "But you'll receive power when the Holy Spirit comes on you;..." From that moment on, the worldwide expansion of the gospel began through the witness of the church.

2. The great miracle of Pentecost

Ask: Have you ever witnessed a miracle or an amazing event? What is a miracle? A miracle is an unnatural event. It's something extraordinary where the power of God intervenes. The Bible tells us of many miracles like those performed by Jesus and the ancient prophets.

It can be said that what happened on the day of Pentecost is the most important miracle in the history of the Christian church. The Holy Spirit came upon believers to abide permanently in them, purifying their hearts from sin, and filling them with power for service.

Some miraculous signs accompanied the coming of the Spirit to the upper room. Those supernatural things filled those present with astonishment. In verses 2 through 4, these three extraordinary events appeared in order of succession:

a. "Suddenly a sound like the blowing of a violent wind came from heaven and filled the whole house…" (v. 2).

b. "They saw what seemed to be tongues of fire that separated and came to rest on each of them" (v. 3).

c. "All of them were filled with the Holy Spirit and began to speak in other tongues (languages) as the Spirit enabled them." (v. 4).

Ask: What were the wind and fire? They were symbols of the powerful cleansing presence of the Holy Spirit.

Ask: Why do you think they spoke in other languages? It was a sign to unbelievers and a way to get their attention, as well as a means of communicating the gospel to outsiders.

But the central miracle of Pentecost was the filling of the Holy Spirit. "All of them were filled with the Holy Spirit...". The word "filled" means "fullness", and it speaks of total consecration to God (sanctification).

What the filling of the Spirit does was later described by the apostle Peter in Acts 15:9 as the "purification of the heart." The cleansing of the heart is the great miracle that takes place in believers through the baptism with the Holy Spirit. The disciples received the power to live holy lives.

3. The Pentecost message: salvation for all

Jesus gave the command to his disciples to preach the gospel to every person. This command is known as the Great Commission (Matthew 28:16-20; Mark 16:14-18; Luke 24:36-49; John 20:19-23).

The coming of the Holy Spirit on the day of Pentecost, precisely, began the movement of expansion of the church to the whole world.

The disciples were mostly people of little knowledge and culture, but the Holy Spirit used them that day to communicate "the wonders of God" in the different languages of the foreigners gathered in Jerusalem. According to a biblical commentary, "the wonders of God" would refer primarily to the resurrection of Jesus Christ from the dead.

Through Pentecost, God not only made known "the wonders" or miracles of the gospel and the life of Jesus, but promoted the spread of the message to all the nations of the known world (Acts 1:8).

It's logical to think that many of those foreigners who received the witness of Pentecost, and who were among the first converts of the church, later took the good news of salvation to their places of origin.

The power that the Holy Spirit brought upon the church at Pentecost enabled those in the upper room to be faithful witnesses of the Savior, our Lord Jesus Christ.

Ask: What is the result of Pentecost in your own life? Have you received that power that allows you to be a faithful witness of Jesus?

Review/Application: Divide your students into groups and have them write the meanings of the following phrases or words. Then have them share their meanings with the class.

- **Pentecost** (Fulfillment of the promise.) Acts 1: 8

- **Speaking in other tongues** (They spoke in other languages.) Acts 2:4

- **The message of salvation** (Salvation through Jesus Christ is for everyone.) Acts 2:8-11

- **When Pentecost came** (They were all together in one place.) Acts 2:1

Challenge: Plan a personal evangelism time for the class in the neighborhood or community where your church is located. Before the activity, schedule time for group prayer to seek guidance from the Holy Spirit.

Message of Love

Objective: That students analyze the events of the birth of Jesus as the fulfillment of the prophecies.

Memory Verse: *But when the set time had fully come, God sent his Son, born of a woman, born under the law.* Galatians 4:4

Connect | Navigate

Introductory Activity (12 - 17 years).

- Materials: Printouts with the following Bible verses.
- Instructions: Organize your students into two groups. Direct each group to choose a moderator and a secretary. Next, have them read carefully and attentively the following Bible verses and identify the fulfilled prophecy related to Jesus.
- Micah 5:2. Place of Birth (Bethlehem).
- Isaiah 7:14. Description of mother (A virgin).
- Isaiah 9:7. Reign on who's throne and over who's kingdom (David's).
- Isaiah 9:1. He would live in (Galilee).
- Hosea 11:1. He would spend time in (Egypt).

  Share the conclusions with the rest of the group.

Introductory Activity (18 - 23 years).

- Materials: Paper, pencils or pen.
- Instructions: Organize your class into three groups, according to the number of students you have. Ask them to appoint a moderator and a secretary. Give each group two sheets of paper and pens. Ask them to divide a sheet into two columns. In one they'll list all the gifts they've ever received at Christmas time, in the other, the gifts they've given. The secretary will record all the group's contributions. When they've completed this part, have them read John 3:16, and answer the following questions What was God's gift to mankind? For what purpose did he give that gift? Ask them to share the answers with the other groups.

Connect | Navigate

One of the wonderful stories in the Bible that impacts us the most is the one that has to do with the birth of our Lord. It's the mystery of the incarnation (John 1:14; 1 Timothy 3:16).

1. The birth of Jesus fulfilled biblical prophecy

It's impressive how the ancient prophecies that announced the arrival of the Redeemer of humanity were fully fulfilled in the person of Jesus. From the proto gospel, the first announcement about a Savior, in Genesis 3:15, until the resurrection mentioned in the Messianic Psalm 16:8-11, they were strictly observed. Nothing was left out. Everything was accomplished.

In that sense, the statement that Paul made in Galatians 4:4 is beautiful, alluding to God's time. It indicates that He was and is in control of everything.

If we look at the context and the historical circumstances surrounding Jesus' birth, one might think humanly that they were just coincidences of life or history. But when we think of God as the Lord of all, whom nothing takes by surprise, and we exercise our faith, we realize that He was always in control and that He used the decree of an empire as pagan as the Roman one, to fulfill His Word and his holy purposes.

Luke, the physician and historian, gives us the details of this event (Luke 2:1-7). An edict was issued (v. 1). Legally speaking, it was a mandate or decree published with the authority of the emperor, Augustus Caesar, and therefore, it was mandatory for all the inhabitants of the empire. The decree stated that: "everyone should be registered". The word translated "census," literally means "registered" or "enrolled." When referring to the whole world, it was understood that it was the entire Roman Empire.

"And everyone went to their own town..." wrote Luke in Luke 2:3-5, referring to the city of their ancestors. The Jews established the custom that each person should go to the city of their origin. Then Joseph, who was from the house and family of David, went from Galilee, from the city of Nazareth, to Judea, the city of David, called Bethlehem.

"Bethlehem was a place rich in historical memories. It was the city of David, the home of Ruth, and the place where Rachel was buried. Just 25 kilometers to the south was Hebron, home of Abraham, Isaac, and Jacob. 15 kilometers to the northwest was Gibeon, where Joshua had stopped the sun. 20 kilometers to the west was Soco, where David had killed Goliath, the Philistine giant. 10 kilometers to the north was Jerusalem, the magnificent capital of David and Solomon, seat of David's throne for 400 years." (Handbook Compendium of the Bible. Henry Halley. Moody, Nineteenth Edition, p. 434).

Well, Joseph arrived there to be registered with Mary who was betrothed to him and who was pregnant. It's interesting to note that God chose the place where his Son would be born and his earthly parents. The chosen parents lived about 100 miles away from Bethlehem. Providentially, they had to make the journey. It must have been a difficult and tiring journey, especially for Mary who was about to give birth.

"...the time came for the baby to be born..." (Luke 2:6). This has to do with Mary's nine months of pregnancy, but also with God's timing. Divine providence had brought them to Bethlehem, and while there, the days of his birth were fulfilled.

We aren't given the date; tradition established it as December 25, but there are no historical or biblical bases that give certainty about that. The date was set for convenience and with certain pagan influences.

2. A demonstration of God's love

A. Made the incarnation possible

The incarnation of the Word, of the Son of God, expresses in an unmistakable way how God loves us. Both the Father and the Son agreed for the second person of the Trinity to become man and shed all that was of his own, of all his eternal glory, to come, live and sacrifice himself for us.

We cannot separate the divine act of this incarnation from the salvific purpose that motivated it. It was so that God would have the opportunity to connect with human beings, draw near to them and save them (John 3:16).

B. It is love with purpose

The well-known text of John 3:16 teaches us of that great love of God. The heavenly Father gave up the most precious thing, his Son, to give us salvation (Romans 8:32). How shocking this is!! He loved us so much that he gave us his Son! The reflection and question is, who were we to deserve such great love? Because of our sins we deserve nothing but death, but, He loved us and came to our rescue (Romans 5:8). Because of his great love, he was willing to give everything up for us, and he did.

His purpose was to give us salvation and eternal life. "... that whoever believes in him shall not perish but have eternal life" (John 3:16). God's love made it possible for human beings to access this type of present and eternal life.

C. It is eternal love

Since the sad and unfortunate fall of mankind, and although God disciplined them by throwing them out of the garden, God continued to love them. Human beings, even in their most rebellious times, continued to be subjects of God's love. Although He had to punish them on several occasions, He always showed them the opportunity for repentance to turn to Him. God's rebellious people in the Old Testament knew of the greatness of the Lord's love for them (Jeremiah 31:3).

3. A response of humanity

God did his part. The biggest and most important part. He took the initiative of reconciliation by sending us his only begotten Son, the only one of his kind. The Son was humanized, clothed in weakness, born in a humble manger, and died for our sins.

Throughout history, humanity has been faced with two alternatives: believe or not believe in the Lord, receive or reject him, choose eternal life or eternal death, serve him or serve self.

The ideal and most beneficial thing for everyone is to receive the Savior in their hearts, to surrender their life completely to Him and ask forgiveness for their sins. But we all have the freedom to do it or not. Those who reject him will be lost forever, but those who receive him will obtain great blessings. The main one is that they'll become sons and daughters of God. Christ Jesus grants them that status, blessing and privilege. Sons and daughters of God! (John 1:12-13).

The best demonstration of our gratitude to the Lord is with selfless and committed service. Let's acknowledge his greatness and power. Since He loved us so much, the least we can do is offer Him devoted and committed service. So much love demonstrated by God deserves to be reciprocated by everyone (1 John 4:19).

The Lord Jesus deserves that all of us offer him service with quality and warmth, and thus we'll not lose our reward today, and in the world to come, life with him (John 12:26).

The person and message of Jesus must be brought to all people and places where they don't know him. Let everyone know about Him and have the opportunity to have Him in their hearts. Let's not skimp on time, energy, or money, doing all we can to ensure that Jesus Christ is known to people of all ages in all places.

Review/Application: Organize your students into two groups. Have them read the following Bible verses: Isaiah 7:14; Micah 5:2; Hosea 11:1; Isaiah 9:1-2, 11:1; Jeremiah 31:15; Matthew 1:22-23, 2:5-6, 2:16-18, 2:22-23, 4:12-16. Have your students divide a sheet of paper into two columns. On the left side, place the Bible verse that contains the prophecy, and on the right side, the verse that talks about the fulfillment.

Biblical Prophecy	Fulfillment
Isaiah 7:14	Matthew 1:22-23
Micah 5:2	Matthew 2:5-6
Hosea 11:1	Matthew 2:15
Isaiah 9:1-2	Matthew 4:12-16
Isaiah 11:1	Matthew 2:22-23
Jeremiah 31:15	Matthew 2:16-18

Challenge: Write down your thoughts on what Christmas means to your life and share them with our class the next time we meet.

Objective: That the students will consecrate their lives to the Lord in this first class of the new year.

Memory Verse: *"Therefore, I urge you, brothers and sisters, in view of God's mercy, to offer your bodies as a living sacrifice, holy and pleasing to God—this is your true and proper worship".* Romans 12:1

Attention!
Allow time for students to share what they wrote in response to last week's Challenge.
Accept

Connect | Navigate

Introductory Activity (12 - 17 years).

- Materials: Cardstock cards (10 x 15 cm) and pencils.
- Instructions: Briefly explain the importance of having a "life project," and the opportunity to be in the first class of the year. Before making any plans, we must ask the Lord for his direction so that we can be guided by him.

  Ask the question: What would you like to be when you grow up, and why?

  What would you like to be and do for the Lord in church?

  Give them about 5 minutes to write and then share what they wrote.

Introductory Activity (18 - 23 years).

- Materials: Paper and pencil for each student.
- Instruction: Once paper and pencils are given to each student, they should write down their answer to: What did you plan to do at the beginning of last year? What achievements did you achieve on a personal level? What achievements did you achieve at work, school, and in service to the Lord? Discuss the answers for a few minutes.

  The New Year. It would be good for the young people who belong to our congregation to consecrate their lives to the Lord, and those who have already done it can evaluate how they are doing.

Connect | Navigate

The new Year. It will be good if the young people who belong to our congregation would consecrate their lives to the Lord and those who have already done it can evaluate how they are doing.

1. Consecrating our physical members

The writer to the Hebrews wrote about the discipline of God, the purpose of which it to aid the maturity of his children (Hebrews 12:5-8). Any child of God who remembers the difficult moments that they had to live this last year will be able to consider that everything that they experienced helped them in some way to grow towards perfection and maturity in their spiritual life.

After this topic, the author of the epistle asked his readers to do the following:

A. Raise your fallen hands

Ask: According to Hebrews 12:12a, what can we do with our hands? Praise God, point to the Most High and God's work in nature and in us.

Also with our hands we can extend help to the needy: to widows, orphans, immigrants, street children, the sick, people with disabilities, etc.

With our hands we can carry out human development projects that benefit society in an integral way towards the full life that Jesus offers us.

B. Don't let your knees get paralyzed

The exercise of walking moves one forward (Hebrews 12:12b). In addition, in order not to become paralyzed, it's necessary to exercise, run, jog, move our legs. Ask: How can we use our knees and therefore our legs to extend the Kingdom of God? We can go to visit friends who don't know Christ, visit hospitals and prisons, go to help new works or missions that are spreading in our districts and outside of it. When we advance and do different ministries, we see the possibilities of service, and in the midst of service, God can call us to do missions in our country or to be missionaries to other cultures and beyond our nations.

C. Make level paths

"Make level paths for your feet" (Hebrews 12:13). It's important that we are examples in the walk of our daily life, as good Christians who live according to the commands of his Word.

Holiness should be reflected in our walk: "But just as he who called you is holy, so be holy in all you do..." (1 Peter 1:15). This verse calls us to a different way of living (holiness) at all times and in all places ... a life of integrity, not only in our relationships with Christians in church or when we congregate, but also at home, work, school, university, etc.

D. So that the weak will not leave the way

"… so that the lame may not be disabled, but rather healed." (Hebrews 12:13). One's behavior can motivate others. Many can be won to Christ without words. But also some misconduct can be a stumbling block for the weak in faith, for those who are in danger of turning away from the Lord. Let's remember a popular saying: "Actions speak louder than words."

Jesus said: "If anyone causes one of these little ones—those who believe in me—to stumble, it would be better for them to have a large millstone hung around their neck and to be drowned in the depths of the sea" (Matthew 18:6). God helps us not to be a stumbling block to our neighbor. Let's ask God for help so that we can live exemplary lives and show Christ in everything we do.

2. Consecrating our relationships

A. "Live in peace with everyone"

God always asks that we take care of our relationship with our neighbor (Luke 10:27). It's important that Christians lives in peace with their fellowmen or their neighbor (Hebrews 12:13a). And the closest neighbor is in our home ... our parents and siblings ... and continues outside our house with friends, neighbors and colleagues.

When we talk about relationships and keeping the peace, we refer to what Jesus said when teaching about anger (Matthew 5:23-25).

Sin disturbs relationships, therefore it must be ended quickly (Ephesians 4:26). Put an end to your anger during the day; this means that conflict resolution must be immediate.

There are young people who make their anger last until it turns into rage, and that leads to other sins. Don't let your anger last beyond twenty-four hours; learn to ask for forgiveness and forgive. This will make your relationships with others harmonious.

B. "Without holiness no one will see the Lord"

Continuing with relationships, holiness has to do with the condition of the Christian as a result of their relationship with God. It's up to the individuals to consecrate their life, as Hebrews 12:1 instructs us, putting off sin. What a good opportunity to start the new year and fulfill the instructions and requirements that the verse demands!

3. Perseverance and conservation

It's interesting that many start the year with a lot of enthusiasm, but as the days, weeks and months go by, they don't continue with the same motivation and they abandon their goals as time goes by. Then, at the end of the year, they realize that they didn't do what they wanted and didn't reach their goals or objectives. To have a blessed and fulfilling year, it's important to have clear objectives and goals for individual and social life. Once one begins the journey of life in a new way, they must be persistent. Perseverance must be accompanied by constant monitoring and evaluation so as not to deviate. This will result in being able to carry out the decisions made.

As children of God, when we make a decision to make changes, we must continue in them.

Conservation

It's important to take care of what one has, what we've cultivated for years. We must be careful not to commit the same sin as Esau, who exchanged his birthright for a bowl of lentils, which the writer describes as profane. In other words, it's belittling sacred things for temporary ones. The same writer to the Hebrews tells us: "...how shall we escape if we ignore so great a salvation?" Hebrews 2:3a.

One keeps something when they know that it has significant value. It may be a gemstone jewel that they acquired or received as a gift, an object, stuffed animals, letters from a loved one, etc.

Jesus paid a great price for our sins by shedding his blood on the cross for our salvation and sanctification. We were bought with Jesus' blood, which is of incalculable value. We must not neglect or underestimate it.

At the end, let's remember what the Apostle Paul said: "...you were bought at a price. Therefore honor God with your bodies" (1 Corinthians 6:20).

Review/Application: Allow time for your students to answer the following questions:

1. What does it mean for you to consecrate yourself to God?

2. How could you consecrate:

   - Your personal relationships?

   - Yourself physically?

   - Yourself intellectually?

   - Yourself socially?

   - Service to the Lord

3. Why is monitoring and evaluation important in reaching goals?

4. How will you stick with your commitment today?

5. What am you going to do to achieve it?

Challenge: During the week, pray that God will help you understand His plan for your life, and that from this plan, you can have clear objectives for your future. Write down the ideas that come out of this prayer time.

Ingram Content Group UK Ltd.
Milton Keynes UK
UKHW032035140323
418553UK00013B/720